I0749134

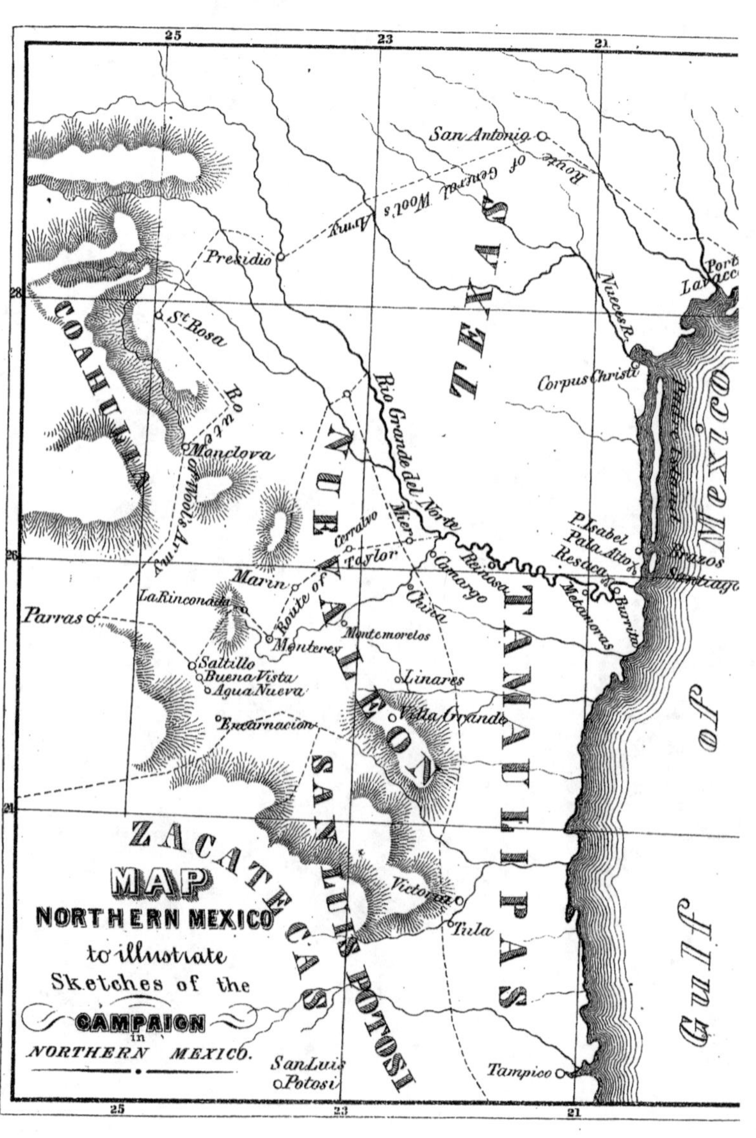
MAP
NORTHERN MEXICO
to illustrate
Sketches of the
CAMPAIGN
in
NORTHERN MEXICO.
COAHUILA
TEXAS
NUEVA LEON
TAMAULIPAS
SAN LUIS POTOSI
ZACATECAS
Gulf of Mexico
San Antonio
Route of General Wool's Army
Presidio
St Rosa
Monclova
Rio Grande del Norte
Nueces R.
Corpus Christi
Padre Island
Cerralvo
Mier
Taylor
Camargo
Reinosa
P. Isabel
Palo Alto
Resaca
Metamoras
Burrita
Brazos
Santiago
Marin
La Rinconada
Parras
Route of
China
Monterey
Montemorelos
Saltillo
Buena Vista
Agua Nueva
Linares
Villa Grande
Encarnacion
Victoria
Tula
Tampico
San Luis Potosi
25
23
21
28
26
24

SKETCHES

OF THE

CAMPAIGN IN NORTHERN MEXICO.

IN

EIGHTEEN HUNDRED FORTY-SIX AND SEVEN.

BY AN OFFICER

OF THE FIRST REGIMENT OF OHIO VOLUNTEERS.

NEW YORK:

PUBLISHED FOR THE AUTHOR BY

GEORGE P. PUTNAM & CO., 10 PARK PLACE.

1853.

TO THE

NON-COMMISSIONED OFFICERS AND PRIVATES

OF

THE FIRST OHIO VOLUNTEERS,

THIS VOLUME

IS RESPECTFULLY INSCRIBED

AS A

TRIBUTE OF RESPECT.

INTRODUCTION.

If the time has not yet come for the grave and impartial summing up by the historian, of that interesting event—*the Mexican war*—it is believed that a sufficiently remote period has arrived for the publication of those Notes and Memoirs which have been prepared, and are designed, not so much to gratify any existing popular interest, as to "serve the cause of History." The writer of the following pages is aware that his subject lacks the charm of novelty. A strong and experienced corps of intelligent officers and literary camp-followers, armed *cap-a-pie* for the campaign, have taken the field before him. Still, as the same landscape or picture, when observed from different points of view, will not unseldom present new and attractive features; the reader may perhaps discover in these Sketches, some lights and shadows to which his attention has not heretofore been directed. The history of the First Regiment of Ohio volunteers (incorporated with the narrative) may be interesting to many of his fellow-citizens; and his account of some of the leading events of the war, he trusts, will not be altogether valueless.

An untrained volunteer in authorship as in arms, the writer—though not indifferent to, nor ungrateful for the approbation of others,—has been more intent upon the performance of his duty, than solicitous for the favorable opinion of his readers. Prompted by a just State pride, and the desire to discharge a merited tribute to the constancy and courage of the gallant men to whom the volume is inscribed, he has endeavored to recite plainly and briefly those interesting events in which the troops of Ohio participatad, together with such incidents of Taylor's campaign as seemed necessary to afford the general reader a clear, connected, and comprehensive view of the war in Northern Mexico. He has quoted only such *Orders, Dispatches* and official documents as were required to elucidate the narrative ; the interest of which he has sought to enhance by occasional extracts from the only history of the war as yet published by Mexicans. To his surviving fellow-soldiers, who are all doubtless content (for the true soldier is never covetous of praise,) with the meager account of their services moldering in the archives of the War-Department, these chapters may serve to recall many scenes which time, perhaps, has already partially effaced from the tablet of memory. An eye-witness of what he describes, the writer confidently claims for it the belief of the reader ; for though his little book be but a trifling contribution to the history of the war, it is one of *facts*,—collected from notes taken almost daily during the campaign.

It has been no part of his purpose to discuss in these pages the question of "*the origin of the war.*" Concerning that, our politicians have scarcely yet ceased to pass resolutions and make speeches. The mists of passion and prejudice still hang like the smoke wreaths of battle over the unfortunate controversy. Time will soon dissipate them, and the impartial pen of some future historian will treat the subject in a manner which its magnitude and interest and justice to both nations require.

However the final decision of the grave question of its *causes* may affect the character of our government, all will agree that its *prosecution* and *results* redound greatly to the credit and permanent benefit of the United States. For, to judge it fairly,—as a military transaction,—the numbers and positions of the forces actually engaged in the field must be regarded, rather than the power and resources of the belligerent countries.

As in all wars, we are compelled to lament among its consequences, the desolation of many hearts and homes ; but it has also extended the blessings of knowledge and of civil and religious liberty to thousands ; it has brought to us States, rivers and harbors, the possession of which was alone necessary for our political and commercial pre-eminence among the nations of the earth. More than this,—it has solved the problem of this country's strength ; and proved to European Powers, what they had previously denied, that the volunteer armies of the United States were competent to carry on extended and offensive operations and to conduct great wars to a successful issue. These are among its fruits ; and it is believed that,—beside the immense accession to our territory and commerce,—the military reputation resulting from it will tend, under Providence, to aid enlightened statesmen in averting greater bloodshed hereafter.

On this subject it will be sufficient to quote, in conclusion, a few lines from the admirable dispatch of our late distinguished Secretary of State (Mr. Everett) to the British and French governments on the subject of the proposed tripartite treaty for the protection of Cuba. In alluding to the great march of events on this continent, he thus speaks of the splendid results of the Mexican war :—

"Without adverting to the difference of opinion which arose in reference to this war,—as must always happen in free countries in reference to great measures,—no person, surveying these events with the eye of a comprehensive statesman, can fail to trace in the main result, the undoubted operation of the law of our political existence. The consequences are before the world. Vast provinces, which had languished for three centuries under the leaden sway of a stationary system, are coming under the influences of an active civilization. Freedom of speech and the press, the trial by jury, religious equality and representative government, have been carried by the Constitution of the United States into extensive regions in which they were unknown before. By the settlement of California the great circuit of intelligence round the globe is completed. Every addition to the territory of the American Union has given homes to European destitution and gardens to European want. From every part of the United Kingdom, from France, from Switzerland and Germany, and from the extremest north of Europe, a march of immigration has been taken up, such as the world has never seen before. Into the United States, grown to their present extent in the manner described, but little less than half a million of the population of the Old World is annually pouring; to be immediately incorporated into an industrious and prosperous community, in the bosom of which they find political and religious liberty, social position, employment and bread."

CONTENTS.

CHAPTER I.

CHAPTER II.

CHAPTER III.

CHAPTER IV.

CHAPTER V.

CHAPTER VI.

CHAPTER VII.

CHAPTER VIII.

CHAPTER IX.

CHAPTER X.

ERRATUM.

On page 273, line 22, read "skirting the *road*."

SKETCHES

OF THE

CAMPAIGN IN NORTHERN MEXICO.

CHAPTER 1.

The Annexation of Texas—Our Army encamps opposite Matamoros—The Mexican Troops cross the Rio Grande and commence hostilities—General Taylor calls for reinforcements—The War recognized by the Congress and people of the United States—Requisition upon Ohio for three Regiments of Volunteers—They are immediately raised and rendezvous at Camp Washington—Organization of the Ohio Brigade—Embarkation of the First Regiment—The Fourth of July—General Hamer's speech.

At the commencement of President Polk's Administration, our country was involved in two very serious disputes with foreign powers: one with England, the other with Mexico; the subject of the former, the boundary of Oregon; of the latter, that of Texas. Although "Fifty-four Forty or Fight" had been the *shibboleth* of the government party in the national election just passed, the Cabinet at Washington did not seem to think it altogether politic to prosecute both of these quarrels with arms. The Oregon question was, therefore, unraveled by negotiation; that of Texas, cut with the sword. Whether the latter could also have been peaceably adjusted, is one of the questions connected with the origin of the war which it is not my purpose to discuss. *Non nostrum tantas componere lites.*

Pending the settlement of the interesting ante-nuptial contracts between "Uncle Sam" (who, besides being a sad old Mormon in his polygamous tendencies, has a decided *penchant* for the dark-eyed daughters of the South) and Texas, and which resulted in their union; the troops of the former were sent to occupy a convenient position in the territory of the latter, with a view of meeting promptly any presumptuous Mexican knights who might approach to forbid the bans. The command of this "Army of Occupation" was entrusted to General Z. Taylor, whose prudence and firmness eminently qualified him for a task of such importance and delicacy. From August, 1845, to March, 1846, he remained encamped at Corpus Christi, a healthful and convenient location on the coast of Texas. Many years had elapsed since so large a portion of our army had been concentrated in the field, and the general commanding availed himself of the opportunity to establish a system of instruction and discipline, which contributed greatly to its subsequent success.

Meanwhile the annexation of Texas—the *casus belli*—was consummated. The "lone star" was added to our glorious banner, and the President announced the event as a bloodless achievement.

But he, and all of us, learned ere long that

"Those who in quarrels interpose,
Must often wipe a bloody nose."

Our government, believing that the limits of the new state extended to the Rio Bravo del Norte, instructed General Taylor to break up his camp at Corpus Christi, and march to the left bank of that river. If, as many have supposed, the design of this movement was simply to quicken the tardy pace of Mexican diplomacy, an unfortunate mistake was evidently committed in estimating the means necessary to accomplish that object. The little army of three thousand men, which General Taylor displayed upon the frontier, rather invited than averted the threatened war. In the presence of a larger force, it is by no means certain that Paredes, the Dictator of "the magnanimous Mexican nation," would have ventured to authorize those bold and offensive operations which led so suddenly to the first shock of arms.

On the 11th of March, General Taylor marched from Corpus Christi. In the latter part of the same month, after establishing a depôt at Point Isabel, he encamped opposite Matamoros; the garrison of which town was soon afterwards reinforced by a strong division of troops from the interior, under General Arista. From that camp, which the Americans hastened to fortify, "the flag of the stars" was unfurled; and the Mexican authorities were informed that the United States claimed all the territory north of the Rio Grande. There, and then, too, was begun that military correspondence in which the American general proved himself an accomplished master, and by which, no less than by his valor and humanity, he won the admiration of his countrymen.

In the following month (April, 1846) were shed the first red drops of the long impending storm, which, it was even then hoped, would pass away like an April cloud. The Mexican cavalry, having crossed the river, succeeded in killing and capturing some officers and small detachments of our army. Encouraged by the good fortune attending these skirmishes, and the comparatively small number of the opposing camp, General Arista, on the 1st of May, passed his army to the Texan bank of the Rio Grande, and displayed there, for the last time, the banner of his arrogant and vain-glorious country. Learning the hostile attitude of the Mexican general, the American commander immediately called upon the States of Louisiana and Texas for troops. In the meantime, he determined to keep open the communication between his depôt at Point Isabel and his camp opposite Matamoros, both of which were now seriously menaced,—Arista having taken an intermediate position, at Palo Alto, with the design of forcing a battle. Notwithstanding the disparity of numbers, Taylor did not decline the combat; but in a characteristic despatch from Point Isabel, May 7th, he informed his government that he should march that day for Matamoros, and adds, "if the enemy oppose my march, in whatever force, I shall fight him."

The Federal government, meanwhile, informed of the critical position of its army, was seized with apprehension for its safety and success; and, on the 11th of May, the President sent a message to Congress communicating the startling intelligence that war existed with Mexico, and this almost before the announcement that annexation was a "bloodless achievement" had ceased to echo through the halls of the Capitol. On the following day, a bill was passed, by large majorities in both branches of the National Legislature, recognizing the war; appropriating ten millions of dollars, and authorizing the President to accept the services of fifty thousand volunteers for its prosecution. It is, perhaps, to be regretted that there was not perfect unanimity in favor of that important measure; and, indeed, for an earnest and energetic pursuit of the war throughout,—all opposition to which should then have been silenced by humanity, if not by policy and patriotism. To abandon or denounce the government in such an alarming crisis, would only serve to prolong the contest. Peace once broken with such a people—ignorant of our power, and boastful of their own—could only be conquered, and that most effectively and speedily, by united councils at home, and resolute and vigorous action in the field. An accomplished historian (Macaulay) has well remarked, that "if there be any truth established by the universal experience of nations, it is this: that to carry the spirit of peace into war, is a weak and cruel policy. The time of negotiation is the time for deliberation and delay. But when an extreme case calls for that remedy, which is in its own nature most violent, and which, in such cases, is a remedy only because it is violent, it is idle to think of mitigating and diluting. Languid war can do nothing which negotiation or submission will not do better; and to act on any other principle is not to save blood and money, but to squander them."

But I have no quarrel with the opponents of the Mexican war bills. According to the venerable Senator from Michigan, they have not been singular in their sentiment of hostility to the cause of their country.* If, however, they, or any

* "I have seen a great deal of this political perversity,—this unpatriotic predisposition, which prompts many men always to take part against their country, what-

who may come after us, shall perchance, in their efforts to arrest the progress of this Republic, either in peace or war, be run over and crippled by that new and powerful American engine ycleped,—"manifest destiny,"—let them not complain if the popular decision should be as usual, "no blame is attached to the company." But a decided majority of the people, as well as of the Congress, of the United States, were far from being averse to a war with Mexico, whose wrongs and insults to American citizens had been greater for a series of years than those inflicted by all other nations combined. Hence, when it was known that American blood had been shed, and that "the question had reached a point where words must give place to acts," the alacrity with which the people tendered their services to the government. Hence the general enthusiasm, the many public meetings, and the generous con-

---

ever be the position in which she is placed. I do not recollect a single controversy in which we have been involved with a foreign power, since I have been on the stage of action, when the whole sentiment of the country was united in the cause of the country. I doubt if there is another people on the face of the globe whose history presents so many instances of this want of true national pride—patriotism rather—as our own. Whether it results from any peculiar political idiosyncrasy, I know not; or whether our party feelings are so strong that we are blinded by them, and led, in their vehemence, to think that all is wrong our opponents do; or, it may be, at any rate so far as England is concerned, that some of the old colonial leaven remains, which leavens much of the lump. Be it one or the other, or whatever else, the deplorable consequence is certain; and the sentiment of Decatur, not less noble than just,—"Our country, right or wrong"—which, being truly understood,—felt rather—means that when embarked in a controversy with a foreign nation, it becomes every true citizen, after the course of his country has been decided by the constitutional authority, to submit to that authority, and to support her cause, and not the cause of her foes. This noble sentiment finds many who repudiate it,—many who possess the character, without possessing the feelings, of American citizens."—*Extract from a speech delivered by General Cass, in the Senate, January* 15*th*, 1853, *on the resolution reaffirming the Monroe doctrine, concerning the Colonization of this Continent.*

tributions for the support of the families of those whose poverty would otherwise have prevented their enlistment.

It was determined by the War Department to call into immediate service but twenty thousand of the fifty thousand men which the President was authorized to employ. Most of these troops were furnished by the Western States,—Ohio, Indiana, Illinois, Kentucky, and Tennessee—as indeed was the largest portion of those subsequently raised. These five States sent twenty-six regiments of volunteers to the field, besides a very considerable number of recruits for both the old and new regiments of the regular army. A requisition for thirty companies (three regiments) was the first made upon Ohio; and Governor Bartley, on the 20th of May, issued a proclamation appealing to the courage and patriotism of the State to render promptly the required aid. Soon afterwards, Samuel R. Curtis, Adjutant General of the State, established a general rendezvous at Camp Washington, near Cincinnati, to which companies were ordered to repair as soon as organized. In less than two weeks after the requisition of the War Department was received in Ohio, three thousand of her people, having gladly responded to their country's call, were marching towards the rendezvous; and before the middle of June, the tents of forty companies were pitched at Camp Washington. I recall with pleasure, and record with pride, the zeal and enthusiasm with which the "young giant of the West" rushed to the conflict, standing, as it does, in favorable contrast with the conduct of other States, whose chivalry and patriotism it is the fashion to applaud.

During the month of June, companies were assembled at

Camp Washington from all quarters of the State. They were chiefly from the rural districts, where the volunteers had followed those manly and laborious avocations that trained them admirably for the fatigues of war. But every trade and profession was represented in the ranks, so that it was no difficult matter, throughout the campaign, to obtain, upon call, a corps of skillful laborers in any branch of industry. There were workers in metal, wood and leather,—men who could make clothes, harness, wagons, mills, bridges, forts, laws, and pills ; all of whom, of course, knew how to make a *charge.* Several more companies than were necessary to fill the requisition, came to the rendezvous, and those last to arrive were sent home ; not, however, without much clamor and dissatisfaction. But in the following year (1847) some new battalions were raised in Ohio, thus affording the disappointed fire-eaters the desired opportunity of "seeing the elephant," or of "reveling in the Halls of the Montezumas," as the phrase went.

Governor Bartley having divided the thirty companies retained at the camp into three regiments, the officers immediately set about completing their organization by the election of field-officers. Though they were naturally desirous of promoting some of their own numbers, yet two of the regiments very disinterestedly conferred their colonelcys upon gentlemen who had not been connected with the volunteers, with a view of securing the benefits of their previous military experience. And here it may be remarked, that the company officers—who were the electors of the regimental officers—had themselves been previously chosen from the ranks, after having been sworn in as privates. Such, at least, was the just and honorable practice, so far as my observation extended. The three regiments organized at Camp Washington, were composed and commanded as follows:

First Regiment, Colonel A. M. Mitchell; comprising companies from Cincinnati, Dayton, Hamilton, Portsmouth, Georgetown, and Sandusky.

Second Regiment, Colonel G. W. Morgan; composed of companies from Athens, Columbus, Mount Vernon, Newark, Logan, Lancaster, Circleville, Chillicothe, and Hillsborough.

Third Regiment, Colonel S. R. Curtis; of companies from Mansfield, Massilon, Wooster, Norwalk, Steubenville, St. Clairsville, Coshocton, Zanesville, and Seneca.

This Buckeye brigade was soon afterwards reviewed by Gen. Wool, (who was then en route to take command of the column assembling in Texas for the reduction of Chihuahua,) and mustered into the service of the United States for one year. Though within the influence of the many allurements of a populous city, but few of the thousands assembled at the camp failed to apply themselves diligently to the task of learning their new profession. The garb and vocation of the citizen were abandoned together; and with his uniform the volunteer assumed the duties of a soldier. Crowds of citizens from all parts of Ohio, attracted by various motives, were in daily attendance at Camp Washington. Among them were many eminent clergymen, who distributed Bibles and frequently addressed the troops. The sermons of those gentlemen were, as a volunteer remarked, "the only rations of religion issued during the campaign;" for in the army there are no Sabbaths, no days of rest and worship, as they who read these pages will not fail to observe.

Contrary to expectation, but little sickness prevailed in the encampment; and there was only one death during the month we remained at the rendezvous. Toward the end of June, our regiment, (the 1st,) having obtained its outfit of clothing and camp equipage, struck its tents, and entered that shining path which leads "to glory and the grave." The streets of Cincinnati through which we marched, to embark upon "*La Belle Riviere*," were filled with a dense multitude of spectators. There were mothers, wives, sweethearts, fathers, brothers, friends, who eagerly scanned the passing ranks for some familiar face; to which, when recognized, they ran to add another blessing and a last adieu. The friendly volleys of artillery that announced our departure from the wharf, shook stout hearts that afterwards remained unmoved, when "death spoke in every booming shot that knelled upon the ear." Many there were in that band of citizen soldiers, who gazed for the last time upon the beautiful "Queen City of the West," then arrayed in the brilliant robes of summer; on her shoulders, a mantle of the richest green; in her hair, fruitful vines and fragrant flowers; her imperial head tiaraed with gems of rural architecture that sparkled brightly in the morning sun.

The Fourth of July found us afloat on the Mississippi, and still many hundreds of miles above New Orleans. The soldiers, who had not then ceased to be sovereigns, were not disposed to let the birth-day of Independence pass by without the usual amount of jollity and speechifying. With a familiarity, and in terms that would doubtless have shocked the martinets of the regular army, several officers were "called out," and addressed the troops. The last, and of course the best speaker, was General Hamer, who possessed an extended and enviable reputation as an orator, but whom it had never been my good fortune to hear until that day; and never before or since have I listened to a more witching speech. His manner was natural; his gestures, graceful; his words well selected from an abundant store; his figures, beautiful and striking; and his voice, clear and musical as a trumpet. As a few of the men had previously evinced a mutinous disposition, he seized the occasion to denounce a spirit so dangerous to the happiness of the soldier and the success of the regiment. He illustrated the importance of subordination and discipline by examples from history; he dwelt upon the privations and sufferings of the men of the Revolution; teaching his hearers that glory was the sweet fruit of toil and danger, not of idleness and pleasure.

> "For sluggard's brow the laurel never grows,
> Renown is not the child of indolent repose."

Such a speech was not without its influence, and proved again the superior efficacy of words wisely wielded, in the conquest of human passions. Hamer was indeed a perfect master of that eloquence which, either in sprightly conversation or grave discourse, went directly to the soldiers' hearts.

Early in July we arrived at New Orleans, whence the regiment immediately sailed for Brazos Santiago, leaving the writer, who had been attacked by fever on the Mississippi, to mend or end his humble existence in that city, not remarkable for its salubrity in the dog days. Two long weeks of solitude and pain there passed heavily by, during which time the sound of artillery and the hurrahs of the crowds that thronged the streets, daily penetrated to his chamber, announcing the arrival of troops from the North, and their departure for the hostile shores of Mexico.

The governors of Louisiana and Texas, upon whom, it will be remembered, General Taylor had called for reinforcements, had long previous complied with his requisition; but their troops, though raised almost as quickly as the fabled battalions of Cadmus, and transported with the speed of steam, arrived too late to share the first harvest of laurels. The battles of Palo Alto and Resaca de la Palma had been fought and won by our gallant little army. The nation, that had awaited the shock with breathless anxiety, was dazzled by the radiance of those brilliant victories. From that hour, "Old Rough and Ready" became the first of living men in the hearts of his countrymen; and as the gloom of war deepened, the glittering galaxy of his manly virtues shone out with that enduring lustre, which no subsequent calumny could obscure. The battles on the Rio Grande opened a compaign, which, terminating with the perilous conflict on the heights of Buena Vista, need not shrink from a comparison with any in our history; and whatever may be the verdict of posterity concerning the justice of the war, it must ever be conceded that it was conducted on our part with great humanity, and waged to a successful issue with a skill and prowess never surpassed in any quarter of the globe.

CHAPTER II.

Departure from New Orleans—Brazos Santiago—" A man overboard "—Scenes on the Island—A fire in the rear—The mouth of the Rio Grande—Volunteers " falling back on New Orleans"—Burrita—Camp Belknap—The cat-fish war—Sickness and trials of the troops—The battle fields of Palo Alto and Resaca de la Palma.

Despairing of convalescence in the atmosphere of New Orleans, and being anxious to join our regiment before the contemplated invasion of Mexico should be set on foot, a brother officer, also an invalid, and myself, concerted arrangements to decamp. Our medical attendant offered no serious objections, either because he thought our chance of recovery as good in one place as another, or agreed with us in believing that the voyage across the Gulf would dissipate the slow, burning fever which his potions had failed to extinguish. We therefore caused ourselves to be conveyed on board the steamer " Alabama," then about to start for Brazos Santiago. In her cabin were assembled forty or fifty officers, and on her decks a crowd of volunteers ; many of whom, like ourselves, were feeble and emaciated from recent sickness, and not very redoubtable looking soldiers certainly. But all were filled with the ardor and ambition of youth, and were hastening with joyful anticipations to range themselves under the standard of the gallant General from whom they were to receive their first lessons in the art of war. We left New Orleans on the 26th of July, 1846, and anchored off the Brazos before daylight on the morning of the 29th. The weather was intensely hot. Not a breath of wind ruffled the smooth glassy surface of the Gulf, and during the three days occupied in the passage, the feverish invalids watched and panted in vain for the sea breeze which we had hoped would invigorate our wasted bodies. Thanks to the genius of Fulton, ours was a steam ship, and, heedless of the calm, glided in triumph over the slumbering sea. Many unfortunate companies, transported in sail vessels, were two weeks on the voyage. An officer of my acquaintance was becalmed ten days, in a filthy little schooner, in which, as he gravely informed us, "the passengers had to fight like terriers to keep the rats from the cabin table." He ever afterwards spoke of the voyage as the veritable purgatory between *heaven* (the United States) and *hell* (Mexico); commencing many a story or jest with the preface—"When I was in purgatory."

At dawn on the 29th, we hastened on deck to see the land which Spanish chivalry and more recently American courage had invested with charms that kindled the most romantic spirit of adventure. Next to the classic shores of the Mediterranean, those of Mexico and Central America, yet so rich in relics of ancient art, had long been most interesting to me. Who, perusing the brilliant pages of Prescott, does not desire to visit the grand and beautiful scenes, he so grandly and beautifully describes? To revel among the intoxicating perfumes and flowery plains of the *tierra caliente;* to wander among the verdant fields and fruits of the *tierra templada;* to gaze upon the magnificent scenery and wonderful exhibitions of Aztec civilization displayed in profusion throughout the *tierra fria!* To conquer the descendants of the Spanish conquerors, and to plant the flag of our young republic upon the capital reared centuries ago above the ruins of Montezuma's palaces! What prospect more captivating to the youthful imagination?

Our first glimpse, however, of the hostile coast, was not particularly fascinating. The country before us, faintly revealed in the glimmering light of the morning, seemed to be but "a dreary waste, expanding to the sky." A narrow belt of sand, stretching northward as far as the eye could reach, lay between us and the main land. This was intersected by shallow channels, which formed *los brazos de San Iago*, the arms of St. James. On one of the Islands thus formed, was located our principal army depôt; and on the opposite side of the broad lagoon, which was spread out between the Island and the main, was Point Isabel.

A number of large transports lay around us, all full of troops, anxiously awaiting their turn to be disembarked. It was five miles from the anchorage to the Brazos, and though a busy fleet of little steamers and schooners was constantly plying between the ships and the landing, the business seemed to progress but slowly. Many hours elapsed before a lighter approached the Alabama, during which time we sat impatiently gazing upon the desolate picture of water and sand, for not a tree could be seen in the distant perspective. A strong breeze had sprung up with the morning, and when the lighter came alongside, there was such a heavy sea on, that it was no easy matter to transfer our troops and baggage to her deck. While all hands were engaged in the work, that startling cry, "a man overboard," rang through the ship. An eccentric little Frenchman, by profession a cook, in the service of an officer of the Maryland volunteers, had thrown himself into the sea. It was supposed at the moment, that he had fallen from the gangway in attempting to reach the lighter, as the footing was very unsteady and unsafe for lands-men. Fortunately or unfortunately for the rash Gaul, his body would not sink, either in consequence of the spirits it contained, or because it was buoyed by the action of the tide under the two vessels, between which he had precipitated himself. He floated like some huge sea-frog upon the surface, but in imminent danger of being crushed between the ships, whose sides were occasionaly grinding hard against each other. Before that, however, could happen, almost indeed before the alarm was given, the mate of the Alabama, seizing a rope, leaped overboard and rescued Monsieur le Cuisinier, much to his dissatisfaction and disgust evidently, and as he was hauled on deck, dangling and twisting at the end of the rope, he looked daggers at the stout and daring sailor who had so gallantly saved him from the sharks. When it was understood that he had attempted "that poor-soul'd piece of heroism, self-slaughter," the sympathy of the crowd was quickly checked, and many of the spectators kindly wished him "better luck in his next effort."

The scene at the landing was a lively and interesting one. Two or three months previous, the Island had been a wild and uninhabited ridge of sand, whose solitude was broken only by the melancholy dirge of the great waves that broke upon its shore. Now, it was alive with busy men; soldiers, sailors, artizans and others, who were running to and fro like ants among the hillocks the winds had whirled up from its surface. Tradition relates that a flourishing village (flourishing after the Mexican fashion, I presume) formerly existed at Brazos Santiago ; and that one morning, after a terrific storm had raged through the night, the amazed inhabitants of the main land looked out in vain for the hamlet that had so long stood firm amid the billows of the Gulf. The last sun had left it gleaming there like a beautiful shell on the shore ; the next, shone upon a sea of foam that danced wildly o'er its walls. The tempest had come in darkness and wrath, and swallowed up the village and its people, not one of whom is said to have escaped. The island was not inhabited again, until General Taylor occupied it, as a favorable position from which to extend his military operations. The harbor is a very poor and unsafe one ; yet perhaps there are not many better on the coast of Mexico, which, though often swept by destructive tornados, offers but few havens to the navigator.

The only house at the Brazos, was a small frame shed, built but a few yards from the water's edge, and which contained the offices of the quarter-master and commissary of the depôt. It was elevated about three feet from the ground, upon Palmetto logs, and beneath it lay more than a dozen volunteers, who, sorely stricken by disease, had sought its welcome shade. Around and near the building were piled great heaps of provisions and munitions of war. The labor of unloading the vessels and rolling barrels, boxes, etc., across the beach to the dry sand hills, was performed by a gang of swarthy Mexicans. These industrious gentlemen were by no means overdressed, their wearing apparel consisting of a *sombrero* alone. Thus lightly attired, they could labor with impunity under the broiling suns of their native land; and, tempted by high wages, had abandoned for awhile the indolence in which they delight. Mechanics, too, were at work on all sides; and sutlers, with their merchandise displayed under awnings, were busily engaged in supplying, at California prices, the numerous wants of men so suddenly deprived of their ordinary comforts. Farther back from the shore, amid the deep hot sands, four or five lately arrived regiments were encamped, awaiting transportation to the less unpleasant banks of the Rio Grande, distant about eight miles from the island.

At that time, and indeed until a very late period in the campaign, there was a lamentable scarcity of wagons, and consequently our troops were long detained in the suffocating atmosphere of that sandy waste at the Brazos, before they could obtain the means of removing their sick and baggage to the more salubrious location selected for the volunteers in the vicinity of Burrita. Many a poor fellow, choked then with sand and parched with fever, will long remember the sufferings that he endured there. To heighten the misery of the 'soldiers, infectious diseases broke out amongst them. I was informed, that at the time of our arrival, one-fourth of an Indiana regiment was sick with the measles; and the only comfortable hospital at Point Isabel being filled with wounded regulars, these unfortunate volunteers lay at their miserable camp, half buried with the drifting sand. Before the termination of the year, however, many convenient hospitals were established, ample means of transportation were provided, and the comforts of life were so multiplied at all our posts, that the volunteers of 1847 suffered but little in comparison with those of 1846. A government, pursuing the wise policy that distinguishes ours in its military establishments, cannot be expected to set an army in the field, or a navy on the sea, in a day; yet, if the Cabinet had regarded the words of wisdom contained in the somewhat famous letter of the Commander-in-chief, General Scott, our privations would have been comparatively few and trifling, while, at the same time, the true interests of the country would have been promoted. The troops would have been accompanied by all the necessary supplies and matérial of war, and hundreds of Americans rescued from inglorious graves upon the coast, to meet the enemy in battle.

I was detained at Brazos Santiago but a few hours, during most of which time I lay on the beach close to a pile of baggage and camp equipage, so arranged as to afford me some shelter from the sun's rays. Much to my surprise and satisfaction, I was enabled to procure some ice, sold from a Boston vessel at one dollar per pound, which costly and fleeting luxury allayed my fever very much. Having ascertained that my regiment was encamped on the left bank of the Rio Grande, about three leagues from "the mouth," and being as yet too feeble for the saddle, I reëmbarked in a small vessel, bound to the river for a cargo of fresh water. That article, by the way, is not to be found on the island; nor was the water brought from the Rio

Grande very fresh or palatable after standing in barrels. Of course, all kinds of liquor were at a premium in that thirsty place. This scarcity doubtless prompted to an amusing trick, whereby, as will be perceived, a tolerably shrewd Yankee got a "fire in the rear," which demolished his calculations for a small fortune. Jonathan had by some means obtained a barrel of cider, with which small stock he determined to "set up" business. To scrape together a few boards and odd bits of canvass, enough to build a small shed, was but the work of a brief hour; to set his barrel on a couple of skids in the back part of the tent, to tap it and to commence retailing the cider at two dimes a glass, occupied but a short time more. Customers flocked in by dozens, and our Yankee was making his "etarnal fortin" at a stride. Some of his patrons complained, that two dimes a glass for cider was an outrageous price; but the times were hard as well as hot, whisky scarce, water bad, the retailer's conscience easy; he had all the cider in the market, and he "ralely could not afford to sell any cheaper."

For several hours the Yankee was as popular as a paymaster, crowds filled his shanty, his cider went off rapidly, and the deep pockets of his short-legged pantaloons contained silver enough to start a free bank in Indiana. But the tide of fortune unfortunately began to ebb before the cider was half sold; his patrons gradually fell off, and by the middle of the afternoon, Jonathan was left alone with his barrel, to whittle and cogitate upon the mutability of trade; speculating it may be, too, as to the time required in that climate to convert apple juice into vinegar. Towards evening, a customer appeared in the tent, and called for a glass of cider. The retailer hastened to draw the desired potation. The customer, after drinking, took out his purse and inquired the price.

"Two dimes," said the Yankee.

"Two what?" exclaimed the customer.

"Two dimes," coolly replied Jonathan.

"Two devils," snarled the customer; "why I can get just as good cider here for five cents a glass."

"No you can't," drawled the Yankee; "there aint a pint of cider 'cept what I've got in that are barril this side of Orleans, I'm darned if there is."

"I know better," indignantly retorted the purchaser; "I bought a glass not an hour ago, and only paid five cents for it."

"I'd like to know just where you effected that small transaction?" inquired the Yankee.

"Right round here," was the answer.

"I guess it was—*right round here;* right round *where*, I'd like to know?" continued the cider seller.

"Why, close by here somewhere, just back of your place:" rejoined the customer.

"I'll bet you tu drinks you did'nt," said the Yankee, "and we'll go right round and see."

"Done," responded the customer; and off they started.

Sure enough, "*right round there*" they found another establishment in full blast. A second Yankee had rigged an awning behind the first Yankee's shed, had tapped the rear end of the aforesaid cider barrel through a board, and was retailing it at five cents a glass to a perfect rush of customers.

We had a short but rough passage from Brazos Santiago to the mouth of the Rio Grande; as the Gulf, long so calm, was then lashed into fury by the winds. In attempting to enter the river, our little vessel was driven upon the bar, and remained through the night in that dangerous position; the surf breaking, at intervals, completely over her. A schooner, which lay aground quite near us, was compelled to give the most valuable part of her cargo to the ravenous ocean, that, in truth, seems to be "at eternal war with man." Old Neptune was evidently propitiated by the gift, for soon afterwards, much to our joy, the wind abated, and with the flood tide of the morning we entered the celebrated Rio Bravo del Norte.

It is quite a narrow river at its mouth, not more than three or four hundred yards wide, but in the wet season disembogues an immense volume of water. On the right bank at that place, is a small collection of mud and reed huts, occupied by Mexican fishermen and herdsmen. The latter pasture large herds of cattle in the marshes, which extend many miles back from the coast on both sides of the river. This miserable village was, I believe, called by the natives, Resguardo; but among our people it was known as the City of Bagdad. When we revisited it, on our return to the United States in the following year, it had been somewhat improved and Americanized. The few poor brown and bare-legged fishermen having been initiated into some of the mysteries of our elective system, were then engaged in an animated canvass for the high office of Alcalde. A Yankee, perhaps the sharp cider dealer of Brazos Santiago, was the democratic candidate, and treated the sovereigns to bad liquor and worse stump speeches alternately. As we were told by those who listened to one of his harangues, that he took good care to represent himself as the only disinterested friend and obedient servant of the people; and denounced his opponent, who, by the way, was some poverty-stricken and ragged Mexican, as an aristocratic whig; in short, a despot in disguise; it is probable that Jonathan was triumphantly elected, and the country saved from the sword and chains of a tyrant.

We landed on the Texan bank of the river, opposite Bagdad, where was located another of our army depôts. At that place, which was known throughout the war as "the mouth," we beheld the same scenes of uproar, confusion, and bustle, that had been witnessed the previous day at the Brazos. Soldiers, sailors, and sutlers, clerks, cooks, and camp-followers—a motley multitude, all "full of strange oaths and bearded like the pard," were crowded along the shore among barrels, boxes, tents, wagons, and artillery. The naked Mexican laborers appeared to be the only people silent and really at work. At "the mouth" we met the army of "three months' volunteers," who had hastened to join General Taylor at the commencement of hostilities; and who were then, as one of their number jocosely remarked, *falling back on New Orleans.* It is a fact, which certain gasconaders, who engage in the poor business of estimating the amount of blood and sweat that each section of our Union expended in the war, will do well to bear in mind, that six regiments of Louisiana volunteers, one of Texas (foot), a battalion of Alabama, and one of Missouri Infantry, retired from the frontier without firing a gun or even seeing the foe. Of all those mentioned, but one company (Captain Blanchard's, of Louisiana) remained. The residue, declining to extend their term of service to twelve months, were discharged by order of the War Department.

After a short detention, caused by the usual parley with the quarter-master of the post, we obtained transportation on a small river steamer to the village of Burrita, around which the volunteer army was encamped. The village is situated on the first inland elevation ; and is but eight miles from the coast by the road, though fifteen by the river,—so crooked is the course of the stream, as it doubles through the intervening plain. It was the middle of the rainy season, and the swollen Grande poured along with such an impetuous current, that we were nearly four hours in reaching our destination. All of that time our boat was paddling to and fro across the marshes, with, as it appeared to me, one or the other broadside constantly turned toward the village and camp, which were in full view all the way. The appearance of Burrita, composed of a score of mud hovels, ludicrously recalled the glowing panegyrics with which some of our editors, a month previous, had announced the capture of that *stronghold* of the Mexican nation. "GLORIOUS NEWS FROM THE ARMY! ANOTHER TRIUMPH! BURRITA HAS FALLEN! THE ENTIRE CITY REDUCED TO ASHES!!" Such was the startling caption of the extras which the news-carriers thrust under the spectacles of peaceable and nervous old gentlemen in our cities, and who, as they read, doubtless in imagination saw—

> "High towers, fair temples, goodly theaters,
> Strong walls, rich porches, princely palaces,
> Fine streets, brave houses, sacred sepulchres,
> Sure gates, sweet gardens, stately galleries,
> All these (oh, pity!) now turn'd to dust."

My regiment had spread its canvas on the Texan bank of the Rio Grande, opposite Burrita, among some scrubby trees and bushes; which, however insignificant as specimens of the vegetable kingdom, relieved the eye, and afforded some protection from the clouds of scorching sand that, rising on the gulf shore, often rolled inland upon the breeze like pillars of fire. This location was called "Camp Belknap,"—the name of an officer of the General Staff, who had selected it. On entering the camp, and finding myself surrounded by so many familiar faces, I really felt like one who had just reached home after a long absence. From that hour my pertinacious fever began to succumb, though it was several weeks before it released me from its grasp. Many of our men, in their acclimation, suffered in a like manner—their fevers appearing to rise and go down with the sun, thus daily and gradually consuming the strength, and sapping the constitution of the most robust. Young troops, entering upon the duties and dangers of an active campaign, are not subject to ennui; and though during our stay at Camp Belknap much sickness prevailed, our life was one of cheerful excitement and bustle. The officers and men were attentive and industrious, and earnestly commenced upon a thorough system of instruction and discipline. On entering the field with the troops of other

States, a desirable *esprit du corps* had been awakened. A kindly feeling also existed between the officers and soldiers, which was strongly cemented by the common trials and triumphs of the campaign. There were some accomplished and agreeable officers in the First Ohio regiment, whose unassuming manners, united with happy social qualities, cheerful wit and humor, rendered them pleasant companions, and enlivened many a dreary scene. The legal profession was well represented among them, as indeed it was in every corps—so numerous as almost to verify Dryden's verse,

"Soldiers the lawyers, and the bar the field."

I have thought that a green bag would have been no inappropriate banner for the volunteer army.

The evening of my arrival at Camp Belknap, I received from our adjutant (who, if reports be correct, did not, on the occasion, place himself in the way of sharing very largely in the beatitude promised the peace-makers,) an amusing account of a difficulty that had occurred between our regiment and the Baltimore battalion, originating in *the larceny of a cat-fish* belonging to our colonel; and which trifling cause had nearly resulted in a disgraceful fight between the two regiments. At that time, Colonels M. and W., the commanders of the belligerent battalions were absent, having gone to head-quarters at Matamoros in consequence of the affair. Various accounts of the row reached the newspapers at home; and in the dearth of more interesting intelligence, their readers were regaled with some entertaining reports of the "cat-fish war." It is to be regretted that the ill-feeling aroused by this quarrel, was permitted, by one of the parties concerned, to manifest itself at a subsequent interesting period.

Between Camp Belknap and the river was a swamp, about a mile in width, through which, from the want of wagons, the men were compelled to wade for all their provisions,—the tent of the commissary being pitched upon the banks of the Rio Grande. All our water, too, was brought from the river; for the ponds in the vicinity of our camp were salt, and the few wells that were dug were as bitter as the fountain of Marah. These supplies were carried in barrels, swung on poles, the ends of which rested upon the aching shoulders of the volunteers, and sinking them knee-deep in the mire. Much of the sickness that so thinned the ranks of the army on the coast was perhaps induced by the severity of these necessary labors. To their ignorance of the art of cooking, however, must be attributed many of the common and painful complaints with which the soldiers suffered, for at that time they had not penetrated far into the mysteries of the culinary science. After a few weeks' practice, when they had learned how best to prepare their food, that class of diseases disappeared. While we lay at Camp Belknap,—nearly two weeks—about one hundred of the eight hundred, rank and file, contained in our regiment, were daily reported on that melancholy catalogue, the surgeon's morning return. Many were at once disabled, and discharged from further service. Indeed I do not think we could have mustered more than six hundred bayonets at Camargo, and scarcely five hundred at Monterey, so rapidly did the climate, like a skillful anatomist, designate and discard all the unsound men. The great number of lives lost by disease in Mexico has caused a very general belief among our people that the country is unfavorable to health. But it must be remembered, in this connection, that our army landed there at the very worst season, and, indeed, the only unpleasant one of the year. The low grounds were overflowed, and the whole country saturated with water, the exhalations from which were quickened by the heat of summer into pestilent malaria. For weeks (until September) it rained every day; not continuously, but at intervals, in sudden and drenching showers, each followed by a burst of melting sunshine. These deluging rains cooled the enthusiasm of a few modern paladins, who found but little romance in the privations and sober realities of the camp.

Among the little *désagréments* attending our sojourn on the lower Rio Grande, not the least were caused by the venomous insects and reptiles that swarmed on those burning sands, and allowed us no repose. Our camp was infested by snakes, tarantulas, ants, centipedes, lizards, horned toads, scorpions, fleas, spiders,—*et id genus omne*. Of these, the ants were, I think, the most annoying. They not only found their way into our food, but attacked our persons boldly, crawling into our blankets or clothes, and stinging with remarkable severity. But the far-famed tarantula was most dreaded. Our assistant surgeon was bitten by one of them, and his was the only case of the kind in our regiment. The effect of the poison was immediate and alarming. So violent were his spasms, that the united strength of several men was required to confine him to his tent, from which he had deliriously rushed soon after receiving the wound.

The consecrated and still ensanguined fields of Palo Alto and Resaca de la Palma, were not many leagues distant from Camp Belknap; and during our stay there, many of our people took occasion to visit them, in company sometimes with those who had witnessed, and could communicate many thrilling incidents of the battles. It was well ascertained that the enemy had at least five thousand fighting men at Palo Alto, while General Taylor's effective force did not much exceed two thousand. Many officers with whom I conversed on the subject united in attributing their success mainly to the artillery. In the action of the 8th of May, was first demonstrated, in the practical operations of war, the wonderful perfection of our light field-batteries. The prairie upon which the hostile forces met, was admirably adapted for their evolutions, and they made terrible havoc in the Mexican ranks. The distinguished *Guarda Costa* battalion of Tampico, is said to have been almost extinguished by the artillery, so boldly and brilliantly manœuvered by Duncan and Ringgold. It is also affirmed that, by a single discharge of one of these batteries, an entire band of Mexican musicians was exterminated, while executing one of their grand martial bravuras.

It is not improbable that General Arista, perceiving at Palo Alto how a complete knowledge of the artillery arm equalized the strength of armies differing so greatly in numbers, was thereby induced to fall back on the morning of the 9th to the broken and covered ground at Resaca, where the bayonet and sabre should decide the combat. But there again his *quantity* yielded to what General Taylor calls in his official report, "the superior *quality* of our officers and men;" and the Mexicans were completely routed, "horse and foot." Confused and panic-stricken, they fled to the Rio Grande, and hundreds escaped the wrath of the battle only to perish in its waves. A few days before, that scattered and flying army had crossed it elated with hope and assured of victory. Nothing can be more conclusive of the confidence which General Arista had in the result, than the fact that he, a soldier of considerable talent and experience, unprovided with pontoons, should decide to hazard a battle with a deep unbridged river in his rear; a position from which, in the event of defeat, would result the loss of his army, and open the northern frontier of his country to our victorious arms. The entire Mexican army had crossed to the Texan bank in two small boats, thus causing a delay of twenty-four hours, by which Arista had been prevented from attacking Taylor on his march from Fort Brown to Point Isabel, on the 2d of May, as he intended. Under the circumstances, it is not strange that the Mexican army, on reëntering Matamoros, should be diminished to one-fifth of its original strength; or that it should be wary of again offering battle in the open field. We shall see how strongly and judiciously it was posted in the next engagement of the war. The Mexican historians ascribe the loss of the battles of the Rio Grande to the distrust and jealousy which existed between Generals Arista and Ampudia. It was currently reported among the Mexicans that General Don Pedro de Ampudia was the first to abandon the field of Resaca; and from his conduct in subsequent battles, there arises a suspicion that Senor Pedro is duly impressed with the conviction that

> "Timely running's no mean part
> Of conduct in the martial art."

CHAPTER III.

The Mexican Army under General Ampudia prepares to defend Monterey—General Taylor's order regulating the movement to Camargo—Departure from Camp Belknap—The valley of the Rio Grande, its people and productions—A Sabbath in Matamoros—Reynosa—A Fandango—The Stag-dance—Death of a Volunteer—A pleasant interchange of visits with a Mexican family—Arrive at Camargo—A glimpse at Head-Quarters and General Taylor.

After the two sanguinary engagements on the northern bank of the Rio Grande, General Arista solicited an armistice, which was refused by General Taylor, who stated in reply, that a month previous he had proposed one to the Mexican General, which had then been declined; that circumstances were now changed; that he was receiving large reinforcements, and could not suspend operations which he had not initiated or provoked. Perceiving that the Americans were determined to crown their victories with the conquest of Matamoros, the broken and dispirited battalions of the Mexican army evacuated the town at twilight on the 17th of May, and retreated to Linares, which place they reached on the 28th, suffering every misfortune in their mournful retreat. We are informed that "many of the soldiers perpetrated suicide; and that General Garcia, a chivalrous man and an illustrious citizen, died during the march of profound grief." *

* These facts are stated upon the authority of a Mexican history of the war, entitled, "The Other Side, or Notes for the History of the War between the United States and Mexico;" written by a *junta* of Mexican officers, and translated by

In the month of July the remnant of that unlucky army was united with fresh troops at Monterey,—a city situated at the base of the Sierra Madre, near the entrance of the principal pass leading up to the table lands of the interior. The Mexican government, learning the disastrous result of the conflicts at Palo Alto and Resaca, and desiring, as usual, to throw the blame upon the unsuccessful general, deprived Arista of the command of the army of the North. He was succeeded by General Mejia. Soon afterwards, however, the Central Government was itself overthrown, and Mejia was in turn superseded by Ampudia, who undertook, as "Governor General-in-chief," the defense of Monterey.

Meantime the American regulars had occupied Matamoros, while the tents of the rapidly arriving volunteers dotted the banks of the river, at various points, between that town and the Gulf. In the latter part of July, General Taylor began to push forward the regular troops to Camargo, a town situated near the head of steamboat navigation on the San Juan, a tributary of the Rio Grande. To that point, by water, it was no difficult matter to transport men and supplies. But beyond it, in consequence of the limited resources of the country, but a small force could be taken with our inadequate means of land carriage. Yet such was the anxiety of the government to hasten operations, that General Taylor determined to march from Camargo upon Monterey with but six thousand men,—half regulars and half volunteers,—unpro-

---

Colonel Ramsey, of the 11th United States Infantry. In that book, to which the reader's attention will occasionally be invited in the following pages, the frightful disorders and hardships of the retreats from Matamoros and Buena Vista are vividly portrayed.

vided with a siege train, and with scarcely transportation enough at the command of his Quarter-Master for a single division. But in Taylor's hands, enterprises of great pith and moment were not to be balked by ordinary obstacles. When the number of troops intended for the reduction of Monterey was made known, a strong desire was manifested by the volunteers to learn which of the regiments would be selected for that honorable service, as all were averse to an indolent garrison life on the frontier. That interesting question was not decided until after our arrival at Camargo; nor were the volunteer troops organized into divisions and brigades until we reached that place. The following communication, however, which was received at Camp Belknap early in August, indicated with tolerable clearness to some anxious spirits that they were not to be included in the glorious six thousand. Being an important order, it is quoted in *extenso*, as it will explain not only the disposition first made of the volunteers, but may also serve to inform the reader of the numbers, commanders, and States of the various regiments in the field.

Orders No. 93. } *Head-Quarters, Army of Occupation, Matamoros, July* 30, 1846.

1. The commanding General being about to leave for Camargo, the following arrangements for regulating the movements of the troops, and the service generally, in the rear, are announced for the government of all concerned.

2. Four companies of artillery, under the command of Brevet Major Brown, now under orders for Camargo, will be

the first to ascend the river. They will be followed, as rapidly as transportation can be provided, by the following corps, in the order named:

Louisville Legion, (1st Kentucky regiment,) Col. Ormsby.
Baltimore and Washington battalion, Lieut. Col. Watson.
Ohio brigade, Brigadier General Hamer.
Second Kentucky regiment, Colonel McKee.
Mississippi regiment, Colonel Davis.
First Tennessee regiment, Colonel Campbell.
Alabama regiment, Colonel Coffee.
Georgia regiment, Colonel Jackson.
Second Tennessee regiment, Colonel Haskell.

3. The Indiana brigade, and the regiment from Missouri and Illinois, will remain below until further orders. The regiments of Texas volunteers will receive particular orders for their movement.

4. Brigadier General Hamer is assigned to the command of the Ohio brigade. He will designate one of the regiments to proceed immediately by water to Matamoros, and take such position as may be indicated by Colonel Clarke, commanding in the town, to whom the Colonel of the regiment will report for orders.

5. The first four corps destined for Camargo, viz:—the Louisville legion, Baltimore battalion, and two regiments Ohio volunteers, will send their heavy baggage forward by water, with four companies of each regiment and two of the Baltimore battalion. The remaining companies of each corps, with their light baggage, will take up their line of march for Camargo as soon as provided with wagons by the Quarter-Master's Department,—say by the 10th of August.

6. The other corps destined for Camargo, viz :—the Tennessee, Mississippi, Alabama, and Georgia regiments, and the Second Kentucky regiment, will move forward by water as rapidly as practicable, in the order prescribed in the second paragraph.

7. Brigadier General Twiggs will remain at Matamoros in command of all the troops in the vicinity until the last volunteer regiment shall pass up by land, when he will move forward with the dragoons and horse artillery to Camargo. On his departure, Colonel Clarke will assume command of all the troops in and near Matamoros, on both banks of the river. Colonel Clarke will receive special instructions for his government in this command.

8. The artillery and train of the third brigade, with the rear companies, will march by the 5th of August, under Lieutenant Colonel Garland.

By order of Major General Taylor:

W. W. S. Bliss,
Assistant Adjutant General.

In accordance with the foregoing order, General Hamer designated the Third Ohio regiment, Colonel Curtis's, for the garrison of Matamoros. The First and Second Ohio regiments, Mitchell's and Morgan's, proceeded to Camargo in the manner mentioned in the fifth paragraph. It was my fortune, being yet on the sick list, to go by water with the four companies detached from our regiment. A frail and filthy little steamboat was provided for our transportation; and on the 8th of August, after exchanging adieus with our companions who were compelled to take the weary land route, we pushed off from Camp Belknap, and commenced the ascent of the Rio Grande.

Owing to high water, the ignorance of pilots, who, being unaccustomed to the river, were unable to steer at night, and the fact that our boat was chartered by the day, we were more than a week in getting to Camargo. It had not been long since the first steamboat ascended the river, and, to the natives, it was yet an object of intense curiosity. At all the *rancherias* on the banks, a throng of people—women, children, and even old men tottering with infirmity—were assembled to stare at our boat as it struggled slowly up against the rushing and roaring stream. At that period, but few woodyards had been established, and we were sometimes compelled to take the troops ashore to gather the pickets inclosing the fields, to be used as fuel. Occasionally, too, we were detained at places where the river, in its whole length brimfull, had overrun its banks and covered the country for miles, forming wide lagoons in which our pilots had to sound for the channel. In these bayous were to be seen large flocks of water-fowl; and not unfrequently the bloated carcases of animals, navigated by piratical-looking vultures, floated slowly through the circling eddies.

Mexico—bare, dry, and mountainous as it is, for the most part—was naturally enough called "New Spain," by the conquerors, from the resemblance of its principal features and productions to those of the Peninsula. It is particularly deficient in good harbors and navigable streams. Of the latter, the Rio Grande is the most important; but the people have not availed themselves of the facilities which even that affords. The river, as it meanders through the *tierra caliente*, offers but few beauties to the eye of the traveler. Nothing is hazarded in asserting that it is the most crooked stream on the continent, since it far surpasses the Mississippi in the number and magnitude of its curves. For hundreds of miles, its yellow waves, pent in by muddy banks, roll through a lonely champaign country, undiversified by majestic cliffs or shadowy woods. Like a great serpent which has lost its brilliant and varying hue, it fails to charm. If it were but straight, its homeliness would be complete. So far as I could hear or observe, it has not a single tributary between its mouth and the Rio San Juan; a fact suggestive of arid wastes, which the mind, touched by remembrance, did not fail to contrast with the many bubbling brooks and enchanting groves that beautify and refresh the Atlantic slope of the United States. As there are no forests on its banks, there are of course no snags or sawyers to excite the fears of the voyager; and its navigation is far more tedious than hazardous. The country, however, is well clothed with *chaparral;* and groves of the more lofty *mesqueet* are abundant in the valley. The former, as the reader is perhaps aware, is a low evergreen thorn; the latter, a tree resembling the peach somewhat in appearance, and of not much larger growth.

The valley of the Rio Grande abounds in fine, nutritious grass, which, after the wet season, dries upon the stalk, and becomes excellent hay. It is but sparsedly populated, yet these plains, interspersed with clumps of mesqueet, gave to many places the appearance of high cultivation, when viewed from a distance. The broad and verdant lawns skirting the river, afford good pasture throughout the year to the large herds of cattle roaming over them. The cattle far exceed in size any of the common herds of the United States; owing, perhaps, to the fact that they never experience any cold or starving winters, but grow and fatten from their calfhood. The quality of their flesh, however, is much inferior to that of our northern stock. This wild beef, together with salt pork, beans, and hard biscuit, constituted our rations. But they were dainties to a campaign appetite,—hunger furnishing a better sauce than epicure ever invented. At some spots along the river, we noticed a few beautiful flowers and luxuriant plants, whose broad and glossy leaves told of an exuberant soil, stimulated by the great heat and moisture of the season. Mexico, from its remarkable terraced formation, enjoying every variety of climate, is said to possess the richest and most diversified Flora to be found in any country on the globe. The soil is not generally poor,—the nakedness of the interior plains being caused by the scorching sun and absence of water, rather than by any natural barrenness. The banks of the Rio Grande are in places chequered with patches of maize, sugar-cane, and cotton, whose large stalks attest the fertility of the soil; and of these products, two crops may be raised annually in all situations where irrigation can be effected. An industrious, well-governed people could make the valley "stand so thick with corn that it would laugh and sing." But the Mexicans, naturally indolent, are oppressed by a government that fosters neither agriculture nor any of the productive arts which are the surest source of public and individual prosperity. Nay, so far from encouraging enterprise, it imposes severe restrictions upon it, and, together with a numerous and avaricious priesthood, is continually and corruptly sapping what little of energy yet remains among the people. Is it strange, then, considering this vampirism of church and state, that the principal productions of the country should be *pronunciamiéntos*, *priests*, and *prickly-pears?*

The cultivation of the soil, in northern Mexico, is slovenly in the extreme. Agriculture there is yet the veriest drudgery; as it always must be when not pursued with system and intelligence. The labors of the farmer, in our country, now rendered comparatively light and pleasant by the improvements which science and the inventive genius of our people have suggested, are there performed, of course, at a great disadvantage, with the most antiquated implements of husbandry. At a rancho on the Rio Grande, near which we landed for wood, we had an opportunity of examining for the first time a Mexican plow. It may be best and briefly described as a forked stick pointed, with a huge ox horn as a substitute for a share. Not a particle of metal was employed in its construction, and probably it was only serviceable for scratching the alluvial borders of the river. It was just such an implement as has been used for centuries on the banks of the Nile; and was fashioned much like that curious specimen of eastern art—the Syrian plow—which was exhibited, in the midst of many beautiful modern American tools, like a senseless mummy, among the active and useful agents of agriculture, at the Ohio State Fair, held at Columbus in 1851.

Domestic animals are numerous in Mexico, but they are

very inferior to ours. The mustangs possess scarcely more than half the size and strength of our northern horses, and are entirely unsuited for farm work or military service. Many of them exhibit marks of fine blood, but from the effect of climate or food, neglect or close breeding, they have sadly degenerated from their famous Andalusian ancestry. The Mexicans are a nation of horsemen, or mulemen,—even the beggars are mounted. I never saw one traveling *a pied.* None are so poor as not to have a riding animal; they throw the lariat too well for that. With them, the mule and ass are literally "beasts of burden," and often made to carry immense loads. The ox is generally used for draught at the plow, and may sometimes be seen clumsily attached by the horns to a heavy, unwieldy sort of tumbrel, with low, thick wheels of solid wood, and which, though a sufficiently picturesque object, would be considered a decidedly slow coach by our go-ahead people. The fact that the Mexicans have existed so long on the boarder of "the universal Yankee nation," without profiting by any of the useful inventions of our country and age, is evidence of a sloth and degeneracy, which, if not soon arrested, must, at no very remote period, terminate in the ruin of their republic and race.

In contemplating the entire *status* of the people,—their political, religious, social, and intellectual condition—no attentive observer, even among themselves, has failed to foresee and lament the fate of the country. It must gradually sink, from its complication of fatal diseases, into the tomb of the Acolhuans and the Aztecs. And not only Mexico, but the whole of Spanish America, will probably pass from the dominion of the original conquerors into the possession of the enterprising blue-eyed Saxon—the chosen people of the age; who, by the way, are even now "prospecting" in the rich basins of the Amazon and La Plata. So few are the wants of man in those soft and genial climes, that they are easily satisfied by fitful and desultory exertion. And as long as the people do not feel the pressure of that necessity which makes intelligent and industrious citizens, they will continue to be vagrant herdsmen and shepherds. The man, too, who merely wanders over a country with his flocks, rarely forms the same attachment for it, and is seldom as able to defend it, as he who mingles the sweat of his brow with its soil as it is upturned by his hands.

The inhabitants of the valley of the Rio Grande are chiefly occupied in raising stock; the wool, hides, and tallow of which constitute the exports of the port of Matamoros. But a pastoral life, generally so propitious to purity of morals and strength of constitution, does not appear to have produced its usually happy effect upon that people, Poets, from the earliest days of their art, have been most gracious and complimentary to all engaged in that primative and innocent occupation. Those men were shepherds too, who, "as they watched their flocks by night, all seated on the ground," were made the honored recipients of the most joyful tidings ever communicated by shining angels to sinning man. But neither poets nor seraphs, I ween, would tune their harps to the praises of these vile rancheros; the majority of whom are so vicious and degraded that one can hardly believe that the light of Christianity has ever dawned upon them. Many of the country people are in quite as "parlous a state" as shepherd Corin, whom that rare fellow, Touchstone, makes the subject of some exquisite fooling. They are just such "*natural* philosophers," and know simply "that the property of rain is to wet, and fire to burn; that good pasture makes fat sheep; and that a great cause of the night is lack of the sun." Never elsewhere have I seen such an idle, ignorant, and unenterprising a community. Their habitations are constructed of the most flimsy materials, and utterly devoid of taste or comfort. Along the river we saw some formed of hides, fastened to a light frame work, and many of reeds placed upright in the ground, and interwoven and thatched with leaves or grass. These domiciles are decorated with rude crucifixes, and perhaps a few wretched prints of the Virgin, or "Our Lady of Gaudaulupe," the greatest of the native Mexican saints. How striking was the contrast everywhere with the United States, in which personal comforts of every kind are inconceivably multiplied and brought within the reach of all!

The population of Mexico is said to be about eight millions; more than half of whom are pure blooded Indians, and the remainder of every cross and color. Three-fourths or more of the inhabitants of the Northern States are of unmixed Indian blood. With scarcely an exception, the country people are brown, broad, and big-headed bipeds; and it is only in the towns that the traveler sees the fair complexion, regular features, and graceful forms of Castilé. In regarding the aspect, bearing, and manners of modern Mexicans, it is difficult to believe that many of them can be the descendants of that chivalrous Spanish race which once gave laws to both hemispheres; or, of that fierce Aztec tribe, which, after centuries of warfare, pushed the boundaries of their empire from a little village of reeds in the marshes of Lake Tezcuco, to the shores of the Atlantic and Pacific. The sad and sinking steps by which our sister republic—the oldest, and once the strongest and wealthiest, power on this continent—has arrived at her present low estate, and her people made the bondman of even the bold barbarians on her borders, are known to every reader.

> "'Twere lŏng to tell and sad to trace
> Each steps from splendor to disgrace."

Now, instead of subjugating neighboring tribes, extending the limits of their territory, and enriching themselves with crowds of prisoners, the Mexicans are unable to defend their own provinces from Indian invasion; and it is stated that there are not less than four thousand of their women and children at this time enslaved by the wild warriors who wander over the vast plains and hills washed by the waters of the Rio Grande. How applicable to Mexico the words of the prophet: "Wo to thee that spoilest, and thou wast not spoiled; and dealest treacherously, and they dealt not treacherously with thee! When thou shalt cease to spoil, thou shalt be spoiled; and when thou shalt make an end to deal treacherously, they shall deal treacherously with thee!" We commend those unhappy captives to the *generous* and *disinterested* sympathies of our ardent Flibustiers, and trust that their next foray in the cause of freedom and the rights of mankind will be to the Camanché country, instead of Cuba.

The towns on the Rio Grande are few and insignificant.

Matamoros, the largest of them, is about fourteen leagues by land from the coast. We did not reach it, however, until the afternoon of the day after our departure from Camp Belknap. On passing "Fort Brown," which is rather below the city, our men greeted the star-spangled banner, that then floated in triumph o'er its battered walls, with many hearty cheers. The fort, as well as the village, Brownsville, that has since sprung up around it, takes its name from the gallant Major who was killed while defending it. Though but a common and hastily constructed field-work, it had sustained successfully for one hundred and sixty hours a severe cannonade of shot and shells. We landed near the Mexican Fort Parades, on the southern bank.

Matamoros is situated on a beautiful plain, half a mile from the river, and from the landing it presented a very picturesque appearance. But a short walk toward it, proved that distance had lent its wonted illusions to the view. The beautiful suburban gardens and cottages that we had so much admired in our first glimpse of the town, were found upon a closer inspection to be cow-pens and contemptible huts. Around the Plaza—for every Mexican village has its public square—and on some of the principal streets, there are a few respectable dwellings of two stories, built of *adòbes*, or large unburnt bricks. The doors and windows are small, and most of the latter are protected by stout iron bars, which cause the houses to resemble so many prisons. Nor were the sulky and swarthy faces peering through some of them at the passers by, in the least calculated to remove the impression. The streets are narrow, unpaved, and, at that season, were very muddy. The town had not suffered in the bombardment, owing to its distance from Fort Brown, and the small calibre of our guns. At the American hotel, in the *calle de Terran*, we were shown some balls which had been thrown by Bragg's battery into the adjacent garden. Such souvenirs of those perilous days in May were interesting to us, who had yet to hear

> "The death-shot hissing from afar—
> The shock, the shout, the groan of war."

In our stroll through the streets, we saw many *senoritas*, sitting at the windows—a favorite position—chatting and smoking; for all the women, even of the most polished circles, use the fragrant weed. They are all alike, too, in having large dark eyes and black glossy hair; the last, it is intimated, is not unseldom frequented by those "ugly, sprawlin, crowlin ferlies," which the Ayrshire poet once observed upon a lady's bonnet, and so humorously addressed. In this, as in many other respects, did some of our young and adventurous soldiers, in whose minds romance and poetry had painted glowing pictures of Spanish beauty and grandeur, suffer a disagreeable disenchantment in the city of Matamoros.

Of course, the foregoing remarks will not be understood as referring to the *upper tendom* of Matamoros. But the women of Mexico,—superior in all classes to the men—even of the best society, do not contrast very favorably with their sex in our country, either in their mental or personal charms. True, their tresses may be like the raven's wing; their eyes may "shame a night of starlight gleams;" but among them is rarely seen

> "That purity and modesty of mien,
> The mind, the music breathing from the face,"

which so enhances loveliness in woman, and stamps her—angel. Give me the blue eyes, fair locks, and snowy hands, of our northern clime.

During our stay at Matamoros we visited the market plaza, where we saw a goodly quantity and variety of fruits and vegetables,—some of them quite new to us. But little space was devoted to butchers' stalls, from which, and subsequent observation, I inferred that the people consumed much less meat than we carnivorous Americans. The crowd of men and women assembled there, citizens and rustics, were all smoking. The towns people were generally pretty well dressed; but the costume of the countrymen was plain, and peculiar enough to be interesting. Scandals of thick hide, coarse cotton trowsers, the unsightly national *sombrero*, with the indispensable blanket, comprise their raiment. Some wear jerkins and pants of leather, both ornamented with jingling bell-buttons, which, with their huge iron spurs, cause a great rattle and clatter at every movement. To the Rancheros, who wear this economical apparel,—so suitable to their occupation in the thorny chaparral—the Texans have given the expressive name of Greasers. One has but to see them clad in their leather armor, shining from grease and long usage, to be satisfied of its propriety.

In one corner of the market square, were some stacks of fresh grass and fodder, which, as they seemed to possess the power of locomotion, attracted the attention of my companions. Great was the merriment when, on approaching one of them to penetrate the mystery, the half smothered bray of an ass broke upon our ears. The immense and well-packed burden, sweeping the ground on every side, so completely concealed the patient little donkey, that, like his brother of the fable who assumed the lion's skin and regal dignity, he might have preserved a successful *incog* but for his foolish and betraying bray.

Among other places, we visited the office of "The American Flag," a spirited little tri-weekly paper, the publication of which was commenced soon after the capture of the town. Its editors, Fleeson, Peoples & Co., kindly offered us late files of New Orleans papers. There was a great number of patriotic typos in the volunteer army; and newspapers were established in the course of the war, at every important point occupied by our troops. Thus, in addition to the "Flag," we had subsequently in Northern Mexico, the "Pioneer," at Monterey, and the "Picket-Guard," at Saltillo. The native population of the town is said to be about three thousand, but at that time the place was full of soldiers, and adventurers of every description. For the consideration of some of these last, the following polite and pointed advertisement (which is copied from the "American Flag" of that date—Sunday, August 9th, 1846) was probably intended:

"TO GENTLEMEN OUT OF EMPLOYMENT.

"I wish to hire two industrious gentlemen to work in my stable. Those who have no business of their own, that can work without getting drunk, and obey instructions, can obtain immediate employment and good pay by applying in time to ISRAEL B. BIGELOW."

That particular calmness which distinguishes the Sabbath in all God-abiding communities, and by which the holy day is intuitively recognized under all circumstances, did not appear "to brood with dove-like wings" over Matamoros. Stores and drinking-houses were open in every street; and it was evident, from the angry shouts and sound of breaking glass that issued from some of the latter, that they were doing *a smashing business*. In consequence of the disorders arising from intoxication, General Taylor, before starting for Camargo, had enacted a stringent anti-liquor law, to take effect as soon as the stock on hand should be exhausted; but it is probable that the adroit smugglers never permitted that event to occur. *

A theater had also been opened by an enterprising histrionic company from New Orleans, whose bill for that evening

---

* Orders No. 94. — *Head-Quarters, Army of Occupation, Matamoros, August* 2, 1846.

No spirituous liquors will be permitted to enter the river or the city of Matamoros, for the purposes of barter or traffic, on account of any person whatever, whether sutlers in the army, or private dealers. Any liquors found in violation of this order, will be confiscated and sent to the Quarter-Master in New Orleans, to be sold: one-half of the proceeds for the benefit of the informant, the other half to be applied to the support of the hospital department. The merchants in Matamoros will be permitted to vend the liquors they may have on hand, but to receive no new supplies.

The Commanding General issues this order under the sanction of the General Government, and calls upon all officers to give their aid in executing its provisions. The Quarter-Master's Department, and Colonel Clarke, will take the necessary measures to have it communicated to the persons interested, particularly to the dealers in Matamoros, and the masters of all public transports, or other vessels, in the river. Any steamboat captains, or other hired persons, that are found violating it, will be at once discharged from the service.

By order of Major General Taylor:

W. W. S. Bliss.
Assistant Adjutant General.

was quite in keeping with the place, if not with the day. The manager posted the public that, "On Sunday evening, August 9th, will be presented for the first time, 'The Dumb Girl of Genoa,' and 'The Forest Rose,' together with a great variety of singing; the whole to conclude with a dance in wooden shoes, that will be a caution to corns and cockroaches."

At Matamoros, our men first tasted that inebriating beverage, *pulque*, the whisky of Mexico. Whether in consequence of their indulgence in it, or some other cause, some of them were reported as "absent without leave," when we left the town on the 10th of August; and, by their disobedience, were compelled to measure with fatiguing steps the land route to Camargo.

The next village of any importance above Matamoros, is Reynosa. There we found a small garrison of regular troops. It is very prettily situated on a commanding elevation, about a mile from the right bank of the Rio Grande, and contains some substantial stone houses; but its general appearance, like that of almost everything else in the country, indicates dilapidation and decay. A short distance below the landing, we passed a number of women bathing in the river; the length of their hair and tongues disclosing their sex. In the course of our voyage, we encountered several parties of natives washing themselves in the discolored stream, many of whom were as destitute of modesty as of clothing. From the custom, not uncommon among the lowest class, of wearing pantaloons only, their tawny bodies have been dyed by the sun and air, many shades darker than their legs. Hence the droll mistake of one of our volunteers, who gravely insisted with his comrades that these swimmers were dressed in "yallar buckskin tights."

Some of these borderers were quite friendly, and often hailed our boat, desiring to sell chickens, eggs, melons, and milk. With the view of obtaining supplies of these rare delicacies, we generally stopped at dark in the vicinity of a rancho; though, sometimes, we were compelled to "tie up" at places where, apparently, the foot of man had never trod. Near one of the landing places between Matamoros and Reynosa, our soldiers had an opportunity of witnessing that novel scene of revelry—*a fandango*. Such social assemblies are of frequent occurrence, and afford the common people their chief amusement. A smooth, well-beaten circle in the open air is generally the *salle de danse* on these festive occasions. This is illuminated with torches, and surrounded by tables for gaming, to which the Mexicans seem passionately addicted. There are tables also for the sale of the vile liquors, and other products of the country, which are pleasantly termed *refreshments*. A swarthy and sweating crowd, of both sexes, engaged in waltzing, gambling, smoking, drinking, etc., I understand to be a *fandango*.

One night our boat was moored near a solitary hut, in which dwelt an old Mexican fiddler. As soon as the musical talents of its occupant were discovered, the men sought permission to spend the evening ashore, for the purpose of enjoying, what is termed in our western parlance, "a stag dance." Accordingly, the whole detachment landed—except the sick, and a few elderly men who had no taste for such boisterous mirth—and soon the fun grew "fast and furious." It was a singular spectacle, as revealed to us by the light of a huge fire on the bank, at which some hungry soldiers were roasting a goat; and the ruddy glow emitted by the smoldering furnaces of the steamer, as she lay with bows inclined to the shore. Those who heard that "brisk awakening viol," or witnessed that "gay fantastic round," certainly were not inclined to think, that

> "They saw in Tempe's vale her native maids,
> Amidst the festal sounding shades,
> To some unwearied minstrel dancing."

In front of the cottage of the musical shepherd, sat one of our fifers and the new-found son of Apollo. Though they could communicate with each other only through those *dulcet* symphonies,—compared with which "*language* is said to be faint and weak,"—yet they formed an amiable orchestra; and, aided by the hoarse blasts of steam which were occasionally suffered to escape from the boat, succeeded admirably in "making the night hideous with discordant sounds." One would have supposed, from the energy and evident delight of the two artists, thus strangely brought together, that they, at least, imagined themselves possessed by the spirits of Pan and Paganini. The dancing, too, it must be admitted, was eminently suited to the music, and became stronger in proportion as the wild strains grew louder. As the performers trod the measure not upon "the light fantastic toe" alone, but with their whole *soles*, the clatter of their heavy shoes, like the sound of many cymbals, united to swell the din. The soldiers, glad to be released from the crowded quarters to which they had long been confined, vied with each other in the extent and singularity of their saltations. They danced in couples, but without much regard to time or order; and at intervals the whole party indulged in a promenade or rather *gallopade* of two or three *heats* around the hut. A heavy rain terminated the sport at a seasonable hour, and the men returned to the boat much amused and refreshed by their exercise.

We suffered much while cribbed upon the narrow decks of the steamboat, from the great heat of the weather, and the mosquitos that nightly environed us like a legion of foul fiends. To the sick (and there were many on board) those roasting days and restless nights were particularly trying. We lost but one man during the trip,—one of the Dayton volunteers, Co. B. His death had a very depressing effect upon the invalids who were stretched around him on the cabin floor, and who seemed not to have anticipated the sudden invasion of the King of Terrors. Late in the afternoon of the day of his decease, we landed to perform the sad funeral rites of poor Dix,—for such was his name. "No useless coffin inclosed his breast," but wrapped in his blanket, the dead volunteer was borne in the arms of his comrades to a grave which had been prepared in the chaparral, close by the shore, and where the last honors were performed by a corporal's guard. Attracted by the volleys of the funeral escort, and understanding their import, a very respectable old Mexican, whose *hacienda* was near by, came down to the boat. He was accompanied by his wife, a fine specimen of the Spanish matron, in manners and appearance. They were closely followed by a timid female slave, who carried in her arms a neatly dressed child. Pleased with the superior air and bearing of this family group, and gratified by the confidence they exhibited, we invited them to the cabin, where we passed a pleasant half hour in conversation with them. The old gentleman was well informed on the topics of the times; and far better acquainted than most of his countrymen with the power and resources of the hostile republics. He confessed that he saw but little prospect of success for Mexico in the pending struggle; acknowledged that his country was badly governed; and that he did not care much how the war terminated. These remarks were received with some *grains of salt*. His wife—a handsome woman, with pleasing manners, and quite *fair* as well as *fat* and *forty*—seemed pleased with the visit, and gracefully acknowledged the respectful attentions of our people and their kindly notices of her child.

As our boat-captain was anxious to clean out the boilers, in which much mud had accumulated, we determined to remain all night at the place; and informed Senor ——, when he arose to depart, that we would take pleasure in returning his visit after supper. We did so at the time appointed. On arriving at the house, or *houses*, (for there were several small tenements clustered around the principal building,—the former occupied by the *peons*,) we were politely received by our host, and offered cigaritas and seats in the open air. The Mexicans generally are skillful fabricators of *cigaritas;* little cigars made of fine cut tobacco, with wrappers of thin corn-husk or paper. These materials they always carry about their persons,—the tobacco frequently tied up in the corner of the pocket-handkerchief, and the husk in the *sombrero*. Our host was a capital cigar-maker, and while engaged in earnest conversation, manufactured the pleasant little *rolls* as fast as three or four persons could consume them. He was a man of considerable substance, and in addition to his *casa de campo* (country house) owned, as he informed us, a dwelling in the town of Reynosa. On his large estate, which extended for many leagues along the river, were grazing a great number of mustangs, mules, cattle, sheep and goats; the tithe of which, he said, were sometimes stolen by the Camanches, at one fell swoop. Fifty of his best pack-mules had recently been hired to the American quartermaster at Camargo; and he informed us that many others were being sent there by the Mexicans, to be employed in transporting our baggage and supplies to Monterey. In the course of conversation, Senor —— asked us, how many *voluntarios* were coming to Mexico? He was told in reply, that we did not know what number had been ordered to the Rio Grande; but certainly enough for present purposes; and that nearly every man in the United States capable of bearing arms was ready, if required, to join Taylor's army. From the incredulous air with which the latter part of this response was received, it was evident that the old man knew more of the opposition to the war at home, than had been supposed. Possibly he may have been *enlightened* by some of the "Stars" and "Torchlights," or other equally luminous and rabid anti-war prints published in Ohio; whose editors, not content with opposing the cause of their country, engaged in the pitiful business of abusing those who dared not only to differ from them, but to take part in the strife.

The road from Matamoros to Camargo was not far from the river at that point; and we were informed that a column of American infantry had been seen passing up that day. From the vague and incoherent description given of it by one of the *peons*, we were led to suppose that it was composed in part of the remaining battalion of our regiment. In this, however, we were mistaken; although, as the distance between the two places is more than twice as great by the sinuous Rio Grande as by the road, it would have been possible for active and healthy troops to march it in less time than our slow boat could steam it,—traveling as we did only during daylight. Before our departure from the *hacienda*, we were invited to enter and partake of some goat's milk; which—upon observing a fold near the house containing some hundreds of "the bearded people"—we had expressed a desire to taste. The patriarchal beverage was delicious. An unusual number of weapons were hanging upon the walls of the apartment; and which, the old gentleman remarked, were used by his household against the Indians, who, since the commencement of the war had become very bold and troublesome; that but the week previous a large and daring band of Camanches had invaded the neighborhood, and driven off a number of horses and fat cattle, besides killing three Mexicans in the foray.

It was night when we returned to the boat, for in that latitude the twilight is so brief as to be scarcely perceptible. The sun disappears, and darkness almost immediately "broods over the still and pulseless world." But those southern nights are enchantingly beautiful. Nothing arrested my attention more, during the many weary vigils of the campaign, than those glittering hosts, which at set of sun, were ever seen in regular and stately march through that pure, unclouded firmament. No where else have "the lights that rule the night" appeared so brilliant or lovely. On reaching the steamer, we mounted to the hurricane deck to enjoy the night breeze, that laded with fragrance stole across from the Texas bank. The scene around us that night, forms one of those interesting pictures of the campaign which the memory has retained more faithfully than the pen can delineate. On one side of us, the restless and turbid stream, rolled moaning to its ocean-bed; on the other a vast expanse of prairie and chaparral, o'er which comes the howl of wolves and the answering bark of watch-dogs at the ranche. The silent sentinels pace with ghost-like tread upon the shore, as if fearing to disturb the last long sleep of their departed comrade, over whose fresh grave the thick bushes bending mournfully in the breeze, weep their dewy tears. Stretched in slumber on the decks are whole ranks of men, many of them with their greasy haversacks drawn over their faces, to protect them from the mosquitos that swarm out from the shore. But even these are not secure from the insidious assaults of the pigmy enemy. For see how often they start and wake,—how they shake their suffocating masks as impatiently as hungry cavalry horses toss their empty nosebags,—how they smack right and left at the gray-coated gallinippers, "then swear a prayer or two, and sleep again." While these are "dreaming of breaches, ambuscadoes, Spanish blades," a party of officers in the cabin are drinking *healths, five fathom deep.* And still below them on the boiler deck, a number of soldiers are making merry over a certain fatted calf, found *couchant* near the landing; and whose peaceful ruminations have been interrupted by a single well-directed bayonet thrust.

Long before dawn of the following day, the steam was hissing like an angry serpent through the cleansed boilers and pipes; and with the first light we were again upon our winding way to Camargo, which place we reached at noon on Sunday, August 16th. The town is situated on the right bank of the San Juan, about a league above its confluence with the Rio Grande. As all our men were wearied, and many indeed sickened, by a long confinement on the comfortless steamer, it was with unusual satisfaction that we beheld our boat gliding, at an unexpected moment, into the mouth of that beautiful little stream. Its limpid waves flowing between high banks (for draining a country of comparatively limited extent, its flood had subsided) formed an agreeable contrast to the dark, swelling tide of the Rio Grande. The water of the latter is, however, more palatable and more healthful, when its 20 per centum (literally as well as *figuratively*) of mud is precipitated. The American camp, with its right resting on Camargo, extended for a considerable distance along the river. The soldiers who loitered on the shore filling their camp-kettles, or stood knee deep in the water, washing their shirts, engaged in the usual skirmish of wit with our men, as we passed slowly up. On reaching the village, we pushed our prow into the landing where a company of Texas Rangers, with all the boisterous merriment of undisciplined troops, were engaged in cleaning their horses. Just above them, a party of the village women were coming to the stream for water, with the most primitive-looking earthen jars upon their heads.

Having sent an officer to the quarter-master's office, in quest of wagons with which to transport our equipage to the camp, we set out to report at head-quarters the arrival of our detachment. In our walk thither, we were overtaken by an officer wearing the uniform of a brigadier general, who, after exchanging salutations, informed us that he was General ——, of the State of ——. Learning our destination and object, he politely offered to accompany us to head-quarters and introduce us to General Taylor. Passing on through some narrow streets and lanes, and between gardens surrounded by mud walls, on the top of which grew many varieties of the luxuriant cactus plant, we arrived in a few minutes at a little grassy lot just without the town, in the center of which were pitched three soiled and ragged tents. A small guard of dragoons was posted near by. The spot was remarkably quiet, being removed from the noise and bustle of both the camp and village. Under an awning in front of the tents, sat a solitary man, dressed in linen coat and trowsers, twirling a straw hat between his fingers, and apparently conversing with or dictating to some one within. The first glance assured us that it was the old hero, with whose name and fame the country was then ringing; and as we approached, we recognized the mahogany complexion, piercing eye, iron-grey hair, and stout frame, which we had been told distinguished the commanding general. As he arose to greet us, I was struck with the benevolent expression of his face, and the affability of his manner. He was invested with no silly pomp or ceremony. There was no ice to break in approaching him; but the natural grace and kindness of his reception at once placed us at ease, and during the time he gave us audience, our respect and admiration for the sturdy old republican general momentarily increased. His first question was concerning the health of the men, about which he seemed extremely solicitous; and he expressed his anxiety to hasten his army forward into a more salubrious region. He conversed with a stammering voice. But if slow of speech, no man could be more prompt in action than *Old Rough and Ready*. On arising to take leave, which we did at the earliest suitable moment, he desired us to report to General Worth, who, he said, was in command at the camp.

Returning to the boat, we had the satisfaction of finding the wagons already laden with our sick and baggage. The road to camp led us through the town,—if piles of crumbling clay and straw might be so called. A short time previous to its occupation by our troops, Camargo had been inundated, and many of the houses being built of soft sun-dried bricks, had partially dissolved. The roofs of some of them were yet clinging mournfully to one tottering wall. The little church and a few buildings around the Plaza, were in tolerable preservation. These were occupied as store-houses by our quarter-masters and commissaries. But few Mexicans remained in the town, the population of which could at no period have exceeded one or two thousand.* A brisk march of half an hour brought us to the left wing of the emcampment, where we pitched our tents and patiently awaited the arrival of the remaining battalion of our regiment.

* The village of Camargo probably derives its name from Diego Munos Camargo, a native, and the historian of the celebrated Haskalian tribe, which was associated with the Spaniards in the conquest of the city of Mexico. Camargo lived in the latter half of the sixteenth century, was educated in the Catholic faith, and composed his "*Historia de Hascala*" in the Castilian language.

CHAPTER IV.

Camp scenes at Camargo.—General Worth.—The review.—The regular troops sent forward to Cerralvo.—Great sickness and mortality in the volunteer regiments.—Character and conduct of the natives.—Our treatment of them.—The Proclamation.—The Army and Church of Mexico.—Their influence on the government.—Eager and enthusiastic spirit of the Volunteers.—The Rangers.—Brigades organized for the field.—Limited means of transportation.—The Mexican jockeys and our Horse Market.—Something of a shower.—General Hamer's brigade crosses the San Juan preparatory to marching for Monterey.

A stroll through the encampment, on the morning after our arrival at Camargo, afforded me,—a raw volunteer,—much pleasure and instruction. It was the first of any magnitude, and by far the most beautiful one I had ever beheld. Never before, indeed, had I seen a battalion of our regular troops, either in camp or garrison. But there, in the same field, were horse, foot and artillery; not in great force, it is true, but perfect in all their appointments and discipline. Four light batteries, of six guns each, a few squadrons of dragoons, and four brigades of infantry, (comprising the divisions of Twiggs and Worth,) in all about three thousand men, comprised the regular army of General Taylor. The tent of every officer and private was pitched in its proper place, so that knowing a man's rank and company, his quarters could be almost as easily found as any number in the streets of our principal cities. In front of the camp was a vast and well smoothed parade-ground; along the edge of which was a row of fading fires, at which breakfast had just been prepared. The long lines of white canvas and stacks of burnished arms, interspersed with umbrageous rose-wood and mesqueet trees; troops of splendid horses, standing with the calm dignity of veterans at their pickets; batteries of artillery, their bright muzzles gleaming from beneath tarpaulins like watch-dogs peering from their kennels; these assisted in forming one of those impressive martial spectacles that swell the veins and give fresh vigor to the step. Militia camps and parades I had often witnessed, but though every man wore the lace, and feathers, and gaudy trappings of a Field Marshal, they presented but a sorry mimicry of war. Here, however, was Mars himself; in repose, yet armed *cap-a-pie* and ready for action. The very calmness and order that pervaded the camp would have told plainly enough that it was no holiday affair, even if many of the quiet men around us had not exhibited upon their persons and bronzed faces the marks of recent battle. It was one of those scenes that sent the mind wandering back through many a bright old page of history, until it dwelt again with all the delight of boyhood, upon those vivid and magnificent camp and battle-pieces with which the Prince of Poets has adorned his Iliad. And I am inclined to think, that the appearance of Achilles himself, brandishing in triumph his bloody spear, and dragging behind his chariot the body of some vanquished enemy, would not, at the moment, have in the least astonished me.

At the quarters of the 3d infantry, I was courteously received by an officer to whom I had brought a letter from a mutual friend, and through whom I at once became acquainted with other gentlemen of that gallant corps. He politely proposed accompanying me to the quarters of General Worth, to whom I had been prevented by sickness from reporting in person, on the previous evening. We paused in our walk to witness the morning drill of Captain Bragg's excellent company of artillery. The horses, as well as men, seemed to understand their business perfectly; and being of "fine bone and blood," they whirled the guns and caissons over the plain with wonderful rapidity and ease. These light field batteries, in which the canoneers ride upon the gun carriages, ready for action at any moment, are very efficient for quick work; and with sufficient horse-power, are certainly the most formidable auxiliaries that science has ever given to war. Captain Bragg, a skillful and courageous officer, is, I understand, distinguished for his attention to the minutiæ of his profession; a merit to be esteemed no less than heroic daring, when it is remembered what disasters may result in critical moments from the most trifling casualties, such, for example, as the loss of a horse-shoe or linchpin.* He was in Fort Brown during its long bombardment. There, his light pieces were of little service as battering guns. So at Monterey. But in the open field of Buena Vista, our horse-artillery exhibited its terrible power. There, in fact, (as General Taylor states, in his report of the battle) *it saved the day.* "Moving rapidly over the roughest ground, it was

---

*Cæsar, whose great sagacity and conduct put success as much out of the power of accident as human reason could well do, remarks in the third book of his Commentaries: "*Fortuna quæ plurimum potest, cum in aliis rebus, tum præcipue in bello in parvis momentis magnas rerum mutationes efficit.*"

always in action at the right place and the right time; and its well-directed fire dealt destruction in the masses of the enemy."

We found General Worth, in this, my first and only interview with him, pacing his tent with much the air of a caged lion. He had that morning received orders to hold his division in readiness for a movement in the direction of Monterey; and was most anxious to hasten events. He informed us that he would march on the 19th, and was to establish himself at Cerralvo until the arrival of the other divisions at that place. Colonel Duncan had just returned from a reconnoissance to Puntaguada, and reported that the roads, which it was supposed had been made nearly impassable by the summer rains, were in good condition, and that water was not so scarce as on the route between Matamoros and Camargo. This was cheering intelligence, and the ambitious and chivalrous spirit of Worth, chafed at missing the glories of Palo Alto and Resaca, now burned to press forward and pluck from the hights of Monterey a laurel as fresh and green as that which crowned his rival.

It will be recollected by the reader that, in consequence of a disagreement with General Twiggs concerning rank, (Twiggs being the senior colonel, and Worth a general by brevet) he had resigned his commission and returned to the United States before the battles on the Rio Grande were fought. When the unexpected and startling news of those actions reached him at Washington, he withdrew his resignation and immediately repaired to Mexico, where he added greatly to his reputation as a soldier, by the brilliant manner in which he fought his division throughout the war. The blow upon his fame,—from which he was then evidently suffering,—like that of Achilles, had been self-inflicted by his voluntary retirement from the camp. And like the Grecian hero, he was destined to learn that "those wounds heal ill, that men do give themselves." The countenance, address and manners of this distinguished General, were exceedingly prepossessing. His features were strikingly handsome, and his face possessed that bright, healthy hue which contrasts so well with the gray locks of age. His appearance and bearing were imposing and knightly; his person and gait erect and military; his voice clear and pleasing; his utterance very rapid yet distinct. His manners were at times, perhaps a little ostentatious; and in that regard as well as in other respects, he differed greatly from the commanding general. Most soldiers in comparing these two generals, (whose charters Death has already given over to the impartial pen of History) would probably have concluded that, while no one,—not even Murat or Macdonald—could lead troops in a charge more fiercely than the fiery and enthusiastic Worth; yet that upon the deliberate courage, unbroken composure and unconquerable will of Taylor, it would be safer to rely for success in all the varying chances of a campaign. Worth, with all his ardor, united great military skill and judgment; but though a more brilliant soldier, of acknowledged talents and courage, he never inspired the volunteer army, at least, with the same confidence and admiration as did Taylor. Yet was he an extraordinary man, and his untimely death has caused a blank in the American army which will not soon be filled.

I was much pleased with the visit, and felt gratified, proud indeed, that my country possessed such a general. Before leaving his tent, he courteously invited the officers of my battalion to attend a review of the regular troops, which was to take place that afternoon.

I have ever regarded myself as very fortunate in reaching Camargo in time to behold that review, which was decidedly the most imposing of the campaign. That man is little to be envied whose heart would not swell with gratitude and patriotism, in contemplating such an army; whose valor and firmness had recently saved the periled honor of his country. Though there were hardly three thousand troops in the line, the display was admirable and gratifying. The men were in excellent condition and looked invincible. The officers, young, brave and intelligent, were (it may be safely asserted) superior to any Europe can boast, in professional skill.*

Soon after the formation of the line, the generals, attended by a brilliant staff, rode down from right to left. Taylor

---

* In common with every candid observer of events in Mexico, I would cheerfully testify to the incalculable benefits derived by our country from its Military Academy. Not only did it give to the regular army nearly all its efficiency, but its advantages were realized to a considerable extent, in every volunteer corps connected with the war. To the thorough military training and knowledge which it imparts, the nation is much indebted for a series of splendid victories; any one of which would more than compensate it for all the expenditures at West Point. That will be an unfortunate day for the Republic, when Congress, influenced either by motives of fancied economy or the vile appeals of the demagogue, shall consent to abandon an institution which has already done much to establish the reputation and extend the borders of the country; and which is constantly spreading among us that intelligence and skill by which *the people*—in their freedom from the burden of a large standing army—may at any time be converted into the grandest host o soldiers that ever battled in any cause or clime.

clad in plain undress, was conspicuous in the glittering group. Every eye was fixed upon him as he passed from corps to corps, acknowledging the salute of each. After he had taken a favorable position in the field, the line was wheeled into column of companies, and then with a grand and inspiriting burst of music from the bands, that glorious little army passed in review, moving as one man across the reverberating plain. Floating high o'er the column was that splendid "standard of the stars," to which Drake has ascribed so poetical and beautiful an origin, and which he has described too, in lines that few Americans can read without feeling their hearts beat within them as at the sound of a trumpet. Ah! the imperial eagles of Rome and France were not more secure in the midst of the immortal "Tenth Legion" and the unyielding "Old Guard," than is that heaven-born banner there!

> "Flag of the brave! thy folds shall fly,
> The sign of hope and triumph high!
> When speaks the signal trumpet tone,
> And the long line comes gleaming on,
> Ere yet the life-blood, warm and wet,
> Has dimmed the glistening bayonet,
> Each soldier's eye shall brightly turn,
> To where thy meteor glories burn,
> And as his springing steps advance,
> Catch war and vengeance from the glance!"

It was indeed a soul-stirring scene, and we earnestly wished that every volunteer in the army could witness and would emulate the soldiership it exhibited. A distinguished officer of the 3d infantry, who shortly afterward expired under the walls of Monterey, pointed to us, during the review, the various battalions and commanders in the field; and related some interesting incidents connected with the history of many of them. In reply to a remark of mine concerning the troops, he said—"Yes, this is very fine, certainly; but our boys always look better in a blaze. You will soon see what stuff is beneath those blue jackets."

The day after the review, (August 19th) General Worth marched with his division for Cerralvo,—a town about mid-way between Camargo and Monterey. No serious opposition was anticipated short of the last named city. Bold and strong indeed must that Mexican force have been, which could have dared to face that splendid van-guard, led by the keenly excited genius and angry courage of Worth. The remaining brigades of the regular army soon afterward passed to the left bank of the San Juan, and were pushed forward in rapid succession. Meanwhile detachments of volunteers were being daily brought up by the boats, but it was not until a week after our arrival that the marching column (composed, as the reader has seen, of six companies from each regiment) reached Camargo. General Twiggs, who marching rapidly up from Matamoros with the Dragoons and Flying Artillery, had passed the column on the road, reported, with his usual sportive and mirth-provoking humor, that the volunteers were in exceeding bad plight, that their patriotism was oozing out at their toes, and that their officers were compelled to encourage them forward by stirring speeches, at least thrice a day. At the commencement of the campaign it was a standing joke among the regulars, that the officers of volunteers found it necessary to enforce every trifling order with a stump speech; and that therefore the discipline of each regiment depended pretty much upon the eloquence of its colonel. At this jest, and its accompanying illustrative anecdotes, we have laughed as heartily as our good-natured brethren of the old line; and, indeed, considering the character of our people, there may have been some room for such innocent raillery. It certainly was calculated to do more good than any severe and unkind professional criticism; which would have engendered much ill-feeling between the old and new troops. None knew better than the regular officers, that the volunteer regiments contained the best material in the world, from which to mold an efficient army; but it required time, tact, and much forbearance, to accustom those independent spirits to the yoke of military discipline. The volunteers, unlike the mass of the regular army, had always been their own masters, and it could scarcely be expected that they should abandon at once all their habits of free thought and free action, and become passive and obedient instruments in the hands of others. Their good sense, however, aided by a little experience, and the example of all who valued the reputation of their regiments, and the honor of their states, soon rendered most of the volunteers quite equal to the regulars, in the prompt, cheerful, and full discharge of every duty.

On the 23d of August, our regiment was again concentrated by the arrival of the six companies which had marched from Camp Belknap under Lieutenant Colonel Weller. The journey, performed under midsummer suns, and through a country but scantily supplied with water, was a severe and trying one to our unripe troops. Several of the wagons came in laden with sick and dying men, among whom we were pained to find Lieutenant S., of Company B, (Dayton volunteers,) one of the most energetic, reliable, and useful officers of the 1st Ohio regiment. His death, which occurred on the morning of the 26th, was, to many of his comrades, one of the most distressing events of the campaign. Lieut. S. had already displayed an activity, and tractable disposition, that won him the confidence and esteem of his superior officers, while his cheerfulness, and the good humor with which he bore every privation, had made him a favorite with all. He possessed, too, all those sterling qualities of the soldier, which, had fate permitted, would have gained him an enviable reputation.

The mortality in our camp at Camargo was appalling. The dead march was ever wailing in our ears, and even at this distant period, I can scarcely look back to our brief stay there without a shudder. At almost every hour of the day, funeral escorts of various regiments might be seen following the bodies of departed comrades to that vast and common cemetery, the chaparral, where officers and men, "in dust, without distinction lie." The large hospital-tents were constantly full—the dead being removed at sunrise and sunset, but to make room for the dying. The groans and lamentations of the poor sufferers during those sickly, sultry nights were heart-rending. Upon our arrival at Camargo, we had been informed by the natives that it was the most sickly place in the valley, but the appearance of the country did not indicate it, nor have I ever heard it attributed to any satisfactory cause. An examination of the circumjacent country might perhaps, have led to the discovery of some swamps or pools of stagnant water, left from the overflow of the San Juan.

General Taylor, though busied with the many important arrangements upon which his subsequent success would depend, yet frequently found time to visit the hospitals, and cheer their inmates with kind and sympathizing words. In a communication to the adjutant general, dated Camargo, Sept. 3d, 1846, he says, "I have used every effort to extend the hospital accomodations and the medical force, but the service is suffering greatly in this latter particular. There has been great sickness and mortality in some of the volunteer regiments. Great numbers are taken into the several general hospitals, and no exertion is spared to ameliorate their condition." The deficiency of medical officers here alluded to, was seriously felt in many regiments. But "the laws of the land," said the surgeon general, in reply to General Taylor's complaint of the scarcity of surgeons, "awarded two medical officers to a full regiment of 750 men," and as there were more than that number serving with the Army of Occupation, *ergo*, the complaint was groundless, and the surgeons in the field were censurable for not performing their duty. Our regiment was fortunate in securing at the onset two skillful surgeons, and in being generally concentrated. But there were others, which, being divided and sub-divided for garrison and escort duty, often suffered sadly, in consequence of what the surgeon general asserted to be "military propriety, and the customs of the service."* It

* "I have given all in the way of medical aid which military propriety, and the customs of the services in like cases, and the wants of the army seem to require;

is due to the chiefs of the various staff departments of the army, to remark that they did all, and often more than "the regulations" required from them; but they should have been neither disappointed nor dissatisfied when gently reminded by the general commanding in the field, that the very nice calculations made at Washington, did not altogether meet the exigencies of every climate and service.

At Camargo we were tolerably well supplied by the Mexicans with fresh provisions, for which they took care to exact exorbitant prices. These native hucksters were a morose and knavish set. Taught to hate all foreginers, and especially "*los Yankees*," they looked—even when pocketing our dollars—as sour as their own bitter oranges when the green rinds have received the first tinge of sickly yellow. As they were allowed to enter the camp at all hours, they of course kept their friends at Monterey well advised of our condition and movements; while, in their dealings with us, they were close-mouthed and professedly ignorant beyond example. Nothing scarcely could be extracted from them save the price of the articles they offered for sale, and which they uttered glibly enough. To every question touching their roads, country, towns, troops, etc., even when put in the purest Castilian, the usual reply was, "*no entende, Senor*," (don't understand you, sir.) It appears that General Taylor, up to this time, had failed to obtain any very reliable information con-

---

but if they desire more medical officers, they shall have them—with myself to boot, if acceptable—and I am borne out in the measure by the government. Far be it from me to withhold aught that will contribute to the comfort of one of those gallant souls who so valiantly fought and so signally triumphed on the battle-fields of Palo Alto and Resaca de la Palma."—*From the Letter of the Surgeon General to the Adjutant General.*

cerning the designs of the enemy, or even of the country beyond the points to which he had pushed his reconnoitering parties. On the eve of marching for Camargo, and but two weeks before he fought the battle of Monterey, he remarked in a letter to the government, "We have no very recent intelligence from the interior, nor have I yet satisfactory means of judging whether our occupation of Monterey and Saltillo will be disputed."

Such indeed had been the barbarian policy of the Mexican government, and the plundering habits of the Mexican people, that travelers and traders had been discouraged from visiting the country; and but few of our citizens knew more of its interior than what could be seen along the great thoroughfare between Vera Cruz and the city of Mexico. Though lying immediately upon the borders of the most enterprising and inquisitive nation under the sun, Mexico had remained, up to the commencement of the war, almost a *terra incognita.* The great wall of China could not have offered a more effectual barrier to Tartarean invasion, than Mexican legislation, insolence, and intolerance have presented to American industry and genius. The reader, therefore, will not perhaps be surprised to find the quarter-master general (who, like the surgeon general, found it necessary to vindicate his official conduct,) writing as follows, in reply to one of General Taylor's letters: "As to the complaint in regard to the want of land transportation, it is proper to remark, that there was no information at Washington, so far as I was informed, to enable me or the War Department to determine whether wagons could be used in Mexico."

Soon after the beginning of the war, our government had announced its intention of conducting it in a spirit of liberality and forbearance; and it may be safely asserted that no people were ever more kindly treated by an invading army. Rarely indeed, in time of peace, have the Mexicans extended to Americans the same respectful consideration. It appears that the Cabinet at Washington entertained a hope that the mass of the natives might be propitiated, and, in some measure, convinced, that, "the war was waged not against them, but a faithless government of military despots, who had both deprived them of their liberty, and wronged and insulted us." To that end, the government had furnished General Taylor with a proclamation to the inhabitants of Northern Mexico, (a copy of which is subjoined) indicating the policy it intended to pursue in prosecuting hostilities, and which many persons in our army, in view of the characteristic treachery and deep-rooted enmity of the Mexican race, roundly condemned at the time.* Even if the statesmen of the United

---

*A PROCLAMATION.

BY THE GENERAL COMMANDING THE ARMY OF THE UNITED STATES OF AMERICA.

To the people of Mexico:

"After many years of patient endurance, the United States are at length constrained to acknowledge that a war now exists between our government and the government of Mexico. For many years our citizens have been subjected to repeated insults and injuries; our vessels and cargoes have been seized and confiscated; our merchants have been plundered, maimed, imprisoned, without cause and without reparation. At length your government acknowledged the justice of our claims, and agreed, by treaty, to make satisfaction by payment of several millions of dollars; but this treaty has been violated by your rulers, and the stipulated payments have been withheld. Our late effort to terminate all difficulties by peaceful negotiation, has been rejected by the Dictator, Paredes, and our minister of peace, whom your rulers had agreed to receive, has been refused a hearing. He has been treated with indignity and insult, and Paredes has announced that war exists between us. This war, thus first proclaimed by him, has been acknowledged as an existing fact by

States had interpreted the character of the enemy aright, they yet greatly over-estimated the influence of the people of the *republic!* of Mexico, if they supposed that their wishes would be in the least regarded by the central government. Arms and religion govern Mexico. The soldier and the priest control her destinies. The priesthood—perhaps foreseeing disastrous results for their church, in the conquest of their country by the free-thinking Yankees—promptly brought to the aid of the Dictator all their potent, pecuniary, and spiritual resources. Though quite shrewd enough to know that it but little concerned our government whether Christian, Jew, Turk, or Infidel possessed the land, yet these holy gentlemen,

---

our President and Congress, with perfect unanimity, and will be prosecuted with vigor and energy against your army and rulers; but those of the Mexican people who remain neutral will not be molested.

"Your government is in the hands of tyrants and usurpers. They have abolished your State governments, they have overthrown your federal constitution, they have deprived you of the right of suffrage, destroyed the liberty of the press, despoiled you of your arms, and reduced you to a state of absolute dependence upon the power of a military dictator. Your army and rulers extort from the people, by grievous taxation, by forced loans and military seizures, the very money which sustains the usurpers in power. Being disarmed, you are left defenseless, an easy prey to the savage Camanches, who not only destroy your lives and property, but drive into a captivity, more horrible than death itself, your wives and children. It is your military rulers who have reduced you to this deplorable condition. It is these tyrants and their corrupt and cruel satellites, gorged with the people's treasure, by whom you are thus oppressed and impoverished; some of whom have boldly advocated a monarchical government, and would place an European prince on the throne of Mexico. We come to obtain reparation for repeated wrongs and injuries; we come to obtain indemnity for the past, and security for the future; we come to overthrow the tyrants who have destroyed your liberties; but we come to make no war upon the people of Mexico, nor upon any form of free government they may choose to select for themselves. It is our wish to see you liberated from despots, to drive back the savage Camanches, to prevent the renewal of their assaults, and to compel them to restore to you, from captivity, your long-lost wives and children. Your religion, your altars and churches, the property of your churches and citizens, the emblems of your faith and its ministers, shall be protected, and remain inviolate. Hundreds of our army, and hundreds of thousands of our people, are members of the Catholic church. In every State, and in nearly every city and village of our Union, Catholic

pretending to believe all the clap-trap uttered in the United States, about the wealth of the country and the mint value of certain "golden images" and "silver candelabras," aroused the people with stories of our avarice, and avowed that the sacred and dearly-prized emblems of their religion had been offered as a bounty to American volunteers. Thus did the priests forestall our proclamation. If there was any disaffection in the land, it added but little strength to our cause. The people generally placed no confidence in the amicable intentions we published among them, and with the exception of the small spy company of Dominguez, which

---

churches exist; and the priest performs his holy functions in peace and security, under the sacred guaranty of our constitution. We come among the Mexican people as friends and republican brethren, and all who receive us as such shall be protected; while all who are seduced into the army of your dictator, shall be treated as enemies. We shall want from you nothing but food for our army, and for this you shall always be paid, in cash, the full value. It is the settled policy of your tyrants to deceive you in regard to the policy and character of our government and people. These tyrants fear the example of our free institutions, and constantly endeavor to misrepresent our purposes, and inspire you with hatred for your republican brethren of the American Union. Give us but the opportunity to undeceive you, and you will soon learn that all the representations of Paredes were false, and were only made to induce you to consent to the establishment of a despotic government.

In your struggle for liberty with the Spanish monarchy, thousands of our countrymen risked their lives and shed their blood in your defense. Our own Commodore, the gallant Porter, maintained in triumph your flag upon the ocean, and our government was the first to acknowledge your independence. With pride and pleasure we enrolled your name on the list of independent republics, and sincerely desired that you might, in peace and prosperity, enjoy all the blessings of a free government. Success on the part of your tyrants, against the army of the Union, is impossible; but if they could succeed, it would only be to enable them to fill your towns with their soldiers, eating out your substance, and harrassing you with still more grievous taxation. Already they have abolished the liberty of the press, as the first step toward the introduction of that monarchy which it is their real purpose to proclaim and establish.

"Mexicans! we must treat as enemies and overthrow the tyrants, who, while they have wronged and insulted us, have deprived you of your liberties; but the Mexican people who remain neutral during the contest, shall be protected against their military despots by the republican army of the Union."

joined General Scott's army, remained faithful to their tyrants.

Notwithstanding the temper and conduct of the natives, the pledges of the Proclamation were as scrupulously observed as circumstances would allow. Our army in its early marches through the country, moved like a rich and powerful benefactor, scattering with a lavish hand, unheard of wealth among the rabble in its path. But ignorance, pride, jealousy and bigotry, were not to be thus overcome. Estimating over much their own resources and the ability of their numerous army, or perhaps encouraged to believe from the division of opinion in the United States on the subject of the war, that we would eventually withdraw from the contest—their government, without the prestige of a single victory, continued to prosecute an active and relentless system of hostilities. At length, when it was discovered that our generosity and mild treatment had failed to produce the desired effect upon the population, and that they frequently committed the most savage outrages upon our troops, the Secretary of War instructed General Taylor to draw supplies from the enemy without paying for them; and thus, by making them feel the weight of war, become interested in the restoration of peace. Beginning to understand the character of the foe, and perceiving the effect of the policy previously avowed, he says in his letter: "It is far from being certain that our military occupation of the enemy's country is not a blessing to the inhabitants in the vicinity. They are shielded from the burdens and exactions of their own authorities, protected in their persons, and furnished with a most profitable market for most kinds of their property. A state of things so favorable to their interests may induce them to wish the continuance of hostilities." But General Taylor never availed himself of this authority to levy contributions, and we continued to pay liberal prices for everything obtained from the enemy.

How differently would the dissolute and brutal soldiery of Mexico have conducted themselves in an enemy's country! How differently, indeed, did they often act in their own. We have the authority of their historians for asserting that their marches through their native provinces were sometimes marked by the worst excesses and crimes; that, "they left behind them, by their unbridled license, an imprint of horror in the towns through which they passed; seizing upon vineyards, sacking shops, and even murdering poor poulterers to take away their fowls." So disgusted was an intelligent Mexican whom I knew, with the arrogance and extortion of his own troops, that he did not hesitate to admit frankly, that he preferred the presence of the American army to his own; since from the former he was sure of obtaining a fair compensation for his property. To a standing army, and an established national church, does Mexico owe most of her troubles and her poverty. Her government, existing only by the consent of the army, is in turn compelled to sustain that army at all hazards and sacrifices. It is now well understood that the recognition of the independence of Texas had been deferred, and the war with that state nominally prolonged by the various military rulers of Mexico, merely as a pretext for the exaction of supplies, which were afterward squandered in the maintenance of their ill-gotten and much-abused power.

The government, being supported by bayonets, always totters, when, from its want of credit, and miserable domestic policy, it suffers the pay of the troops to fall in arrear. Woe to it in such dark hours, for then thrives that baleful mushroom, the *Pronunciamiento*. Nearly all their revolutions, since their independence from Spain, have been conceived by ambitious generals, and achieved by a greedy soldiery.* In these civil wars, the church, of course, is careful to side with that party most favorable to its interests; and it has been truly remarked by one of our envoys to Mexico, that, "no political movement can succeed there, to which the priesthood is opposed."

The Mexicans have a very well written constitution; but what is the best system of government worth to those who have not moral and intellectual power enough to compel its observance? Where the minds and hearts of the people are not properly educated, there can be no real freedom; and to

---

*Even mercenary motives have sometimes been wanting to excuse the disloyalty of the army—as witness the following passage of history from the Mexican "Notes of the War:"

"During the last month of the administration of Paredes, in consequence of the reverses suffered by our troops on the other side of the Rio Bravo, it was agreed to organize the same expedition which Santa Anna afterward resolved upon. To realize it, pecuniary resources were wanting, and a contract was accordingly made with the church for $1,000,000, which sum was estimated as being more than sufficient for the division that should march from the city of Mexico. The state of internal politics, and the fear, above all, of abandoning his prey, detained Paredes in this city, even after Congress had given him permission to march from Mexico, with the forces that were in garrison, and to place himself at the head of the troops of the North. This delay began to consume, without profit, the loan from the clergy, which, being for the most part wasted, obliged Paredes at last to take the forces and relinquish the government, at the end of July, for the purpose of joining the army of the North. Then he made payments for the march to all the corps, to all the officers and chiefs; with which, a few days after, they flew to the citadel to proclaim a new revolution; and assisted by the very money that ought to have served to march to Monterey. Infamous intrigues, to which we owe principally the unfortunate issue of our contest at the North."

attempt the establishment of a republic among them, is the very folly of building upon sand. Until directed by wisdom and virtue, all popular efforts in Mexico, as in France, will terminate in a military despotism, or in the crime and folly of a Reign of Terror. In the words of the leading Democratic paper of New York—which in April, 1853, announced the return of Santa Anna to his native shores—"What is chiefly wanted in Mexico, is virtue and intelligence among the people; an intelligence which can not be bamboozled by priests, and a virtue which will subject the military to the civil power; together with such practical energy as will convert the generous resources of nature into the food of industry, instead of the nutriment of idleness and beggary." Whether these wants will ever be supplied, whether the military will ever be made subject to the civil power so long as she perseveres in what her recently exiled President, Arista, terms, "that grand enigma, that squaring of the circle—nationality," is excedingly improbable. For every President constitutionally elected by the people, the army can easily make a half-dozen "*ad interim* Presidents," as the usurpers are called. Look, for example, at the changes of administration in the three years that intervened between the annexation of Texas, and the treaty of Guadaloupe Hidalgo. In that brief period, I believe Herrera, Paredes, Salas, Farias, Santa Anna, Pena and Anaya, were severally at the head of affairs. Was there every such a political whirligig? That certainly was such "rotation in office" as one might suppose would satisfy the most greedy spoils-seeker that ever fought in the ranks of Jacobin or Empire club. Nor has the condition of the country materially improved since the termination of the war. It has been somewhat more tranquil, but it is the calmness of indolence and humiliation. The indemnity, paid in annual installments by the United States, has perhaps been the means of sustaining the government, and of saving her thus long from anarchy.

The future of Mexico is one of the saddest and most embarrassing political problems of the day. That a country of such extent and resources, enjoying a position which commands two oceans, (the advantages of which, by the proposed Tehuantepec road, it has been left to foreigners to demonstrate,) and with eight or nine millions of inhabitants, should be in such a hopeless condition, is a peculiar phenomenon in history. It is scarcely possible that Santa Anna, who has again become "the Supreme Government," can avert, for more than a brief season, her ultimate fate. Even well-informed and patriotic Mexicans now cease to regard, with aversion, the "manifest destiny" of their country. Ex-President Arista seems to look forward to it with hope and encouragement. He says, in a late letter to his government: "I desire the happiness of my country, and to attain it, I see no road but through federal institutions, and, if it be desired, annexation to the United States, in which Mexico will meet an inexhaustible fountain of riches and prosperity, notwithstanding she may lose that grand enigma, that squaring of the circle, called by General Santa Anna, Nationality. The day will arrive when this will happen." There can be but little doubt that a majority of the people of the United States are prepared to annex Mexico at once, and "the rest of mankind" at the proper time; yet a voluntary proposition, on her part, for a peaceful amalgamation of the two republics, would perhaps be but coldly embraced, if not rejected by some of our ardent annexationists, who rejoice in more violent delights. To their palates, stolen fruits are always the sweetest. In whichever manner the Mexican States may come into our Union, it is more to be hoped than expected that they would be at once relieved of the incubus which has so long oppressed them; or that the people, long tantalized by the *mirage* of liberty, would be able to appreciate its living waters when offered to them in all their freshness and purity. Nor is it certain that the connection would be very beneficial to us for sometime at least, especially if the whole of Mexico should be *swallowed at one gulp*—as is sometimes *mildly* proposed by our annexationists. In that event, it is likely that—be she ever so well "licked" before deglutition—we should find her one of those morsels which, "though sweet in taste, prove in digestion sour."*

---

*It will be seen by the following extract from a recent speech delivered by the Nestor of the Democratic party, (Gen. Cass) that the venerable Senator is of the opinion that the gastric juice of the body politic has not been in the least reduced by the digestion of a brace of Mexican states. But considering the fact that those were very thinly populated, it might be advisable to swallow the remaining nineteen or twenty at many, and perhaps smaller meals. This would enable us to manage an island or two *by way of desert.* Meantime the South American states may consider themselves as *in a pen*, fattening for our capacious maws. In good time they will doubtless furnish Brother Jonathan with excellent thanksgiving dinners.

In a speech upon Mr. Mason's resolution (in Senate, December 23, 1852,) calling for the correspondence concerning the proposed tripartite treaty with England and France, for the safeguard to Spain of the island of Cuba, General Cass took occasion to say, *inter alia*—" As to the general subject of annexation, I have no new views to disclose. It is pretty well known that I have a capacious swallow for territory, though I am free to confess that I can wait awhile patiently, if necessary, and spend the time in digesting our last acquisitions. They sit lightly on the

The volunteer army assembled at Camargo was composed chiefly of young men, who had just attained the age at which the enthusiasm of youth and vigor of manhood are united.* The "Young Guard" of Napoleon did not contain in its ranks more energy, valor, and daring, than was to be found in that youthful mass. There were soldiers in various regiments whom I had known when "we were boys together," who contemplated the prospect of an arduous campaign with more pleasure than they ever did a recitation in Thucydides or Juvenal. To many of them, a battery was a more agreeable object than a black-board, and I am convinced that some of my old school-mates would have assaulted a bristling *tete de pont* with more alacrity than they had aforetime evinced in demonstrating the *pons asinorum*.

---

stomach, and promise to promote the health of the body politic to a degree surpassing the most sanguine expectations of those who expected most from the measure."

In the admirable speech from which the above is quoted, the eloquent Senator is particularly severe upon the press and people of Great Britain for their Pharasaical pretensions, and justly denounces the inconsistency with which, after acquiring empires by the sword, on the most frivolous pretexts, they presume to arraign this country for its rapacity.

* "The volunteers of Mexico, were the picked men of the nation, who, devoting themselves to a service more than a thousand miles from home, went to it under the strong impulse of adventure and love of martial glory. They consisted of the young, the ardent, and the brave, who, for the time, renounced all domestic pursuits and marched to the field, animated by the hope of distinction, and disenthralled from all civil cares and engagements. Thus fortified by resolve, stimulated by love of the profession, cheered by loud acclamations of friends, unimpeded by domestic solicitude, and filled with the ardor and courage of the national character, they more resemble the chivalry, which a few centuries ago, assembled around Gonsalvo de Cordova, or Gaston de Foix, in their descents upon the fields of Italy, than they do any army of modern times. The skill, concert, impetuous valor and persevering labor of their assaults, will be the theme of commendation from military critics in centuries to come, while the brilliancy of their victories over such disproportioned numbers, and the rapidity of their conquest of the strongholds of Mexico, will be regarded as the marvels of the age in which they were achieved."—*Hon. J. P. Kennedy.*

Many adventurous spirits who had failed to obtain desirable places in the Infantry, and who were determined to participate in the war even as privates, attracted by the loose discipline and hazardous service of the Texan Cavalry, had become Rangers. There were two regiments of Texan troops with the army, commanded by Colonels Hays and Wood, comprising the brigade of General Henderson. Their knowledge of the character of the enemy and of the military frontier, acquired in their long border struggle, rendered them valuable auxiliaries in the invasion. Of this far-famed corps—so much feared and hated by the Mexicans—I can add nothing to what has already been written. The character of the Texan Ranger is now well known by both friend and foe. As a mounted soldier he has had no counterpart in any age or country. Neither Cavalier nor Cossack, Mameluke nor Moss-trooper are like him; and yet, in some respects, he resembles them all. Chivalrous, bold and impetuous in action, he is yet wary and calculating, always impatient of restraint, and sometimes unscrupulous and unmerciful. He is ununiformed,* and undrilled, and performs his active duties thoroughly, but with little regard to order or system. He is an excellent rider and a *dead shot.* His arms are a rifle, Colt's revolving pistol, and a knife. Unaccustomed to the saber or to move in mass, the Rangers are of course unable to make a charge upon, or to receive one from well-armed and well-disciplined troops. But when an

* Some wag (doubtless the same individual who remarked that the Georgian costume was "a shirt collar and a pair of spurs,") has described the Texan uniform as "a dirty shirt and a five-shooter."

enemy's line is broken by the rapid volleys of their rifles, they then "pitch in promiscuously," and finish the work with the "five-shooter,"—delivering their fire right and left as they dash along at full speed. And it must be confessed that for a chaparral skirmish, or an "up and down and cross over fight" upon house-tops, such as that of the third day at Monterey, the Rangers have few superiors. Centaur-like, they seemed to live upon their horses; and, under firm and prudent leaders, were efficient soldiers, especially for scouts and advanced post-service, where the necessity for unintermitting vigilance left them no opportunity for indulging in the mad-cap revels and marauding expeditions for which they are somewhat celebrated.

Before the end of August, all the regular troops were *en route* for the interior; and intelligence was received from General Worth—who had taken possession of Cerralvo—that the enemy was in force at Monterey, and would probably stand siege. Upon this, General Taylor determined to lose no time in moving forward the volunteers, and bringing the matter to an issue of arms. On the 28th, the subjoined order, decisive of the long debated question, "which of the new regiments and brigadiers will Taylor take to Monterey?" was published.* We of the First Ohio regiment were much

---

* Orders } *No.* 108. } *Head-Quarters, Army of Occupation, Camargo, August* 28, 1846.

1. The limited means of transportation, and the uncertainty in regard to the supplies that may be drawn from the theater of operations, imposes upon the commanding general the necessity of taking into the field, in the first instance, only a moderate portion of the volunteer force now under his orders.

2. In addition to the mounted regiments from Texas, four regiments of volunteer infantry will be held ready for the march, constituting two brigades and one division, to be commanded by Major General Butler. The 1st Kentucky, and 1st Ohio

rejoiced at our good fortune, and heartily condoled with those less successful and loudly lamenting men, who, after coming so far to share in the glory of a campaign, were compelled, by "the limited means of transportation," to remain for weeks and months inactive upon the malarious plains of Camargo.

The reader will perceive, from Order No. 108, that the four regiments of infantry, comprising General Butler's division, were reduced to a strength of 500 men each. These, with the two regiments of Texan Horse, constituted a force of 3000 volunteers, which, with about the same number of regulars, invested Monterey. The allowance of transportation for the march, were as follows:

---

regiments will form the first field brigade, under the command of Brigadier General Hamer; the 1st Tennessee and the Mississippi regiments, will form the second field brigade, to be commanded by Brigadier General Quitman.

3. The regiments designated will be reduced to a strength of 500 men each, exclusive of officers, by leaving behind all sick and disabled men, and all who shall not be deemed capable of undergoing the fatigues and privations of the campaign. These selections will be made under the direction of Major General Butler, in the first, and the brigadier generals in the second divisions—a board of medical officers being convened in all doubtful cases. It is for the good of the service, and the reputation of each regiment, that the selections be rigid.

4. In announcing the above arrangements, the commanding general feels that he is disappointing the hopes of many regiments and superior officers, who looked forward to a participation in the campaign. But they will see that he is controlled by the necessities of the case, and that it is impossible to gratify the wishes of all. The selections have been made solely with a view to promote the interests of the service, and the successful prosecution of the war with present means. The general hopes, that after penetrating the country, and ascertaining its resources, he shall be able to bring forward other corps now unavoidably left in the rear.

5. The volunteer regiments, remaining at this place, will be temporarily brigaded for instruction and camp service. The 2d Kentucky, and 2d Ohio regiments coming under the command of Brigadier General Marshall, and the other regiments or battalions, under that of Brigadier General Pillow, the command will be exercised by Major General Patterson, or, in his absence, by the senior brigadier general, who will take measures to institute a rigid system of police and discipline.

By order of Major General TAYLOR:

W. W. S. BLISS,
Assistant Adjutant General.

To each division and brigade head-quarters,	1 wagon.
To the field and staff of each regiment,	4 pack mules.
To the officers of each company,	2 "
To every eight non-commissioned officers, musicians, and privates,	1 pack mule.

Three wagons in addition were assigned to each regiment, one for the transportation of water, and two for such articles as could not be packed on mules.

Such was the small force and limited means of transportation with which General Taylor took up his line of march for the interior, and which he was careful to place upon record, in a communication, dated September 1st, 1846, to the government. But doubtful as the result then seemed, his bold advance, under the circumstances, had a show of confidence, which, if it did not intimidate the enemy, at least inspirited our own troops. In consequence of the short allowance of mules, a great amount of baggage had necessarily to be abandoned at Camargo. But no complaints were heard on that account; indeed, the troops selected were all too glad to go, to stand upon the manner or order of their going. Such was their enthusiasm, that they would cheerfully have marched in their shirts alone, rather than have missed the *fandango*, as they facetiously termed the anticipated battle at Monterey.

Taking advantage of our wants, a number of native horse-dealers daily visited our camp, offering mustangs and mules at prices previously unheard of in that region. These leather-clad jockeys were the most arrant knaves I ever encountered, and, in selling their animals, rarely failed to sell the purchaser also. The wild, half-broken mustangs generally escaped in a short time to their native chaparral, for, "the Unicorn could not be less willing to serve thee, or abide by thy crib;" or, if detained by strong halters, were often claimed by other Mexicans, who had doubtless shared the purchase money with the vendors. In the prevailing desire to conciliate the inhabitants, and live up to the Proclamation, these false claims of ownership were, in many cases, recognized upon the bare assertion of the claimant, and the property restored; perhaps to be re-sold and re-claimed again by the same villainous confederates. Indeed, it was ascertained that one notorious rogue had sold the same mustang to five different persons; the animal having escaped from each successively, and been re-captured by the same lasso. The writer himself can not deny having been victimized by these Camargo cheats. After purchasing two mustangs—both of which disdainfully curled their noses at the wholesome oats given them, and finally, breaking from their pickets, disappeared in the chaparral—I determined to invest in mule flesh. My speculation in that article, however, was equally unfortunate. Shortly before our departure for Monterey, a Mexican brought a fine mule to my quarters, which I immediately bought. After tying the money carefully in his pocket-handkerchief, the fellow departed, politely wishing me much luck with the mule. He had hardly got out of sight, before another sombrero-covered wretch hastily approached my tent, and with well-feigned excitement, claimed the animal, averring, as usual, that the other Mexican had stolen it from him. Understanding the game, I declined to give up the mule until the thief (*ladron*, as he kindly termed his countryman and colleague in guilt,) was brought back to the camp for punishment. Upon his expressing an unwillingness to aid in the arrest, I bade him *adios*, upon which hint he vanished. I retained possession of the mule until the army reached Cerralvo, at which place I received an order from head-quarters, through a Colonel K., of Texas, who had charge of the mule train, to transfer the beast to him, for the use of the quarter-master's department, to which, it was alleged, the mule had been hired by some Mexican, who claimed to be its owner. As I sought no explanation of the trifling, though not unprovoking affair, I have never learned by what evidence the gentlemen at head-quarters satisfied themselves that the right of property was vested in Mr. Insolent Ranchero; and I have mentioned the incident simply to illustrate the character of the border Mexicans, to show how groundless were their many complaints of ill-treatment, and how over careful General Taylor was of their rights, real or pretended. The writer is clearly of opinion that his government is still indebted to him for the value of the mule aforesaid; and, (between us, good reader,) if the practice of allowing compound interest upon musty old claims, comes to be generally recognized by the Treasury Department, our investment may not prove to be such a bad one, after all; especially if we keep our mule out of Congress for a half century or more. My companions were of course much diverted at the result of the matter, and really I could not but admire the shrewdness displayed by the Mexican jockeys, in hiring the animal to our government, since they well knew that its claim would at once outweigh that of any individual officer or soldier. General Ampudia's proclamation * of August 31st, threatening death to all the natives who continued to traffic with the Americans, did not distress us very much, after our dealings with the Camargo people. Before leaving Camargo, the business of these horse-traders was broken up, in our quarter of the camp at least, in an amusing manner. A party of them having entered our lines one afternoon, were for some time quietly permitted to exhibit their horses and horsemanship, in which last they possessed considerable skill. Their greatest feat, and one which they practiced most, was that of bringing their animals from the most rapid stride to a sudden halt. This, which was properly esteemed as a great accomplish-

* The following is a copy of Ampudia's bulletin, which, (as Gen. Worth remarked in his letter from Cerralvo, transmitting it to Taylor,) "is ingenious, and well calculated through the clergy, to operate upon the fears of the ignorant Mexicans:"

"Considering that the hour has come for taking energetic and timely measures to free the department of the East from Anglo-American rapacity, and that by the laws of nations and of war, every traitor to his country, or spy of the enemy, should suffer the penalty of death; and, finally, considering that it is my indispensable duty to oppose a barrier to the torrent of evils caused by the contraband traffic which has been carried on in the most barefaced manner with the usurpers of our sacred territory, in virtue of the powers confided upon me by existing laws, I have determined to decree:

"1st. Every native or foreigner, who of his own accord, shall give aid directly or indirectly to the enemy, shall be shot.

"2d. Those who, after the publication of this decree, shall continue to traffic with the enemy shall suffer the penalty stated in the preceding article.

"3d. The authorities of every branch of the public administration will take care, strictly, and under the most rigid responsibility, that these provisions be punctually fulfilled.

"4th. This decree is intended to produce action among the people, since all citizens have the right, and are under obligation to denounce any infraction of it, and to apprehend the criminals in order to deliver them up to the judicial authority; and, that it may reach the notice of all, and that none may allege ignorance, I order it to be published and circulated among all to whom it belongs, to see that it be faithfully executed.

"Given at Head-Quarters, Monterey, August 31, 1846.

PEDRO DE AMPUDIA."

ment, by a people much addicted to *halting* and *dodging*, they were enabled to do by means of a ring-curb that is universally used. After the usual preliminary display had taken place, the natives, by preconcerted arrangement, were gradually surrounded by all the soldiers of the regiment not on duty. One of the volunteers—a famous wag—then mounted a barrel, and announced to the crowd that he proposed to sell at auction, "for the benefit of whom it might concern," the collection of live-stock before them. He invited particular attention to it as the most miserable assortment of *spavined*, *sore-backed* and *shoulder-shotten* mustangs, mules and Mexicans, ever seen in any market; and humorously added, that possession would not be guaranteed unless *strong halters* were used upon either the animals or their thievish riders, *especially the latter*. During the delivery of these and other preparatory remarks, the Mexicans—profoundly ignorant of their meaning, and wondering much at the position and merriment of the Americans—were either watching the speaker, with looks of astonishment and alarm, or peering anxiously around for some avenue of escape through the crowd.

The volunteer auctioneer, familiar with all the cant phrases of the horse-market, then proceeded with admirable spirit and wit to sell the animals, some by measurement and others even by the pound, "Commissary weight." This innocent fling at the Commissariat was received with great applause. He pleasantly commented the while upon the various qualities of the stock; now insisting that the ponderous ears of a certain ugly, brown mule, indubitably proved his "*Andrewlusian* blood;" and again, swearing that a shabby, little gray pony was a noble steed, indeed, a perfect Tartar, and would carry any ambitious gentlemen as far as Montezuma's Halls, to the tune of

> "Yankee Doodle came to town,
> Upon a little pony," etc., etc.

At this scene in the farce, some of the grave-looking Mexicans could not refrain from joining in the general laughter caused by the song and comic action of the auctioneer, who, while he sang, continued to saw with his right hand upon an imaginary fiddle in his left. Thus the sale progressed amid much lively and good-natured competition in the crowd surrounding the kicking mustangs and braying mules. Not the least diverting part of the affair, was the dialogue that followed the sale of each animal, between the auctioneer and purchaser, concerning the terms of payment, and which generally resulted in the granting of credit for some indefinite period, or the acceptance of a draft on the Mexican Treasury.

At the conclusion of the sale, the auctioneer remarked, that,—"flattered by the unexampled patronage he had received, and encouraged by the *animated* condition of the market, he would shortly invite the attention of the public to a *small invoice of excellent donkeys* or rather to *some small donkeys in excellent voice*, soon expected to arrive from the chaparral." With these words the wag descended from his stand; the crowd dispersed, leading away their purchases to their quarters, and followed by the excited Mexican owners, who now began to comprehend, though they did not seem to relish the joke. After playing for some time upon the fears of the avaricious jockeys, their animals were restored to them, and they left the camp under whip and spur. Nor did they again venture to traffic within our lines. As to the promised invoice of asses, it may be added that the sale was not allowed to take place upon their arrival, inasmuch as those musical little beasts were daily employed in transporting needful supplies to the camp.

On the 4th of September, General Hamer's brigade crossed the San Juan, preparatory to marching on the 6th. The weather was intensely hot, and we anticipated a thirsty, dusty, and fatiguing journey. We had, I think, but one rain during our stay at Camargo, but that was a memorable one. Though it "overcame us like a summer's cloud," it nevertheless excited our special wonder. It occurred one sultry afternoon in the latter part of August, when the sun was low in the west. Sitting in the shade of our tents, and looking toward the east, our attention was suddenly arrested by a dark cloud that was unrolled from the heavens, like the drop-curtain of a theater, and which completely shut out the distant landscape. It advanced rapidly, and we soon perceived that it was one of those showers, peculiar to the *tierra calienti*, which are concentrated in a single drop,—a mass of water from earth to sky. Their force is soon spent, but most unlucky is the traveler on whom they chance to fall. This cloud began to discharge itself not far from us, and swept directly toward the camp. Rainbows were playing upon its broad surface, giving it the appearance of a vast and beautiful curtain of variegated silk, shaken by the winds; while the sound of the falling water as it broke upon the earth was really terrific. It steadily approached, every moment becoming more fearful and audible, until, like a thousand horse "thickly thundering on," it swept over our camp with a force that almost crushed the awe-struck sentinels to the ground. In a few moments the storm was o'er, the cloud had sunk into the bosom of the earth, and the last glancing rays of the sun shone upon a scene of bright tranquility, as well as upon (to quote the immortal Mantalini) some "demd, damp, moist, uncomfortable bodies."

CHAPTER V.

ARRIEROS.—Packing the mules.—The march commenced.—Trials of the first day.—Cerralvo.—A storm.—Mustard *per se*.—Orders for continuing the march.—Description of the country.—Marin.—The enemy seen and heard from.—A stampede.—Crossing a stream.—A donkey going down stern foremost.—San Francisco.—The army arrives before Monterey.—Encamps at Santo Domingo.

THERE are two very good roads from Camargo to Monterey, on both of which it was supposed that a sufficiency of water, beef, and corn, could be obtained for the marching force. To avoid any inconvenience, however, and doubtless, for other good reasons, General Taylor decided to advance columns on both routes. The mounted troops were sent up the valley of San Juan *via* China to Marin; while the infantry pursued the more westerly route, by way of Mier and Cerralvo. From Camargo to Cerralvo the army marched by brigades; thence to Marin by divisions. At the last named place the entire force—horse and foot—united, and moved in one column upon Monterey.

On Sunday, September 6th, the 1st brigade (Hamer's) of General Butler's division commenced its march and arrived at Cerralvo, a distance of twenty-five leagues, on the following Thursday. The first day's march was the most weary and painful of the campaign. No soldier of our regiment will ever forget his sufferings on that unhappy day. Hoping to reach the first camping ground before noon, the tents had been struck, baggage packed, and every thing got in readiness at dawn. But it was not until the sun had been up several hours, that the muleteers made their appearance with the animals assigned to our brigade.

The mules of Mexico have always been usefully employed in its domestic commerce, and, indeed, appear to be all-sufficient carriers. Like the camels of Arabia, they are peculiarly adapted to the country and primitive condition of their masters. But to persons, fresh from a land in which all the many wonderful inventions in art and science are made subservient to the wants of man, a pack-mule is almost as great a curiosity as a battering-ram, or any other relic of a barbarous age; and accordingly we contemplated with some interest, the little animals, as unbridled and with most provoking and mulish *nonchalance*, they strayed slowly toward us from their pasture in the chaparral. Each of them was covered from neck to tail with a huge, arching saddle, of itself no light burden, upon which was to be packed a load of from three to four hundred pounds. One of the mules was laded with ropes of hide, to be used in fastening the packs. To another, the most staid and venerable member of the drove, was attached a bell. He enjoyed the honor of leading the train, and of carrying the large, smooth stone, upon which the drivers crush corn for their frugal meals of *pan-de-maize.*

The muleteers were stout, athletic fellows, and the most uncouth, as well, perhaps, as the hardiest class in Mexico; where the mixture of various races has resulted in the production of some strange looking species of the *genus homo.* Their features and those of the rancheros generally, are large, but less prominent than those of our Indians; their lips,

6

thick; their faces, smooth; and their coarse hair, like their eyes, black. Their frames are short and thick-set, and seem to be made of sinew and muscle. With great ease they endure fatigues which we northmen, even when seasoned to the climate, scarcely equal. A few *tortillas* (cakes made of corn, coarsely bruised by hand, with an infusion of chili and lime) and a gourd of water, will suffice the *arriero* for a day. If a little muscal or a few cigaritas be added to his allowance, he is perfectly contented. He seems to desire no other bed than the bare ground; and if rains overtake him at night, he will shelter himself beneath one of his large semi-cylindrical pack-saddles, the thick wood and leather sides of which, being bullet proof, make an excellent barricade in the common event of an attack by banditti. His dress consists of a short, close-fitting leather jacket, ornamented often with rows of buttons; and wide buckskin or dirty, white-linen trowsers, open and flaring from the ankle to the knee. The foot clothing consists of sandal-shoes, fastened with rough thongs—stockings being a luxury enjoyed only by some of the towns-people. The heavy, hand-made, party-colored blanket, peculiar to the country, is an indispensable article of apparel, and is at all times fastened about the shoulders. In bad weather it is unrolled, the head thrust through the opening in its center, and its ample folds allowed to fall gracefully around the body. This, with the wide-brimmed sombrero, enables the wearer to defy the storm.

Our *arrieros*, as if to make amends for their long delay, proceeded to pack with commendable celerity and skill. Walking rapidly through the camp, they first examined the amount and character of the baggage. They then divided it into as many heaps as there were mules, each one being a *cargo*, or load; taking care at the same time to place such articles together as would balance well upon the saddle. This accomplished, the mules were brought up to receive their burdens; which were put on by two men working on opposite sides of the animal. The largest articles, bundles of tents, barrels or boxes, were first lashed to the sides of the saddle; then upon those the rest of the load was piled, forming a ridge high above the back, the bulk of the burden being often much greater than the animal beneath it. Each article was securely fastened by cords passing around it, and crossing under the body. The men on either side, bracing their feet against the thick, lower edge of the saddle, and with the rope in their hands, would throw themselves back horizontally, and jerk and pull until the poor mule fairly groaned with the pressure. A few young and restive animals were only made to receive their packs patiently, by the application of a bandage, which the drivers carried for the purpose, to their eyes. The business of packing completed, the sage and distinguished wearer of the bell, carrying a few measures of corn and the primitive mill-stone before mentioned, was led off upon the road. The train obediently followed the well-known sound; while the muleteers walking on flank and rear, urged forward the slow and lazy with their peculiar "*hist! hiss!*"

Thus, after a vexatious detention of many hours, we commenced in the noonday heat, our memorable march. Considering the debility of our men, consequent upon recent sickness, the inactivity of camp-life, or long confinement on transports, I was prepared to witness much suffering on the route; but owing to the late hour of starting and the scarcity of water, it was distressing and lamentable beyond all expectation. Our route lay through dense chaparral which, being a little higher than our heads, shut out every refreshing breeze; and the dust, which was ankle deep, hung in suffocating clouds over the road. The vertical rays of the sun fell like fiery arrows upon the column, and so heated the burnished metal of our accoutrements, that it could not be held in the naked hand without pain. The heat was indeed almost intolerable, as the parched tongues of all momentarily united in asserting. Even the sable descendants of Ham—the servants of officers—drooped beneath it like blasted blades of corn. Before one third of the day's march was accomplished, our then inexperienced soldiers had consumed all the water in their canteens; the contents of which, at later periods, they learned to make suffice for an entire day. Unfortunately no supply of water had been, placed in the wagons, set apart by General Taylor's order, for its transportation, it having been supposed that the canteens would hold enough for the first short march; and had we been able to start in the early morning, we should perhaps have escaped that arid thirst. Many brief halts were made, and parties sent out on the flanks to seek for water. These were all unsuccessful, and the search but added to the fatigue of the explorers. After the first disappointments, the men marched silently forward, determined to brave the trials of the day with becoming fortitude. For some time, their great and increasing agony was endured with calm resignation. Many, whose scorched throats scarcely granted utterance, endeavored to cheer the weak with hopes of speedy relief, which they, themselves, hardly entertained. Our skillful, sympathizing, and attentive surgeon (Dr. Chamberlyn,) passed to and fro among the ranks, distributing pills, cordials, and other needful tonics, with which a mule, led by the hospital steward, was laded. Thus onward, still onward, with feeble steps, staggered our poor, uncomplaining fellows; all hoping to reach water at every turn or descent of the road, if only in some foul mud-hole.

At length, when about two-thirds of the march had been effected, with much pain and suffering, yet in tolerable order, a solitary rancho was descried a short distance in advance. The foremost troops hastened toward it with exclamations of gladness, for there, indeed, we might hope to find the much desired beverage; to us, truly, the precious *aqua vitæ*. Ah! deceitful hope! transient pleasure! The house was deserted, and the well contained not "a drop, to moisten life's all gasping springs." Each man as he arrived, hastened to gaze into its hateful depth, as if unwilling to believe the sad report of the first comers: "the well is dry!" What heart-sickening intelligence to those, whose veins seemed swollen with liquid fire; whose dusky skins and mouths were dry and crisp as ashes! Even at this distant period, the recollection of my own sensations causes some slight aridity in the region of the jugular. The acclimatizing fever—as the surgeon termed the fever with which I had long been daily harrassed—had seized me with renewed violence early in the march; and when we halted at the well, the blood was "boiling like lava within the glowing caverns of the heart." A hundred strange visions floated through the heated brain. Vivid and tantalizing pictures of bubbling springs and limpid streams well known in years long gone by, were again present to the mind. Then the wandering thoughts successively recalled all the horrible scenes of distress arising from thirst, which they had ever contemplated; from the notable case of that certain rich man who, "in hell lifted up his eyes, being in torments," to the latest narrative of shipwrecked mariners casting lots for each other's blood. And when from the crowd around the rancho, there broke forth some expressions of pain and disappointment that could no longer be subdued, the mind reverted to the wanderings of the Israelites, their thirst, and their murmurings against Moses in Rephidim, and to the rock in Horeb smitten by the rod. But the age of miracles was past! 'Twere vain to sigh for that rock and rod, or to expect relief, save by additional exertion. All complaints were soon hushed, and the column again put in motion. For another half hour it continued to drag its slow length along amid a silence that was broken only by the melancholy rattle of empty canteens. Then, when we were not more than a mile or two from water, occurred some touching scenes of human misery. Here and there, the weakest men began to reel from the ranks. Sinking upon the road-side, they declared that their strength was spent, and that they could go no further. Some were still helped forward by their stronger comrades, while others, whom no words of hope or fear could move, begged to be left to their fate. With these, threats and persuasions were alike ineffectual, such was their indifference to danger under the pressure of present pain. Soon all order was lost. The two regiments composing the brigade were mobbed, and the stragglers from both increased at every step. Had we been attacked at the time by a resolute enemy our troops would inevitably have been cut to pieces. This distressing and discouraging march was lengthened about two miles, for the want of competent guides to direct us to the usual camping-ground, which was near a large pond, and some distance from the main road. In our ignorance of the locality, the leading companies passed it and were compelled to retrace their steps. Upon reaching the water, many noble fellows, after satisfying the cravings of their own thirst, filled their canteens, and hastened back to administer to the wants of their weary and straggling comrades. Not more than half of the column reached the camp before dusk. The remainder came in singly, or in small parties, at various hours of the night, and but two of our regiment were reported "absent, and unaccounted for," at roll-call on the following morning. Those two unfortunate absentees never afterward responded to their names, and their fate has often been to me a matter of anxious interest. It appeared that they had left their company by permission, during a short halt early in the journey, to look for water. Failing to return as soon as expected, their captain supposed that they had wandered back toward Camargo; but they never reported themselves at that post, or elsewhere, so far as we could ascertain.

Such was our first day's march, upon the many painful incidents of which I have forborne to dwell. Much censure was lodged at the time against those who conducted it, but as I think, rather unjustly. Prudence should perhaps have suggested the employment of the wagons allowed for the conveyance of water; but I presume it was supposed that the length of the march (about five leagues) scarcely rendered it necessary. The late hour of starting, the unusual (even for that climate) heat of the day, and the physical debility of many of the soldiers, no human sagacity could have prevented. Under ordinary circumstances, the same men could, and frequently did march with ease, twice the distance in less time.

The second day we suffered less from thirst, and having started early, reached our camp before noon, without much fatigue. The country passed over was level and dry, but, in many parts, well supplied with mesqueet wood, and grass. Near our encampment, which was upon the banks of a deep and rocky ravine, one of our soldiers discovered a mineral spring, the water of which nearly resembled that of the Blue Lick, in Kentucky. On the morning of the third day, the men, though still quite foot-sore, took the route with all the cheerfulness of gay and thoughtless youth, and made a good march—more than six leagues—before 11 o'clock, A. M. We ascended the brow of a hill, overlooking Mier, just as the sun pushed his broad disk above the horizon, and poured a flood of rosy light upon the white walls of that pretty and interesting village. We did not enter the place, for our road, the general direction of which had thus far been parallel with the Rio Grande, after bringing us within sight of it, inclined to the south, and led us into a more hilly and broken region. There, too, the mountains of Cerralvo were first discerned in the misty distance, their airy tops so softly blending with the clouds,

> "That the cheated eye
> Forgets or which is earth, or which is heaven."

On the fourth day, we encamped by a clear and rapid stream, near Pontaguada, (in which village, *en passant*, we obtained some delicious dried figs;) and on the fifth we entered Cerralvo, thus making as good time as the Regulars who preceded us. It was gratifying to witness the improvement in the health and spirits of the troops as we approached the mountains. The tender feet of many unaccustemed to such laborious exercise, hardened as they progressed, and each day added to their knowledge in the business of campaigning. In the pure streams of the upper country, they washed away their wasting fevers, and before reaching Monterey, were generally in excellent condition for service. Amid subsequent toils and trials, the hardships of the first day's march were sometimes blithely recalled, and often served to assuage the severity of present privations.

Cerralvo is a smiling little town, of about twelve hundred inhabitants, and is built chiefly of white limestone, which is quite abundant in the neighborhood. The houses, as in all the Mexican towns we saw, were of the old Spanish style; with massive walls, flat cement roofs, and a few narrow, barred, and unglazed windows. The thick inside shutters, substituted for sash, exclude both air and light. Though devoid of all architectural beauty, they are not without their advantages in a warm climate, and are quite comfortable enough for such a people. A sparkling rivulet, fresh from the cool recesses of the mountains, waters the town, and forms, in its passage through some of the gardens, deep, clear, and refreshing baths. One enchanting little spot I frequently visited, where the brook danced and sang through banks of flowers, shaded by luxuriant lemon and fig trees, the interlacing branches of which offered a welcome shade and screen to the bather.

The country around Cerralvo, except on the margins of the streams, appears to be very poor and stony. The stratified limestone lay so near the surface of the hill upon which we encamped, that it was no easy matter to pitch the tents, the pins being broken or blunted in many attempts to drive them. In consequence of this unfortunate geological formation, our canvas was carried away by the first breath of a storm which broke upon us one night during our brief sojourn there. Of all confusions confounded or confounded confusions, but few can exceed that caused in a large camp by high and sudden winds, especially when attended by rain. A squall in the day-time is often sufficiently annoying, but when it occurs at night, when the frail tents are capsized in a twinkling, and the tightened ropes, and flying-pins are made to lash and bruise the prostrate bodies of thousands of sleepers; when, in an instant aroused from profound slumber, loose horses, kicking mules and swearing soldiers, are sent stumbling about among each other, tripping and falling over knapsacks, cooking utensils, and the many articles which the wind has also set in motion; what pen can describe the scene! "The storm fiends," as the poets aptly term certain imaginary gentlemen in the clouds, must enjoy the fun vastly as they ride by upon the blast. It would go hard with pussy and puffy old Æolus, should he venture to make himself visible within musket range of these ludicrous and vexatious scenes. What new dispositions were made at Cerralvo in our little army, will be known by a perusal of the annexed order:

Orders No. 115. *Head-Quarters, Army of Occupation, Cerralvo, September* 11, 1846.

1. As the army may expect to meet resistance in its further advance toward Monterey, it is necessary that the march should be conducted with all proper precautions to meet attack, and to secure the baggage and supplies. From this point, the following will be the order of march until otherwise directed:

2. All the pioneers of the army, consolidated into one party, will march early to-morrow, on the route to Marin, for the purpose of repairing the road, and rendering it practicable for artillery and wagons. The pioneers of each division will be under a subaltern to be specially detailed for the duty, and the whole will be under the command of Captain Craig, 3d infantry, who will report at head-quarters for instructions. This pioneer party will be covered by a squadron of dragoons, and Captain McCulloch's company of rangers. Two officers of topographical engineers, to be detailed by Captain Williams, will accompany the party for the purpose of examining the route. Two wagons will be provided by the quarter-master's department for the transportation of the tools, provisions, and knapsacks of the pioneers.

3. The 1st division will march on the 13th, to be followed on successive days, by the 2d division, and field division of volunteers. The head-quarters will march with the 1st division. Captain Gillespie, with half of his company, will report to Major General Butler; the other half, under the 1st Lieutenant, to Brigadier General Worth. These detachments will be employed for out-posts and videttes, and as expresses between the columns and head-quarters.

4. The subsistence supplies will be divided between the three columns, the senior commissary of each division receipting for the stores, and being charged with their care and management. The senior commissaries of each division will report to Captain Waggaman for this duty.

5. Each division will be followed immediately by its baggage train and supply train, with a strong rear-guard. The ordnance train under Captain Ramsey, will march with the 2d division, between its baggage and supply trains, and will come under the protection of the guards of that division. The medical supplies will, in like manner, march with the 1st division.

6. The roops will take eight days' rations, and forty rounds of ammunition. All surplus arms and accouterments, resulting from casualties on the road, will be deposited with Lieutenant Stewart, left in charge of the depot at this place, who will give certificates of deposit to the company commanders.

7. The wagons appropriated for the transportation of water, will not be required, and will be turned over to the quarter-master's department, for general purposes.

8. Two companies of the Mississippi regiment will be designated for the garrison of this depot. All sick and disabled men, unfit for the march, will be left behind, under charge of a medical officer, to be selected for this duty by the medical director.

By order of Major General TAYLOR,

W. W. S. BLISS,
Assistant Adjutant General.

The small garrison mentioned, in the last section of the foregoing orders, was the only one left on the route. Among the sick and disabled, about one hundred and fifty in number, who remained at this depot, was the captain of one of our German companies. We had one Irish and two German companies in the 1st Ohio regiment. According to Surgeon Chamberlyn's account, the captain, being sick with pleurisy, had swallowed in rather hot haste a quantity of mustard, which had been prescribed as a plaster. Though the condiment thus taken, internally and *per se*, proved as unwholesome as unpalatable, yet it served to season a good joke; and it was even contended by some that it had saved the captain's life, inasmuch as his unlucky mistake prevented him from participating in the battle of Monterey, where his gallant 1st Lieutenant was slain at the head of his company.

On the 15th of September, the field division of volunteers—General Butler's—marched from Cerralvo, and on the 17th reached Marin, where the Regulars awaited our arrival. Nothing of unusual interest occurred between those places. General Torrejou, with about a thousand horse, was constantly in front of our army, but distrusting his own strength, or intimidated by our steady advance, he made no effort to arrest our progress, and contented himself with destroying property likely to fall into our hands. The road led us over a succession of rough and bare hills, which, with the distressingly hot weather, and the length of our column, increased at Cerralvo by the addition of Quitman's brigade, Webster's battery, and the supply train, rendered our progress tediously slow. The country, as far as Marin, presented a more barren and desolate aspect, though better watered than that previously passed. From the summits of the thorn and cactus-covered ridges over which we marched, the *coup d'œil* was dreary and forbidding in the extreme. Far and near, whichever way we looked, the mountains, hills, and plains were glowing with the scorching heat of summer, a few narrow belts of green foliage showing where the streams yet generously moistened the thirsty earth. The rancheros were mean and scattered, and sometimes we did not see a Mexican during the day's march. On the borders of the stream, we alone found their wretched habitations. The intervening wastes appeared to belong to the banditti, judging from the many crosses erected on the wayside; evidences that the land was guilty of many "an arch deed of piteous massacre." The country is, for the most part, bare of trees. This is its great and ever-prominent characteristic. The fig, olive, orange, and lemon, flourish in some locations, but there are no forests, and a few scattered palmettos alone show their tufted heads above the surrounding masses of chaparral. The traveler from the United States finds himself continually looking around, but in vain, for the magnificent groves which diversify and adorn the scenery of his native land. In the vicinity of the water-courses, the student of zoology, ornithology, or botany, may perchance find something to interest him; but among the cheerless hills and plains that lie between the streams, there appears neither life nor beauty. The presence of an army, hastening to the conflict, did not materially enliven the dismal landscape. And yet, without pausing to seek its rationale, the idea most frequently present to my mind, when contemplating the country, was *its remarkable suitableness as a theater for war.* That desolate district, overhung by unclouded skies and burning suns, seemed to invite belligerent men to strife and carnage, as naturally as does the well-rolled turf, the horse-race, or the ring, the wrestling and boxing match. *Bella, horrida bella!* might rage with all her rampant furies there, undisturbed by a single tender appeal from the genius of civilization. There was the stage and all the scenery for war's bloody drama. Enter armies, and the martial spectacle is complete.

The village of Marin, said to contain a population of one thousand, is picturesquely situated on the edge of an extensive and elevated plateau. It commands a vast prospect in the direction of Monterey, and a charming little valley blooms at its feet. Into this we descended, after marching through the village, and directed our steps toward a silvery stream whose murmuring waters, as we approached it, filled our hearts with delight. With what "luxuriant joy and pleasure unrestrained," did the weary men stack arms upon its grassy banks. For an hour or more after halting, none of the usual camp labors were performed, and all resigned themselves to the bliss of rest in such a spot after a toilsome march. Officers enjoyed their cigars *in otio cum dignitate*, while the men, reclining in groups, chatted merrily with each other, or were quietly engaged in bathing their swollen and heated feet in the cool ripples of the brook. In good time, however, tents were pitched, fires kindled, and guards posted, the rustic deities flying the spot as Mars asserted his sway.

Those who have seen large bodies of troops in the field, can not have failed to observe how rapidly and strangely rural scenes are transformed by encampment. There is, perhaps, some favorite landscape which you may have known from childhood. Let yonder army, whose banners and bayonets you descry in the distance, approach and halt upon the familiar spot, the artillery on that broad hill-side, the cavalry in the plain, and the infantry down by the stream, and along the skirts of the silent and shadowy woods. In a brief half-hour an extensive camp is established with a celerity, quietness, and precision, that recall the story of Aladdin's lamp. Rows of tents arise as if by enchantment; these, with batteries, wagons, horses, fires, arms, and men, so metamorphose the scene, that your eyes wander over it almost in vain for a single familiar object.

Soon after encamping at Marin, we learned that the enemy's corps of observation had been seen leaving the town as our pioneers approached it. The absence of any hostile demonstration during so long a march, had induced many of our impatient young soldiers to discredit the report that there was a Mexican force in our front. A lance-head, found in the road, was the only "sign" which our Texan scouts had discovered until reaching the vicinity of Marin. The intelligence, therefore, that a considerable body of the enemy had actually been seen, and had even halted on one or two occasions to exchange shots with our van-guard, satisfied the most incredulous. When, moreover, they were *kindly* informed by copies of a Proclamation,* which the enemy, before evacuating Marin, had industriously scattered about the village, that one Pedro de Ampudia, and certain battalions with long and formidable-looking names at least, might be found at Monterey; all were happily agreed that a fight would be the sequel of the march; and, full of confidence in their brave old General and in themselves, regarded the capture of the city as *un fait accomple.*

While our army lay at Cerralvo, I had heard it stated that the Mexicans intended to fight us at some favorable point on the route; no one seemed to know exactly where. But as we afterward marched to Monterey without opposition, I

---

* "ARMY OF THE NORTH.

"*General-in-Chief, Head-Quarters,*

"*Monterey, September* 15, 1846.

"It is well known that the war carried on against the republic of Mexico, by the United States of America is injust, illegal, and anti-Christian, for which reason no one ought to contribute to it.

"The federal government having been happily re-established, a large number of battalions of the national guard in the States of Coahuila, San Luis Potosi, Guanajuata, Tacatecas, Queretaro, and others, are ready to be on the field and fight for our independence.

"Acting according to the dictates of honor, and in compliance with what my country expects of me, in the name of my government, I offer to all individuals that will lay down their arms and separate themselves from the American army, seeking protection, that they will be well received and treated in all the plantations, farms or towns where they will first arrive, and assisted for their march to the interior of the republic by all the authorities on the road, as has been done with all those that have passed over to us.

"To all those that wish to serve in the Mexican army, their offices will be conserved and guaranteed. PEDRO DE AMPUDIA."

6*

continued to regard the statement as one of the many groundless rumors of the camp, until recently informed by the Mexican history of the war, that General Ampudia at one time *had* decided to leave his intrenchments.* My surviving companions in arms will unite in regretting the counsels by which he was induced to change his plans; for, if on the beautiful plains around Marin, he could have advantageously employed "his well-appointed and numerous cavalry," he would there also have enjoyed the pleasure of witnessing some judicious combinations on our part; and have received gratis, a few West Point lessons, which he might have turned to good account in his subsequent professional career. But the Mexican General, it seems, was overruled by his *prudent* chiefs of brigade, who doubtless entertained a lively recollection of the manner in which our light artillery was handled at Palo Alto, and so—knowing that we brought no siege train—determined to await the issue behind his walls. A wise conclusion certainly, since from the advantageous posi-

* "He (Ampudia) decided to receive the invaders at Marin, by availing himself in the movement of his well-appointed and numerous cavalry. In the event of a reverse he still had a point of defense in Monterey. The advantages which the country from Papagallos to Marin afforded, and other circumstances, confirmed his hopes. With the object of adopting this plan he called a *junta*, composed of the chiefs of brigade. In it he espoused the project, and it was perceived that in Monterey could be counted, *beyond the corps already mentioned*, the 3d and 4th Light, 3d of the Line, the active battalions of Agua Calientes, Queretaro, and San Luis Potosi, *of infantry*; and the regiments of Guanajuato, San Luis and Jalico, *of cavalry*.

"General Mejia answered to the project of Ampudia, that he was ready to execute it, but the answers of the chiefs of brigade not being equally satisfactory, frustrated the plan. It was then agreed to prosecute the fortifications of the first line, and to undertake the second or interior intrenchments, and to so distribute the work that all could labor with indefatigable strength. The enemy, with their characteristic energy threatened us with a strong indication of a quick advance."—*Mexican "Notes of the War."*

tion of the enemy, do the scenes at Monterey, which I shall presently attempt to describe, derive their sanguinary coloring. The same numbers, in a fair, open field, could scarcely have withstood the first charge of our impetuous and enthusiastic battalions.

At *Retreat*, at sunset, on the evening of our arrival at Marin, the following orders were read to the troops, from which it will be perceived that the order of march was prudently changed as we approached the point of resistance:

Orders, }
No. 119 } *Head-Quarters, Army of Occupation,*
Camp near Marin, September 17, 1846.

1. The corps of the army will march to-morrow in the direction of Monterey. The following will be the order of march:

The advance, consisting of McCulloch's and Gillespie's companies of rangers, and a squadron of dragoons, will march at 5½ o'clock. The pioneer party will be broken up, and the pioneers will return to their regiments.

The 1st division will march at 6 o'clock, followed immediately by its baggage and one half of the ordnance train. The head-quarters will march with the 1st division.

The 2d division will march one hour after the 1st, followed in like manner by its baggage, and the remainder of the ordnance train.

The 3d division will march one hour after the 2d, followed by its baggage and the general supply train. The rear guard to be composed of two companies of regulars, one from each division, will follow the supply train, and close the march.

2. In case the Texan volunteers, under Major General Henderson, should arrive in time, they will be thrown in advance, except four companies, which will form the rear-guard instead of the infantry above indicated. The dragoons in that case will march with the first division. Four men from Captain Gillespie's company will be attached to each of the rear divisions—2d and volunteers—to be employed as expresses, etc.

3. The habitual order of battle will be as follows: The 1st division on the right, the 2d division on the left, and the volunteer division in the center. The chiefs of divisions will organize such reserves as they may deem necessary. The above order is not invariable, but may be controlled by the nature of the ground.

By order of Major General Taylor,

W. W. S. Bliss,
Assistant Adjutant General.

At dawn on the 18th of September, the slumbering camp was aroused by the gay notes of the *reveille* from drum and bugle. In a few minutes, the thousand tents which had checkered the verdant little valley disappeared, the morning meal was eaten, and the foremost troops began to cross the stream and march toward Monterey, still eight leagues distant. It was an animating spectacle, that gallant little army of ours, pressing boldly forward to the mountain peaks that had long guided our steps, and which stood like giant sentinels around the city that was soon to rock and ring with the shock of contending arms. But doubtless there were some sad countenances and heavy hearts among the villagers, who, from their lofty situation, watched the column as it uncoiled from the valley, and stretched, like a huge serpent over the hills. Far away to the south-west, a moving cloud of dust told the position and progress of the advance corps. For a long distance, the road could be traced by the bright bayonets that heaved and flashed like breaking waves, over the dark, green thickets, while near at hand, battalions and batteries were wheeling successively into column, as prompt to execute, as to hear the loud, quick words of command.

Hamer's brigade being the last to march that day—the brigades of the volunteer division led by turns—we did not get in motion till 9 o'clock. Just before that hour, and while the companies were standing at ease, awaiting further orders, a fat, greasy-looking Mexican, mounted upon a little sway-backed mule, came galloping up the valley toward us. Though the animal was goaded to the top of its speed with whip and spurs, the rider yet continued to use his arms and legs so industriously, that it was evident that his progress was not satisfactory, or at all equal to his notion of the importance of his errand. As he drew near, it was perceived that the man was badly frightened. The mule, too, seemed to participate in his master's fears, and was honestly doing his *petite possible* in the race. To the many questions, in mingled English and Spanish, with which he was greeted as he came within ear-shot, his only reply was, "*Canales! Canales!*"* ycleped at every jump, as he dashed

* The name of a partisan leader of some celebrity among the border Mexicans, and who, according to their many and conflicting rumors, was *ubiquitous*. He owes the newspaper notoriety which he gained during the war, more to the extra-

through the camp, and splashed across the stream, not pausing for explanation, in his anxiety to place as many troops as possible between himself and the dreaded pursuer.

Our drummers immediately beat "to the color,"* and the companies ran quickly into line. Those who had heretofore complained of their tedious position in the rear, then rejoiced at being in the post of honor. All were anxious for an encounter with the much talked of Canales, the Bayard of the Greasers, and every eye was turned in the direction whence the flying Mexican had come. Soon the tramp of horses, and the clatter of arms, informed us that a large mounted force was rapidly approaching. A few moments of anxious interest and unbroken silence ensued, terminating not, as all expected, in the shouts of angry defiance that hung upon every tongue, but in cheers of friendly welcome, as the advancing party was recognized to be the Texan regiments of Colonels Hays and Woods. They passed us at a rapid trot, to gain their position in the column. The terrified Mexican, not knowing that the principal part of our cavalry was advancing on the lower or China road, had taken General Henderson's brigade for the troops of Canales, an interview with whom, he, being a muleteer in our service, reasonably supposed would not be very agreeable just at that time.

---

ordinary fear with which his name inspired some of the country people, and the hyperbolical representations of our letter-writing corps, than to any success as a *guerrilla*. As, for a long time after our arrival in the country, we had only *heard of* him, and almost of *him alone*, I had begun to regard Senor Canales as a "man in buckram," and every Mexican account of his audacity and courage as a mere myth.

* The signal to form by battalion.

The army marched five leagues on the 18th, and before dusk had encircled, with its camp, the little village of San Francisco, which, like all others on our route, was nearly deserted. During the day, the men traveled merrily and briskly, their ardor increasing at every step which brought them nearer to the foe. The jest and repartee flew rapidly from rank to rank, and the songs were more frequent and vociferous. The few old campaigners, in the regiment, had already taught their young comrades some merry, marching-ballads, the measure of which chimed well with the swinging route step. Thus they went on, laughing and singing, over hill and plain; and, in the light-heartedness and unconcern of youth, extracting mirth from every trivial incident or accident of the march. Of course, in such a campaign, laughable as well as lamentable events were of frequent occurrence; and the former, by affording amusement, served to lessen the fatigues of duty. A scene, so ludicrous that it has not yet escaped from my memory, was witnessed between Marin and San Francisco. It was one of those that should be seen to be enjoyed; and which the pencil of Hogarth or Cruikshank could describe more faithfully than the pen of Dickens or Thackeray.

In the progress of the march we came to a creek, or rather what our western woodsman call a *swale;* the boggy banks and muddy bottom of which had been much cut up by the trains in advance. It was a sluggish stream of disgusting mire, which the wheels and feet of preceding battalions had scattered far along the road, causing it to look, as a sergeant remarked, "like the slimy track of an army of mud-turtles." A short halt was necessarily made, in order that the men might cross as comfortably as possible, during which the companies successfully passed over under a lively cross-fire of wit and ridicule, drawn forth by the little accidents which befell many in the ford. One of the first to scramble up the opposite bank, was a stout, good-natured son of the Emerald Isle, who possessed a full share of all those qualities which have given the Irish a deservedly high reputation as soldiers in all quarters of the globe; for what land has not witnessed their constancy and courage? After attempting to shake off the brown mud that incased his legs, he turned and shouted to those behind: "Ah! my jolly chaps, ye'll all be Quakers by the time yez get through that swate bog-hole?" Then, after another survey of his nether integuments, "upon me sowl, it's as lovely a drab as ever was dyed!" "Come on, boys," he continued "never fare the Red Say; sure, and was'nt it the Israelites thimsilves that made yer pantaloons?" This allusion to the Jew tailors of Cincinnati—who, it was supposed, had *taken in* some of the companies in their clothing contracts—and the idea that any such saving virtue as that insinuated, should linger in their threadbare garments, convulsed all with laughter. A short man, whose uniform was exceedingly ragged, waded the creek at my side, holding to my stirrup-iron, while I carried his musket. He, less fortunate than his long-legged comrades, was plastered from waist-belt to brogans, *usque ad nauseam*. On taking his gun he remarked: "that's first rate mud, sir it's patched all the holes in my trowsers." But the odor, I suggested, might not be quite as agreeable as that of spring flowers. He laughingly replied that he thought it would not be so bad when it became dry, and with great good humor turned away to take his place in the ranks.

Among the foremost to reach the stream was the bugler of one of our flank (rifle) companies. He had obtained a donkey somewhere and somehow on the route; one of the most deformed of its ugly species. Its head was nearly as large as its body, and supported a pair of ears that the prince of asses or of darkness might have envied. The little animal was quite a pet with the men, and had been made to play a part in many comic scenes. It was unusually lively and musical withal, and seldom failed to lend its melodious vocal accompaniment to the instrumental performances of its master. The wags of the regiment pretended to regard it as the chief musician of the corps, and to incense the drum-major, sometimes offered mock obedience to its bray. This wonderful production of the animal kingdom the bugler had been permitted to ride during the march, much to his own satisfaction, and the amusement of others. When near the bank of the muddy creek, the donkey "smelt a rat"—a muskrat, perhaps, in that situation—and halting, suddenly braced himself back in the usual manner of his stubborn race; and which graceful attitude was understood to signify: "here's one donkey that won't go it." Without pausing—in the words of a popular comic song—"to give him some hay, and ax him to go," the rider, by the prompt application of a stout cudgel, compelled him to enter the water and advance a few steps from the shore. While in that situation, one of the heaviest men in the battalion mounted behind the musician, and humorously insisted upon being "*toted*" across. The little animal, already overladed, sank deep in the mire under the additional weight, and becoming seriously alarmed, stretched its head toward the dry land and brayed both loud and long. In vain did the merry bugler coax, or the soldier *en croupe*, prick with his bayonet. The beast of Balaam was not more immoveable. The predicament of the pet donkey, naturally enough, elicited many amusing remarks from the men, as they waded across. "Well, Bob," said one to a comrade, "I always did admire music on the water, and that ere jackass is a full brass band—*he* is." Another hailing the bugler, politely desired to be informed "whether he intended to run all night?" A third ventured to tell him that if he wished to stop, he could do so by "pulling the strings." The hind quarters of the poor animal were, by this time, setting rapidly in the bog, while its ears stuck out like the masts of a stranded ship. "Twig him now," shouted some one, "he's going down stern foremost." "Throw your guns overboard!" "Take to the life boats!" and many other such exclamations were made by the crowd. The bugler's donkey was finally brought over, as were the wagons, by dint of much laborious pushing and pulling. After a general scraping off we again moved forward, and though halting "to noon" at the village of Agua Frio, reached camp at San Francisco before sunset.

Such scenes as that I have attempted to describe, often enlivened our march to Monterey; and toward the close of it, the regiment was in excellent health and cheerfully encountered every labor and difficulty. To our young troops, even the dangers and the duties of the service had a romance in them that was particularly fascinating. Owing to the absence of sufficient means of conveyance, or the negligence of the rear-guard, many tents and much private baggage—mine included—had been left by the muleteers at Cerralvo; and it was not until many days after the battle of Monterey that we recovered them. My friends made themselves merry over my misfortune, especially as they knew that the mule which I had purchased at Camargo had been claimed for the public service, and probably had aided in the transportation of their own baggage. But I had remaining a good saddle-blanket, and as the ground was dry and the weather clear, suffered no great hardship.

The scenery, which daily became more interesting and charming, was an ever-present source of pleasure to some of us. Before reaching Marin, the road, deflecting to the west, had brought us almost imperceptibly into a broad valley which was inclosed on the one side by the gigantic Sierra Madre, and on the other by the Cerralvo range. The mountains, first seen from Mier, floating like clouds in the distance, now reared their bold and rugged peaks far into the sky, showing

> "How earth may pierce to heaven, yet leave vain man below."

These massive palaces of nature increased in hight and grandeur as we advanced; the gorge or pass through the Sierra Madre, at the mouth of which Monterey is situated, expanding as we approached, daily, almost hourly, disclosed new beauties to the eye.

> "Thus, from afar, each dim-discovered scene,
> More pleasing seems, than all the past hath been."

The mountain scenery of Northern Mexico is singularly striking and grand. The Sierra Madre chain differs from all that I have seen, in the abruptness with which it rises, like a vast wall, from the bosom of the plain. And a most suitable boundary it is, for the wide and wild expanse that lies between it and the coast. The great Appalachian range of the United States, having its feet buried in numberless broad and high-rolling hills, does not so fill the eye or the heart. Unlike our mountains, too, the Sierra Madre wears no forest drapery around its majestic form; a few pines and cedars alone fringing its summit, or crowning the pinnacle of some jutting crag. Yet the rough, weather-stained rocks upon its sides, deeply set in moss, and half overgrown with shrubs, vines, and the bright-flowering cacti, make it a beautiful object, and one which the lover of scenery will ever "clasp firmly in the mind's embrace." I have gazed upon it at all hours and seasons, and always with increased delight. View it when you will—and 'tis ever attracting *the musing eye*—either when night melts into morn, and the growing light disrobes it of the cloudy garment it sometimes wears; when glowing at midday in the soft light of serenest skies; when twilight lingers o'er its craggy sides, "beautiful as dreams of heaven;" or when the silvery moon, at evening bright, walks o'er its dewy crest; it is always grand and enchanting. Even now, it rises before the mental vision, its towering peaks and richly tinted slopes looming through the mellow haze of that entrancing climate like a shadowy specter, called up by some magician's incantations.

At San Francisco, after taking a hearty supper, composed,

as usual, of coffee, hard biscuit, and tough beef, (the stereotyped bill of fare, to which sometimes was added a kid or chicken,) a friend and myself climbed upon the flat roof of one of the village houses, to enjoy the view and evening breeze from the mountains. The prospect was an agreeable one, and amply compensated us for all the bruises and scratches attending the ascent, caused by thrusting the hands and feet into the holes which Mexican masons leave in the outer walls, as the only means of reaching the roofs of such buildings. The surrounding country was flat and uncultivated, slightly descending toward the Sierra Madre in our front. We turned our eyes in that direction, hoping to obtain a glimpse of Monterey, knowing its position between the now prominent *Saddle* and *Miter* mountains*—peaks which had long been to our march, as the cloud to the path of Israel. But the advancing shadows from the Sierra, and the dense foliage of the shallow valley in which it is situated, concealed it from view. In the gardens and streets of the hamlet, and in the few green fields around it, lay our army, just then busied with the last labors of the day. On one side of us were the quiet and sytematic blue-clad soldiers of the old line; on the other, the gay and rollicking volunteers, diverse in their uniforms as their states. Many of these last seemed unusually merry, and little thought or cared for the

---

* These lofty mountains, jutting from the main range of the Sierra Madre, flank the city on the east and west, and obtain their names from the very strong resemblance which their peaks respectively bear to the deep-seated Spanish saddle, and a Bishop's miter. They are correctly and beautifully represented in the lithographed views of Monterey, taken from pictures by that accomplished artist, Captain Whiting, of the 7th Infantry.

morrow, on which some of them were to make their last march on earth.

Though the hostile armies were then almost within sound of each other's drums, the Mexicans continued to practice their policy of "a masterly inactivity," and had evidently concluded, rather than get into any disagreeable scrapes, to let us have our own way. An invading army in the United States, I take it, would have fared somewhat less comfortably. The boasted light cavalry of Ampudia, must have been composed of apathetic and most unenterprising fellows, or methinks they would have preferred a dash into our lines, some pleasant night, to the dull amusements afforded by the *fondas* of Monterey. Though there were many favorable positions for ambuscades along our route, yet nothing more formidable than the natural difficulties of roads and climate harassed our march; nothing more alarming than the howl of greedy wolves disturbed the repose of our camps. These animals, by the way, are very numerous throughout the country, and were induced, by the savor of our mess-pans, to give us frequent serenades. They are very bold, too, and great pests to the shepherds and herdsmen. I have occasionally seen them at dusk, prowling within the suburbs of large towns, a temerity encouraged by the absence of a rural population in Northern Mexico; for there, the whole country without the walls of the villages, is surrendered to the beast and bandit. The season was exceedingly propitious for both these animals. The robber accepted a pardon from his government, and took, in addition to his plunder, the pay of a guerrilla; and the wolf not only obtained an unusual share of ox, mule, and horse flesh, but many a human corse found its way into his rapacious maw.

At sunrise on the 19th of September, General Taylor with the mounted troops marched from San Francisco, followed, at intervals of an hour, by the three infantry divisions. The order of march being the same as that of the previous day, we were again in the rear. We had scarcely left the village, when a cannon-shot was heard in the direction of Monterey. Every man instantly, and almost involuntarily, stopped to catch the sound. It was the first hostile gun many of us had ever heard, and for the moment arrested every word and thought.

"But hark! that heavy sound breaks in once more,
As if the clouds its echo would repeat,
And nearer, clearer, deadlier, than before!
On! on! it is—it is the cannon's opening roar!"

The first solitary and rather indistinct report was soon followed by the unmistakable booming of distant artillery, which rolled, on the morning breeze, far over the wide-spreading plain. "Column, forward! *Quick*—march!" shouted the chiefs of battalions, and away the men went at a stride which kept the mounted officers in a trot. Every heart beat high with new and strong emotions, and the most desirable enthusiasm pervaded the various companies and regiments, as they dashed, with their rattling accouterments, through the chaparral, like a swollen and angry torrent through some mountain glen. All supposed that the advance guard had encountered the enemy in force outside the city walls, and, knowing the value of minutes on such occasions, we pressed forward for some miles at the greatest speed compatible with order. The heat and extraordinary exertion were beginning to tell upon the men, when a dragoon—his horse covered with mud and foam—came dashing to the rear, to inform us that the firing was from one of the Mexican forts upon General Taylor and the Texan troops, who had ventured within range of the enemy's guns.

This intelligence allowed a most welcome halt, after which the march was renewed and finished at a more comfortable pace. The road, as we approached the city, had been much broken up by the enemy, and in some places flooded by the damming of little streams that crossed it, so that the soldiers were again compelled to push the wagons through the mire. The army encamped in the beautiful grove of Santo Domingo, two miles from Monterey. A slight elevation, about midway concealed the city from our view. This delightful camping-ground was erroneously called, by the letter-writers, "the *Walnut Springs.*" The grove contains perhaps more than one hundred acres, and is composed chiefly of live oak and pecan trees, whose spreading boughs are thickly covered with the funereal drapery of Spanish moss. It is watered by many clear, gushing springs, the moisture of which has probably caused the remarkable growth of forest trees, so uncommon in that country. The shade and water it afforded, made it a charming spot—just the place, indeed, in which to refresh a travel-worn army for battle.

CHAPTER VI.

The reconnoisance.—Beautiful view of the city and valley of Monterey.—Description of the fortifications.—Worth's division sent to seize the Saltillo road, and attack the western defenses.—Skirmish with the Mexican cavalry.—The action of San Jeronimo.—Divisions of Twiggs and Butler advanced on the north.—Attack of Garland's column upon the north-east corner of the city.—Its result.—Advance of Quitman's brigade.—The Teneria captured.—The 1st Ohio regiment enters the town.—Its operations.—Charge of lancers.—The repulse.—Loss and gain of our army on the 21st of September.—View of Worth's operations on the 21st and 22d.—The hights are stormed, and the castle carried.—The Mexicans retire upon their second line during the night of the 22d.—Street fights on the 23d.—The capitulation of the 24th.—Taylor's letter vindicating it.—Ampudia's proclamation.

The city of Monterey derives its name from the Conde de Monterey, one of the earlier Spanish viceroys of Mexico. It is the capital of the State of Nueva Leon, and the most beautiful city in the northern section of the republic. Say the Mexican historians of the war*—"The houses of Monterey are sufficiently handsome. Buildings of hewn stone, streets regularly intersecting, specious plazas, and a cathedral of magnificent architecture. A river, clear as crystal, flows on one side of the city, on whose borders there are romantic rural cottages, and gardens with thick foliage. The city from its origin had enjoyed repose; even the civil revolutions had many times spared it, sacred to the frontier. After the misfortunes on the Rio Bravo, the whirlwind of war menaced it closely, and the inhabitants anticipated the grievous and mournful conflict." Situated in a fertile valley, in the midst

* "Notes of the War," p. 65.

of lofty and picturesque mountains, nature has invested it with many charms, and blessed it with that mild, dry, and salubrious climate, common to elevated intertropical locations. The city is said to contain a population of twelve thousand. It exhibits no evidences of prosperity, and is chiefly supported by the wealthy landholders of the department, who from social or political considerations have established their residences within its enchanting precincts. It has no manufactures, and but few shops. The bustle of business is seldom seen, the noise of mechanics' tools rarely heard within its walls. Indeed, the modern Mexicans seem to be scarcely superior to the semi-civilized aborigines, in their knowledge of the useful or decorative arts. And, judging from the aspect of the country traversed in our march, they are not even as well instructed in agriculture as those mysterious and most interesting races who formerly possessed the land.

As previously stated, the army encamped before Monterey on Saturday, the 19th of September. During that day, and most of the next, our engineers were engaged in reconnoitering the city. So completely were its batteries, and the whole town, masked by luxuriant gardens and embowering trees, that but little information concerning its defenses could be obtained, though the reconnoisance was wonderfully extensive, at least one fifth of the inquisitive volunteers assisting in it. At the enlivening suggestion of a friend—" ye living men come view the ground, where you must shortly lie"—a few of us, soon after our arrival, had ridden down to the hill midway between the camp and city, and were surprised to find a great number of our soldiers already there. Some of them were strolling far down the slope toward the citadel, which, being situated just outside the northern suburb, was the only fortification distinctly visible. In the general desire to see that as yet unseen biped, a Mexican soldier, they had escaped from the camp, unarmed, and under various pretenses. The conduct of these men must have been no less surprising to the enemy, who were perhaps prevented from making a sally by the fear of some stratagem or ambuscade. In the event of a sudden onset of Lancers, the rash stragglers, defenseless and on foot, would have been slaughtered to a man.*

Of course the Texan brigade was numerously represented in such an adventurous assembly, but the Rangers, being mounted on fleet horses, could in any emergency have retreated safely to the camp. Like boys at play on the first frail ice with which winter has commenced to bridge their favorite stream, those fearless horsemen, in a spirit of boastful rivalry, vied with each other in approaching the very edge of danger. Riding singly and rapidly, they swept

---

* The thoughtless rashness of these men elicited the following order from head-quarters.

Orders No. 121. — *Head-Quarters, Army of Occupation. Camp before Monterey, September* 20, 1853.

The commanding general finds it necessary to condemn the practice which prevails, of small, unarmed parties, and even individuals, straying from the limits of the camp. No persons, except officers, or armed parties conducted by officers, will be suffered to pass the exterior guards, and the several commanders will give the necessary orders to secure an observance of this regulation. An infantry picket will be thrown out from the 1st division upon the Monterey road, at a distance of half a mile, whose duty it shall be to arrest all persons who may be found in that direction violating this order.

By order of Major General TAYLOR,

W. W. S. BLISS,
Assistant Adjutant General.

around the plain under the walls, each one in a wider and more perilous circle than his predecessor. Their proximity occasionally provoked the enemy's fire, but the Mexicans might as well have attempted to bring down skimming swallows as those racing dare-devils. While the marvelous ring performances of that interesting equestrian troupe were in progress, the artillerists of the citadel amused themselves by shooting at the spectators on the hill. But the volunteers kept one eye at least upon the fort, and wisely *scattered* whenever they saw the flash and smoke rise from its battlements. The distance of the battery from the elevation on which we were, about 1300 yards, afforded sufficient time for a change of position before the balls fell hissing to the earth, generally upon the spot where a group of men had been standing. The excellence of the enemy's guns, and the skill with which they were served, were the subjects of mingled admiration and regret.

From the position we occupied, a magnificent prospect met our gaze. In the verdant valley before us, lay the beautiful capital of New Leon, sparkling like a gem in the bright beams of the evening sun. The houses of Monterey, covered with a hard, white stucco that glistened like polished marble, were seen in glimpses through the acacia and orange trees of the suburbs.

"Amid the shade of trees its dwellings rose,
Their level roofs with turrets set around,
And battlements all burnished white, which shone
Like silver in the sunshine."

In the rear or south side of the city, and at no great distance from it, was the Sierra Madre chain, while on the east and west rose those remarkable mountains heretofore described, now seen from base to summit in all their grand proportions. As we looked upon the refulgent and beautiful city, reposing in the green valley, its charms coquettishly hightened by their partial concealment in the fragrant foliage of the gardens, the lofty and insolated Saddle and Miter mountains, along whose sides floated many golden clouds, like ships drifting upon a lazy tide, the whole scene was in such striking contrast to the country over which we had recently passed, that we seemed to have arrived at the very gates of Paradise. A paradise, alas! too soon to be converted into a Pandemonium. But with the roar of a hostile battery in our ears, we did not regard that lovely landscape with the calm delight of pacific and pleasure-seeking tourists. The imposing yet beautiful aspect of the city awaiting the combat, was viewed with feelings rather akin to those with which the keen huntsman, after a long and fatiguing pursuit, suddenly confronts some much-prized and formidable foe, at bay in its mountain lair. Its rare beauty and unexpected strength kindles anew the waning enthusiasm of the chase, and causes him " to hold hard the breath, and bend up every spirit," for the inevitable and doubtful struggle.

Linked in the memory with our first view of Montery, is one of those sublime and fleeting ærial scenes, by which the heavens are often made to declare the glory of God and the firmament to show his handiwork, and whose surpassing grandeur appeals to " every thing that hath breath to praise the Lord." There is a deep and romantic mountain gorge west of the city, through which passes the road to Saltillo, and the interior of Mexico.* As we lingered upon the hill to survey the dangerous charms of our fascinating foe, we beheld a dense cloud far up the pass, rolling rapidly down, like an Alpine torrent, toward the city. It completely filled the gorge, and concealed in its massive folds every crag and shrub as it advanced. It differed from the wonderful cloud we had observed with so much interest at Camargo, especially in the ominous silence attending its progress. Both were presented to our gaze about the same hour of the day, but that seen at Camargo, approaching us from the east, was brightened and adorned by the rays of the setting sun, while this, coming from the west, frowned darkly and fearfully upon us. As it advanced, it continued to rise and spread until it occupied the whole of the narrow valley through which it moved. The slanting rays of light from the west, piercing its thin, upper folds, formed a foam-like crest upon the cloud cataract. It was a mute and magnificent representation of Niagara. The resemblance was more perfect when the cloud, reaching the mouth of the pass, encountered a strong current of air flowing parallel with the Sierra Madre, which, while holding it firmly within its mountain banks, whirled in wild eddies the heavy vapor at its base, and scattered into mist the more elevated and projecting portions of the mass. Like some mighty host suddenly and impetuously assailed when marching in close column through a narrow defile, the broken

---

* Through this gorge, which widens into the pretty little valley of Santa Catalina, is the only practicable route for wagons and artillery to be found in the whole range of the Sierra Madre. There is another pass through the rocky rampart, many leagues to the eastward, leading to Tula de Tamaulipas, but it is rough and precipitous—merely a bridle path.

and tumultuous cloud, unable to extend its front, was dispersed as rapidly as it advanced. In this splendid spectacle, this combat of the elements, the deities of the air had imparted to us a practical lesson in the art of war.

Having loitered around the city until the glimmering landscape faded from the sight, we galloped back to camp. It was a pleasant night, and I did not regret that duty called me to watch through its witching hours. A solemn stillness pervaded the camp, when, soon after our return, I set out to visit the guard. Many of the men, whose tents had been lost on the march, were stretched in sleep beneath the umbrageous trees, dreaming, perhaps, of the kindred and country some of them were never more to see. A few individuals wrapped in their blankets were sitting or standing, silent and alone, their minds, it may be, occupied with dazzling and ambitious hopes of distinction, or obscured by gloomy presentiments of the coming strife. As I groped my way among the many obstructions which then filled the grove, I came upon a party of officers who were discussing in low and earnest tones, the rumored result of the first reconnoisance. In a brief conversation with them, I discovered that they were all greatly disappointed in the strength of the city, and anticipated a sanguinary conflict. One of them, a thorough soldier, asserted that any attempt to take the place without a battering train, would be to convert the army into a forlorn hope. But dark as the prospect was, all had evidently determined to triumph or die, and in passing the canteen, united in the sentiment, that a victory worthy of our arms and country might be gained at Monterey. The volunteers being generally inexperienced in military affairs, yet having blind confidence in their Chief, had no idea that the means in our possession were considered inadequate to the easy accomplishment of the object in view, and I believe that most of them would gladly have stormed at any hour.

But belligerent as man is said to be by nature, and anxious as all were to participate in that most interesting of great events, a battle, yet, probably, there were but few persons in the army who could regard with indifference such a trial as was then at hand. Officers high in rank, or occupying those fortunate positions which secure for them a favorable mention in the official reports, may see bright rewards glittering in the dark and dangerous future. In their ears, the weird sisters may whisper mystic promises of the Presidency, the Senate, and Foreign Missions. But *life* is their stake also, and considering the responsibilities as well as the rewards attending rank and station, it is doubtful whether their minds are as much at ease on the eve of battle, as those of the nameless soldiers, abused in the particular, and applauded in the aggregate, who are destined to die unwept, or live unhonored. To all ranks, particularly to us raw volunteers, the proximity of our enemy, and the certainty of combat, was strangely exciting. How anxiously did the mind at that hour contemplate the future! How busy, too, was memory with the past! How ineffably pleasing to the aroused senses were all the works of nature then! For ourselves we would confess, that when emerging from the shadow of the wood, we entered the open, moonlight plain in which the guard was stationed, the earth and its, "majestical

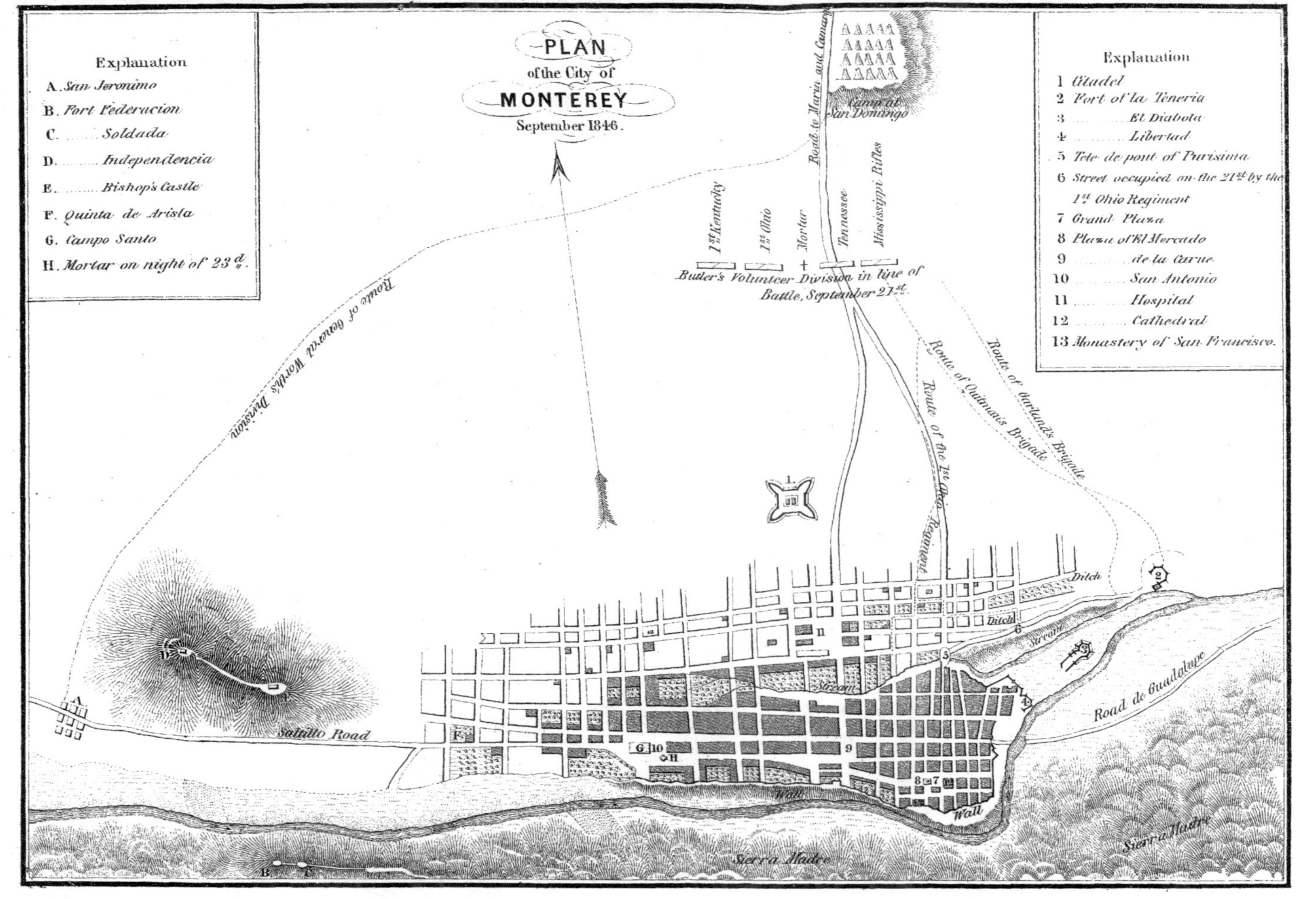
PLAN
of the City of
MONTEREY
September 1846.
Explanation
A. San Jeronimo
B. Fort Federacion
C. Soldada
D. Independencia
E. Bishop's Castle
F. Quinta de Arista
G. Campo Santo
H. Mortar on night of 23d.
Explanation
1 Citadel
2 Fort of la Teneria
3 El Diabolo
4 Libertad
5 Tete de pont of Purisima
6 Street occupied on the 21st by the 1st Ohio Regiment
7 Grand Plaza
8 Plaza of El Mercado
9 de la Carne
10 San Antonio
11 Hospital
12 Cathedral
13 Monastery of San Francisco.
Road to Marin and Camargo
Camp at San Domingo
1st Kentucky
1st Ohio
Mortar
Tennessee
Mississippi Rifles
Butler's Volunteer Division in line of Battle, September 21st.
Route of General Worth's Division
Route of Quitman's Brigade
Route of Garland's Brigade
Route of the 1st Ohio Regiment
Ditch
Stream
Road de Guadalupe
Saltillo Road
Wall
Sierra Madre

roof, fretted with golden fire," seemed more beautiful than ever before.

> "The balmiest sigh
> Which vernal zephyrs breathe in evening's ear,
> Were discord to the speaking quietude
> That wrapt the moveless scene."

The scene was, in truth, divinely calm and fair. Even the stern sentinels yielded to its influence, and like the radiant orbs above them, moved in solemn silence through the night. The large force assembled at the guard-station was unusually quiet, and while the men stood leaning on their arms, ready for any emergency, the thoughts of many had doubtless flown through that pure, serene, effulgent air, back over the wild and thirsty plains of the *tierra caliente*, across the wide and trackless Gulf, and up the great "Father of Waters," to the loved ones at home. From that happy communion, they returned to inspire many a watch-worn and weary soldier with courage and mercy.

The Mexicans, disinclined to night operations, permitted the hours to steal quietly on. Before morning had "dappled the drowsy east," or the *reveille* had pierced the sleeper's ear, the army was stirring; the blazing breakfast-fires dissipated the darkness of the grand old grove, and, though no orders for battle had been issued, the camp began to resound with the din of preparation. Soon the music of the distant church-bells floated sweetly and peacefully to our ears. These familiar sounds, it must be admitted, alone reminded some of us that it was the Sabbath; for the fourth commandment, and indeed almost every other not contained in the "Army Regulations," and "Orders of the Day," seemed to be generally ignored. Two Catholic priests were attached to our army, but what part they were instructed to perform in the campaign is, to the writer at least, unknown. *Quien sabe?* Certainly they never, perhaps for lack of encouragement, observed the divine injunction declared by the Prophet whom the Lord knew face to face—"And it shall be, when ye are come nigh unto the battle, that the priest shall approach and speak unto the people." If, as some believed, their appointment was designed by the government as a master-stroke of policy, it deserves to rank with the admission of Santa Anna to the blockaded port of Vera Cruz. But whatever may have been the motives of the Cabinet in the matter, the worthy ecclesiastics were well received by the army, and treated with due respect by the commanding general, who, unlike the Constable de Bourbon, had no fear that men would say—"Taylor is turned driveler, and rides to war in company with monks." *

At an early hour on the 20th, (Sunday,) I had occasion to visit head-quarters, where I found the General sitting before his tent, as "calm as a summer's morning." I learned soon afterward that an attack would probably not be made that day, and that the engineers under the direction of the gallant and accomplished Mansfield, were again busied with the reconnoisance. The position of affairs at that period, as will readily be seen, was well calculated to inspire the commander-in-chief with the most painful anxiety. No one,

---

* The reverend gentlemen alluded to, were Fathers McElroy and Rey. The former, I believe, remained at Matamoros, but the latter marched with us to Monterey, and was murdered by the Mexicans soon after the capture of the city.

however, who observed the cheerful manner and determined mien with which he received his officers that morning, could suppose that the usual serenity of his strong mind was in the least disturbed. On the bold spirit of Taylor, difficulties operated rather as incentives than discouragements to action. Doubtless, as at Palo Alto, he had resolved to fight the enemy, whenever, wherever, and in whatever numbers he found him. His officers and soldiers were not slow to participate in his courageous impulses and resolute spirit; they, "beholding him, pluck comfort from his looks." But few doubted the issue of the approaching conflict. Situated as was our army, hundreds of miles from reinforcements, with a powerful enemy in front, a barren and hostile country in rear, it became absolutely necessary to beat Ampudia, and take Monterey, cost what it might, and so, "out of this nettle, danger, to cull the flower, safety." Why, after Congress had voted ample means to prosecute the war, our armies in Mexico were so often placed in those fearful straits, from which their deliverance appeared to be almost miraculous, is a question that has frequently excited the attention and astonishment of the American people. The Executive department of the government being of course responsible for the conduct of the war, and the proper application of the men and money granted for its prosecution, has not escaped censure; but a more charitable explanation of the matter, may perhaps be found in the great extent of the line of military operations, the difficulty of obtaining transportation, and the unceasing and wasting inroads of disease. However, many perplexing obstacles might have been avoided, and many lives saved, had the prudent counsels of Winfield Scott, heretofore alluded to, been heeded by the Cabinet.

In order that the reader may have a better understanding of the battle of Monterey, it will be well, before entering on its description, to take a general survey of the fortifications of the enemy, of the position and strength of many of which we were not apprised until we received their fire in the progress of the engagement. The outline of the city, as will be seen from the accompanying map, is nearly that of a parallelogram, the longest sides being on the north and south. The only elevated ground in its immediate vicinity that could be made serviceable in its defense, was the steep and bare hill of the *Obispado*, rising from the western suburbs, and upon which the Bishop's Castle and Fort Independence were situated. Between this hill and a spur of the Sierra Madre, about six hundred yards to the south of it, and which was crowned by the two forts Federacion and Soldada, runs the river and road from the Saltillo pass. The elevation between our camp and the city, already mentioned, could scarcely be termed a *hill*. It was merely a low swell of the plain, within good battering distance of the town, however. On this elevation our Mortar Battery, (save the mark!) was planted. This formidable battery consisted of a single ten inch concern, which looked more like some old witch's soup pot, than one of those—

> " Mortal engines, whose rude throats
> The immortal Jove's dread clamors counterfeit."

It proved perfectly useless in that position, and our old gray-haired chief of artillery, on observing how far short of the city the first shell exploded, gave it a contemptuous kick which almost sent it from the platform.

The fortifications of the exterior line on the north were, first, *the citadel*. It was a remarkably strong work, occupying an area of two hundred and seventy yards square, and inclosing an unfinished church, which, in its solidity, like most others in Mexico, showed a military as well as a religious design. Indeed, the churches have been almost as conspicuous in the wars of modern Mexico, as were the "teocalles," pyramidal temples of the aborigines, in the Spanish invasion. This fortress, standing just on the edge of the plain, commanded every approach to the northern suburbs, which, thinly covered with humble dwellings, environed by luxuriant gardens, stretched from east to west the whole length of the city. Lofty hedges, and rows of fruit trees divided these suburban squares, whose dense foliage served to screen numerous parties of lurking sharpshooters. A small stream flows between the city and this suburb. The Marin road, upon which we advanced, and which is the principal thoroughfare from the north, crosses this stream, and at once enters the city by the bridge of the Purisima, a substantial stone structure, defended by artillery and infantry. All the streets leading in the same direction were barricaded at the stream, down to the edge of which the city is compactly built. To turn these works, therefore, flanked by massive stone houses, full of troops, was out of the question. And no prudent officer, advised of their strength and position, would assault them until he had probed in vain for a more vulnerable point in the enemy's exterior line. Such were the defenses on the north side of the city.

On the west were, *the Bishop's Castle*, situated about midway up the rugged slope of the hill of the Obispado, *Fort Independencia*, crowning its summit, and forts *Federacion* and *Soldada*, on a spur of the Sierra Madre, south of the Saltillo road. These fortifications, with the citadel, were the only military works observable from the plain. Naturally strong, and occupied by the enemy in considerable force, they seemed impregnable, and the troops selected to storm them were generally regarded as *enfans perdus*.*

On the south and east, the walls of the city are washed by a broad and rapid river, which flows from distant and almost inaccessible ravines of the Sierra Madre. Its high and precipitous banks were defended by the redoubts, *La Teneria*, *Diabolo*, *Libertad*, with other smaller batteries, all so connected by houses and fleches of masonry, as to form a continuous line of defense on those two sides. In additon to these works of the first, or exterior line, commanding all the approaches to the city, there was a vast number of interior street fortifications. Every square was defended by barricades, some ten or twelve feet in thickness, and many of

* These hights were, however, carried by General Worth's division, with such trifling loss, that many persons, supposing it the weakest point in the enemy's defenses, have suggested that our whole army should have attacked on the west. But it was (naturally at least) the strongest section of the Mexican line, and its cheap conquest is alike due to the admirable strategy of Worth, and to the extraordinary diversion, made in aid of his operations, by the ardent troops under Taylor, on the opposite side of the city. Had the whole American army been thrown upon the enemy's western defenses, it must be considered that, instead of meeting the garrisons only of the forts stormed by Worth, it would certainly have encountered Ampudia's entire force on the Obispado hill.

them having embrasures for guns, while the flat roofs, surrounded by high and massive parapets, made each house a fortress. At least ten thousand troops, regulars and citizen auxiliaries, with fifty pieces of artillery, held the town, the entire population of which was animated by a spirit of determined hostility. They were fighting, as they believed, for all that could nerve men to the most desperate resistance.

For the reduction of the city, thus fortified and defended, General Taylor had about six thousand men of all arms. Unfortunately he had no artillery suitable for a siege. With the aid of a half dozen heavy guns, it is believed that we could have taken Monterey in half the time, and with a tenth of the lives it eventually cost us.

The following is a list of the corps comprising the Six Thousand. But few of them had more than half their complement of men, and some had even less.

First Division—General Twiggs.

3d Brigade, Commanded by Lt. Col. Garland.	2d Dragoons, Ridgely's Battery, 3d Infantry, 4th Infantry.
4th Brigade, Commanded by Lt. Col. Wilson.	Bragg's battery, 1st Infantry, Baltimore Battalion.

Second Division—General Worth.

1st Brigade, Commanded by Major Staniford.	Duncan's battery, Artillery battalion, (serving as infantry) 8th Infantry.

2d Brigade, Commanded by Col. P. F. Smith.	Mackall's battery, 5th Infantry, 7th Infantry, Blanchard's Company of La. Volunteers.

Third Division, GENERAL BUTLER.

Brigade of Gen. Hamer.	1st Ohio regiment, 1st Kentucky regiment.
Brigade of Gen. Quitman.	1st Tennessee regiment, Mississippi Rifle regiment.
Gen. Henderson.	1st Regiment Texan Rangers, 2d " " "

Webster's battery (two 24-pound Howizers) 1st Artillery.

It was evident from the first that there would be a vigorous defense. The enemy made no petty sallies, or boastful displays of strength, but lay quietly behind their walls, awaiting the attack for which they were so well prepared. The greatest difficulty, that of breaking the exterior line, and effecting a lodgment within the city, was to be encountered at the outset. That accomplished, the enemy's superiority of artillery would be no longer felt, and the rest of the work would be comparatively easy to our skillful troops. Had we possessed a correct knowledge of the Mexican works, there can be no question, it is presumed, but that a night attack would have been advisable under the circumstances. In the want of all reliable information, the battle promised, as indeed it proved to be, a headlong assault of infantry columns over an open plain, within full view and range of the enemy's batteries. It has been remarked by a popular American historian that, "to defend walls, a body of sharp-shooting militia may be as serviceable as the oldest and best trained troops, but to attack them, requires that perfect discipline, and unyielding courage, which neither pain, nor death itself, can unsettle or subdue." Yet courage and discipline alone will not always insure success in such contests. The assailants should have a sufficient weight of numbers to enable them, after deducting the loss necessarily suffered in the long charge, to overcome the force against which the blow is directed.

By the reconnoissance on Sunday morning, September 20th, it was discovered that the enemy's defenses on the west, were not as strong as at first glance they had appeared to be, General Ampudia having placed a delusive confidence in the natural advantages he possessed in that quarter. The commanding general at once determined to seize the Saltillo road, by which route, on the day before our arrival, a *conducta* with a large amount of money and provisions had reached the garrison. The roads on the north and east were already ours, and our cavalry swept the intervening country. By this movement to the west, therefore, we should cut off all communication with the beleaguered city, except by the laborious foot-paths across the steep Sierra in its rear. Brevet Brigadier General Worth, whose splendid division, increased to a force of 2000 men by the addition of Hays' regiment of Rangers, immediately got under arms, was instructed, "to endeavor, by a detour to the right, to reach the Saltillo pass, effect a thorough reconnoissance of the approaches to the city from that direction, to cut off supplies and reinforcements, and, if practicable, carry the hights."

The whole army united in commending General Taylor, for assigning this hazardous and honorable service to Worth, not only on account of the pre-eminent qualifications he possessed for it, but because it gave that distinguished officer an opportunity of healing his fame, which had been so "shrewdly gored," at the commencement of the war. General Worth promptly and cheerfully accepted the important commission, with the remark, it is said, that it should bring him a "grade or a grave." He marched from the main camp at El Bosque de St. Domingo, at 2 o'clock, P. M., September 20th, in high spirits, and at the head of one of the finest bodies of troops ever arrayed under the standard of the United States. A Mexican prisoner, with a hempen cravat about his neck, was led by the Texans as a guide. It was hoped that the circuitous march of the division through the chaparral would not be perceived by the enemy, and Generals Twiggs and Butler were ordered to display their commands in front of the city, in order to divert attention from the seriously menaced point. This *ruse de guerre*, however, was unsuccessful. The large bodies of infantry that were soon seen pressing up the hights to reinforce the garrison of the castle, indicated that Worth's movement had been discovered. Owing to the difficulties of the ground, and the consequent delay in making the route practicable for artillery, the division was occupied the whole afternoon in its march from the camp to the pass. About dark, the Mexican cavalry, which had been favorably posted on the slope of the Miter mountain, charged and forced back some reconnoitering detachments of the Texan regiment. After a brief skirmish between the Lancers and Rangers, the increasing darkness compelled the division to halt, and bivouac for the night, just without the range of the battery of the Independencia. At nightfall also, the troops on the north side of the city were withdrawn to camp, leaving only the 4th Infantry upon the plain, to guard our famous mortar battery, which, some credulous individuals supposed, would, on the morrow, blow the enemy's citadel higher than the Saddle mountain. Thus terminated the operations of the 20th of September.

A gentle shower fell upon us in the night, pattering most melancholy music through our leafy camp. But the morning of the 21st was calm and clear. A fresh and balmy breeze played in the tree-tops, and the sun sent many a warm and kindly glance through the long aisles of the majestic grove. How many then beheld, for the last time, that most common, yet most magnificent and ever joyous spectacle, the opening of "the bright eye of the universe!"

It was understood that General Taylor did not then meditate a serious assault, but wished to make a strong diversion upon the center and left of the town, to favor Worth's distant and detached enterprise against the hights on the right. As soon as breakfast was eaten, the drums called to arms, and the regiments were quickly formed. One company was detailed from each to serve as a camp-guard. This, while it materially reduced our effective force, formed a corps of no great strength. Had there been any union or energy among the country people, they could, while our army was engaged in a distant conflict with the city, have overpowered the guard and plundered the camp. The loss of our stores would have resulted in great inconvenience and suffering, if, indeed, it would not have placed the army *hors du combat.*

A march of twenty minutes brought us to the hill in front of the town, where our columns were deployed; the Regulars (Twigg's division) on the left of the line of battle, and the Volunteers (Butler's division) on the right. The order and calmness which characterized the movements of the former, were in striking contrast with the excited step and irrepressible enthusiasm of the latter. A short time after our regiment had taken its position in the line, and while every eye was fixed upon the frowning citadel, whose time-worn towers were decked with many gaudy flags, a cloud of smoke was seen to rise suddenly from its walls. The next moment, a deafening roar broke upon our ears, and in the next, a shower of round shot came bounding up the hill and crashing over our heads. Startled by this thrilling and unfamiliar melody, this piercing "music of the spheres," our people, much to their subsequent amusement, made an involuntary obeisance to the volley as it hurtled past. The Mexicans managed the heavy guns of the citadel admirably, and their practiced artillerists had been wise enough to obtain the exact range of every part of the plain before our arrival. They had one long and excellent piece, mounted on the north-east bastion, which seemed to carry death in every discharge. "That infernal barbette gun shoots like a rifle," said a friend to me, as one of its balls thumped through the side of an orderly's horse, a short distance from us. A few men were killed and some wounded on the hill. The surgeons, who had already, with their usual professional nonchalance, displayed their glittering instruments and bandages on the grass a few yards behind the line, then commenced their merciful labors. It was remarked that, after the groans of the first sufferers were heard, but few of the soldiers seemed inclined to commit the offense of Lot's wife.

To describe the events of the 21st of September as they occurred, it should be stated that, even before our line was formed in front of the city, Worth had brilliantly commenced operations among the hills and gorges on the right. Leaving his bivouac before "the blabbing eastern scout" had returned to advise the enemy of his movement, he had, at the hamlet of San Jeronimo, encountered the cavalry of Generals Romaro and Torrejou, covered by the batteries on the hights. After a fierce conflict of fifteen minutes' duration, the enemy was completely routed, and driven in disorder up the pass, or compelled to take refuge among the mountains. The Mexican loss in the affair was about one hundred killed and wounded. Among the former, the Lieutenant Colonel of the Jalisco Lancers, Don Juan N. Najera, whose conspicuous gallantry and death-defying courage, elicited the admiration of friend and foe. General Worth, having thus become the master of the Saltillo road, prepared to launch his columns against the batteries on the hights—of which hereafter.

The enemy, after the morning combat of San Jeromino, finding all his communications cut off, prepared, with undaunted courage, to resist the closing of the fatal coil so rapidly and dexterously thrown around him. The citadel maintained a deliberate fire upon our line in its front, which was as steadily returned by Webster's howitzers and the mortar, but without making the least impression upon the enemy. Meantime, the light field batteries of Bragg and Ridgely were compelled to remain inactive in the line, (for they were as useless as muskets in that position,) their strong and courageous horses pawing and neighing with delight at the well-known roar of battle. The preponderance of metal being evidently with the Mexicans, the game of artillery was becoming a decided bore, when Taylor, advancing his left wing, brought on the action.

Lieutenant Colonel Garland commanding a brigade of Twiggs' division, was ordered, with the 1st and 3d infantry, the battalion of Baltimore volunteers, and Bragg's battery of horse-artillery, to make a strong demonstration upon, and, if it could be done without too heavy loss, carry one of the enemy's advanced works in the *north-east* corner of the town.* Major Mansfield, of the Engineers, accompanied Garland's column to direct the attack, which, doubtful and desperate as it seemed, was yet undertaken by the troops with a cheerful and resolute spirit. With what breathless interest did we watch the progress of that devoted column! Though the withering fire of the citadel was at once concentrated upon

* This column of attack included all the infantry of Twiggs' division, except the 4th regiment, which soon followed it into action. The 2d Dragoons (also of Twiggs' division) with Colonel Wood's regiment of Texan cavalry, had been ordered to scour the country on our right flank, and to support Worth if necessary. The writer has never seen a report of Garland's command; but, after deducting the company left by each regiment at the camp, his entire force could not have exceeded seven or eight hundred men.

it, it moved firmly and rapidly down the slope. Undisturbed for the time by the enemy's balls, a profound silence reigned through the volunteer division. The same objects filled every eye, the same sentiment every heart. The tranquil courage of the commanding general was not without its influence on our troops. Motionless as an equestrian statue, he occupied the highest point of the hill, his bronzed face turned steadfastly toward those well-known battalions of Regulars, whose courage and discipline were now about to encounter a trial such as they had never before known. Disregarding, and as if proudly disdaining, the galling fire which was unintermittingly poured upon them from the citadel, they pressed heroically forward upon the Teneria, a redoubt of five guns, full of men, and flanked by other strong works. Now an intervening field of sugar-cane conceals the brigade from our view. Again it appears, still moving rapidly toward those ominously quiet walls, behind which are kindling the fires of death. Now the distance between the head of the column and the Teneria is so short that the cannoneers of the citadel suspend their labors to gaze, like ourselves, in silent expectation on the issue of the charge. Another moment, and—

> "The pause is o'er; the fatal shock
> A thousand thousand thunders woke;
> The air grows thick; the mountains rock;
> Red ruin rides triumphantly."

Artillery and musketry opened furiously and together from the enemy's well protected line, shattering the leading companies, and striking down a number of distinguished officers. The open area in front of Fort Teneria, to which our troops had advanced, was swept with grape and musket balls. So great and sudden had been the loss, especially of officers, that the column was, for the moment, checked and stunned. Had Garland or Mansfield luckily been informed of the enemy's positions, they could then undoubtedly have rushed upon the front of the Teneria with the bayonet. But with the hope of taking the redoubt in reverse, the direction of the column was unfortunately changed to the right, and led immediately into the focus of fire from several batteries. The torn and bleeding ranks, unable to make head against that terrible storm, and unwilling to retreat, halted there, and set the smoke in which they were wrapt ablaze with their volleys. The Mexicans, greatly outnumbering Garland's brigade, being aided by artillery, and concealed behind intrenchments, had every advantage in the combat. The rank and file of the 1st and 3d regiments, and also of the 4th, which had soon advanced to their assistance, was badly cut up. Among their officers slain were, Morris, Field, Barbour, Hoskins, Terret, Irvin, Hazlett, and Woods; for whose precious blood a hecatomb of Mexicans would be but a paltry propitiation. Among those wounded in this assault, some of them mortally, were, the gallant Williams, of the Engineers, Lear, Abercrombie, Bainbridge, Lemott, Graham, and Dilworth. Failing in their attack upon the Teneria, the regular troops, dividing into small parties, and sheltering themselves as much as possible behind some scattered cottages in the vicinity, kept upon an annoying fire upon the advanced works of the enemy.

Meanwhile the division of volunteers had remained quietly

on the hill watching the fierce conflict that raged on the left, at the north-eastern angle of the town. The roar of artillery, mingled with rapid volleys of musketry filled our ears, but the scene of action, at first partially hidden by fields and trees, was soon completely enveloped in smoke, in the midst of which the work of destruction went wildly on. Again did the batteries of the citadel open upon our line. The fire was promptly returned by our *gameful* little mortar, which, if it damaged not the enemy, served at least to diversify the spectacle, for its shells exploding high in the air, formed beautiful circles of smoke that continued to enlarge themselves "till, by wide-spreading, dispersed to naught." The scene, even before the introduction of Butler's division into the affray, was one never to be forgotten by those who so anxiously witnessed it.

Soon from out the dark cloud on the left, reeled solitary soldiers, wounded and bleeding; then came small parties, bearing back officers or comrades gasping and groaning in agony; then staggered out from the fiery edge of the fight, broken and discouraged ranks of men, chiefly volunteers. The appearance of these, and of mounted messengers, whose haste betokened evil tidings, assured us that the attack of the 1st division had failed, yet the continued but irregular rattling of small arms told too, that our gallant troops were obstinately maintaining their ground. Considering the disparity of numbers in favor of the enemy, and his advantage in position and artillery, it is not surprising that some of our troops yielded to that destructive fire. The veterans of Wellington and Bonaparte have faltered in like situations.

General Taylor finding it necessary to support the attack, made at such sacrifice by the Regulars, now ordered General Butler, with three regiments of his division, to march at once by the left flank toward the scene of battle. The Tennessee and Mississippi regiments, constituting General Quitman's brigade, and the Ohio regiment of General Hamer's brigade were selected, leaving the 1st Kentucky regiment, which had been posted on the extreme right of the line, to cover the mortar battery. Our men, hitherto the excited spectators of the conflict, and standing "like grayhounds in the slips, straining upon the start," received the order with loud hurrahs.

The three regiments above named, moving left in front, advanced together in the same direction. Before proceeding far, the Ohio regiment was ordered "to the right," and instructed to enter the town at a more central point, nearer the citadel. Generals Butler and Hamer rode with us to the attack, while General Quitman with his brigade, continued to advance upon Fort Teneria. Profiting by Colonel Garland's experience, that general avoided any movement calculated to expose his command to the cross-fire on the right, and marched steadily upon the front of the redoubt. Arriving within musket range of the work, he extended his column and advanced firing. A terrific and incessant discharge of all arms was encountered from the Mexican defenders, but it neither checked not changed the direction of that blazing line. Manfully breasting the storm, the brigade moved firmly on till within a few yards of the fort, when the order to charge was given. Then the troops rushing forward through the smoke, scaled the low earthen walls, and took the work as Joshua took Jericho, "with a shout."

Captain Backus, of the 1st infantry, who, with a portion of his own and other companies, had previously gained the roof of a house overlooking Fort Teneria, by pouring a destructive fire into the work just at the time when the charge was made by Quitman's brigade, contributed largely to its capture. Too much credit, however, can not be awarded to the Tennessee and Mississippi regiments, for the unyielding courage they exhibited in the attack. In spite of a resistance hardly less vigorous and formidable than that encountered by Garland's brigade, they carried in handsome style, a strong and important position, and thereby secured to us that foothold within the enemy's line of defenses so necessary to our operations on that side of the city. In this assault, the brave Tennesseeans suffered a loss of twenty-five killed, and seventy-four wounded. Of the Mississippians, seven were killed, and forty-two wounded. The garrison of the work fled precipitately as our troops entered it, yet about thirty prisoners, including three officers, five pieces of artillery, and a considerable supply of ammunition, fell into our hands.*

* The Mexican historians give us the following account of the capture of the Teneria in their "Notes for the History of the War." Their complaint of the scarcity of cartridges is altogether unfounded. We certainly thought they possessed a tolerably good supply throughout the battle; and upon taking the town we found many well-filled magazines; even the cathedral contained several tons of ammunition. But to the extract:

"Then there broke forth to the north-east, a vivid flash of musketry and artillery, on the points of the line of General Mejia. A rude, sustained and desperate shock took place in the redoubt of the Teneria, whose limited garrison, with only four pieces, was multiplied by their glowing heroism. The attacks were renewed.

We now return to our own regiment, which, though then numbering less than four hundred, rank and file, was ordered, as the reader will remember, to attack the center of the northern front of the city. Its line of march was over the open plain, within grape range of the citadel, on our right flank; but the guns of that fortress, which had hitherto been trained upon more distant columns, were not soon brought to bear upon ours. The air above us was turbulent with whizzing and bursting shells, and more than once we distinguished a sharp cracking, as of balls driven violently in contact. The regiment advanced in excellent order, but not without loss from the heavy flank fire. Near the edge of the town we passed Bragg's battery, already in very bad plight, apparently indeed, a perfect wreck. A few of his artillerymen, and more than a dozen of his horses, were down in the same spot, making the ground about the guns slippery with their gasped foam and blood. The intrepid Captain and his men, though exposed the while to a galling fire, were deliberately engaged in re-fitting the teams and in stripping the harness from the dead and disabled animals, deter-

---

The impulse of the invader was vehement. The general-in-chief sent the 3d Light to reinforce us. The enemy came close upon the work when we had not one cartridge for the cannons. The assault was plain; but a reinforcement came up, with an order for the Lieutenant Colonel of the 3d Light, to sally forth and charge the enemy. The word to handle the bayonet was answered by enthusiastic *vivas*; to form column and then * * *. The parties say, and different witnesses do not satisfactorily deny it for this officer—with whose name we do not wish to defile these pages—that rushing out through the gorget of the work, he threw himself into the river, taking to flight among cries of scorn and indignation. By the desertion of the Chief of the Light, the enemy took the Teneria. Our soldiers retreated to the 'Rincon del Diabolo,' within musket range of the Teneria, whence they made a courageous resistance, distinguishing among others Lieutenant Colonel Bravo, and Captain Arenal of the artillery."

mined that not a buckle or strap should be lost upon the field. For the safety of this battery, the advance of our regiment was most opportune, as we immediately attracted the fire to which it had previously been exposed. On entering the suburbs, Lieutenant Colonel Watson, commander of the Baltimore Battalion, with two or three of his officers joined our column. That high-spirited and worthy gentleman was killed soon afterward, while bravely fighting in our midst.

We moved rapidly through a labyrinth of lanes and gardens, without knowing or seeing upon what point of the enemy's line we were about to strike. At every step the discharges from the batteries in front became more deadly, while we had no opportunity for burning a cartridge. Nothing discouraged, the regiment went boldly forward, until it had reached a point in the suburbs north-west of the "Puente Purisima," and nearly on a line between it and the citadel. There we met Major Mansfield, who had conducted the first assault upon the Teneria, and who had since been closely examining the defenses in front. He informed General Butler of the failure of that attack, and advised the withdrawal of the Ohio regiment, "as there could no longer be any object in advancing further, warning him at the same time, that if he advanced he must meet a fire that would sweep all before it." * The command was thereupon halted in a broad street, parallel with, and not more than two hundred yards from the enemy's works, at the stream heretofore described. Though screened from view by a dense

* From General Butler's Report

hedge of pomegranate, the Mexicans seemed well informed of our position, and, during the few minutes we stood quietly yet impatiently there, sent some terrific rounds of canister into our ranks. Among those then killed was Lieutant Hett, commanding Company H, whose captain had been left sick at Cerralvo. To stand still and be thus tamely and unresistingly slaughtered, was a severe trial for volunteers. Had the order been given they would willingly have cleared the hedge, and have stormed the barricades in front with indomitable fury.

We had been but a short time in that position when General Butler, who, on receiving Major Mansfield's communication, had galloped back to consult the general-in-chief, returned and gave the order to retrograde, and the movement was accordingly commenced in no very good humor. General Taylor, however, who was near at hand, animating, directing, and watching every shock and charge in the fight, "presenting himself even in the aim and very flash of danger," learning almost immediately afterward that Quitman's brigade had carried Fort Teneria, countermanded the order. At once and again the direction of the column was changed, and we re-entered the streets further to the east, striking at a point in the enemy's line between the tete-de-pont of the Purisima and Fort Diabolo. Upon the withdrawal of the regiment from the point to which it had first penetrated, the Mexicans had been encouraged to throw out parties of light troops, who, being familiar with the ground, followed us with a close and annoying fire. The order to countermarch, therefore, was obeyed with alacrity by our men, who hoped to encounter these skirmishers outside their walls. But the skulking sharp-shooters knew not only how "to fall on pell mell," but, as we perceived, how "to fall back and retreat as well." They retired in haste before our men, whose impetuosity the officers were directed to restrain, in order that the companies might be kept well in hand for the deadly struggle just before us.

Passing now near that quarter of the suburbs which had already been fought over by Twiggs' division, we occasionally heard, amid the roar of combat, the deep groans of the dying, and the cries of the wounded for water.* But in consequence of the oppressive heat of the day, and the quenchless thirst which seizes all in the fever of battle, every canteen was dry, and we were painfully compelled to witness, without the means of relieving,

> "The panting thirst, which scorches in the breath
> Of those that die the soldier's fiery death,
> In vain impels the burning mouth to crave
> One drop—the last—to cool it for the grave."

Among mangled bodies, and these melancholy sounds, the regiment marched quickly on, with shouts that were heard above the din of the fight. Thus for ten or fifteen minutes we groped our way through the streets, turning many corners, and crossing the northern suburbs diagonally toward Fort Diabolo.

At length a large open lot was reached within full view of

---

* General Hamer informed the writer, in a conversation touching these sad scenes, that he saw a soldier of Company G, (from Brown county, Ohio) climb an orange tree, the branches of which were being momentarily torn aad severed by the enemy's shot, and pluck some of its juicy fruit for a wounded comrade.

that battery, which at the time was engaged in a spirited contest with Fort Teneria, then in the possession of our troops. The artillery captured in the last named work was being skillfully served by Captain Ridgely, and as these now opposing batteries were not more than two hundred yards apart, the cannonade just in that vicinity was deafening. This lot or square was separated from the broad area around El Diabolo by a wall and a ditch. Between these two obstacles was a lane, leading, (as we too late discovered,) from an angle of the tete-de-pont on the right. As the regiment entered this open place, we observed a number of the enemy's skirmishers hurriedly taking position behind the wall. The next moment a line of flame flashed above it, and almost at the same instant the diabolical battery in its rear saluted us with a terrible discharge of grape. A few men of the leading companies were killed or disabled, and our colors riddled and cut down by this first discharge. We were now evidently "in for it." There, within sixty yards of us, were some of the olive-colored gentlemen with whom an interview had been so long and earnestly sought. The appearance of the regiment in the square was followed by startling explosions from every house and battery in that part of the town. There, and then, by that bloody baptism, did the 1st Ohio regiment obtain a name to which no pen has yet done justice. Never will the writer forget the gallant bearing of those courageous and obedient young troops at that place and period of the battle. There was no hesitating or wavering, no turning, or even looking to the right or left. A few of the foremost files discharged their pieces at the enemy, and then the whole corps made a dash at the wall, determined to dislodge the foe with the bayonet. No orders were heard in that indescribable din and uproar. The officers, first among whom were Generals Butler and Hamer, led, and the soldiers followed, as American volunteers I trust will never fail to do. One had but to look at their countenances, their set teeth and expanded nostrils, to be assured that those men so recently taken from the gentle pursuits of peace, were now ready for the wildest work of war.

The enemy's fire was, in my inexperienced judgment, particularly heavy. The guns of Fort Diabolo belched forth an unintermitting sheet of flame and smoke as we advanced, but owing to the short distance, overloading, or the excited haste of the cannoneers, they overshot us at times so widely, as to cut off the highest branches of some lofty trees growing thereabout. A thick smoke rolled over our men as they crossed the square, and to the mounted officers, their serried bayonets alone were visible, moving resistlessly on through the flickering canopy like an ærial stream. Before reaching the wall our progress was unexpectedly, though but for a moment, arrested by a wide ditch which was full of water. Into this the men, notwithstanding their ignorance of its depth, did not hesitate to plunge. The water was waist-deep, and flooded the cartridge boxes of some who unfortunately had neglected to raise them while crossing. By this misfortune a part of the corps was rendered temporarily unserviceable at a critical juncture. A few soldiers, who halted in the water to slake their thirst, were there shot. Adjutant Armstrong was severely wounded as he reached its edge, a grape shot passing through his leg, and entering the side of his horse. The enemy retreated from the wall before we succeeded in clambering up to it, and commenced a race for life, which some of them lost. The greater number, however, succeeded in sheltering themselves behind the adjacent batteries.

We were now in the street which unites the bridge Purisima with the Fort Teneria, and which is inclosed at the point where we entered it, by a ditch on the one hand, and a wall on the other. Spreading rapidly to the right and left, the regiment opened a general fire upon Fort Diabolo, and the houses within musket range in front. The more numerous defenders of these poured such a storm of balls upon us that we could not have held our position five minutes, had it not been protected by the wall. Against it, the Diabolo and his imps kept up a knocking that would have put our modern spirit rappers to shame, if not to flight. Some of the Mexicans at first exhibited a daring courage, often leaping upon their barricades to deliver their fire. But the quick and true aim of our better marksmen soon extinguished that vaunting spirit. Of course, in such a fight, most of the wounds given and received were about the head and shoulders, many of them fatal. One of our men, Myers, a soldier of the Rifle company was shot in the mouth, which was fortunately closed at the moment, so that the ball after summarily extracting divers molars and incisors, lodged in the upper part of the throat, whence it was easily removed. The gallant Rifleman, spitting out the teeth and blood, and coolly remarking, (in a voice singularly changed,) that the pill had salivated him, continued with his company for some time after receiving the wound.

Aided by the lively and effective fire still maintained by our friends in the Teneria, we were beginning to hope that we might ere long silence the guns of Fort El Diabolo, when, suddenly as the lightning's flash, and loud as the thunder's peal, a battery was opened close upon our right, and swept the regiment with grape shot from flank to flank. It took all by surprise, and taught some young soldiers a lesson they will not soon forget. It sufficiently explained, too, "why the Mexican engineers had suffered that garden wall in front of the Diabolo to remain for our *protection*." A question which I had asked myself more than once. So dense had been the smoke, and so intent had we been on engaging the enemy before us, that we had not observed on entering the street that it was enfiladed by the tete-de-pont of the Purisima on the right. The same causes, with the uninterrupted cannonade, had probably prevented the garrison of that formidable work from sooner discovering our exposed position. At the Purisima, General Mejia, who was charged with the northern defenses of the city, commanded in person, and his artillerists having us "in a string," kept the street so full of balls that the escape of the regiment from utter destruction seems now, in a calm retrospect of the affair, almost miraculous. But our men displayed much coolness and dexterity in the emergency, and dividing into small parties availed themselves promptly and prudently of such shelter from this new and angry cross-fire, as happened to be near.

It was evident from the moment the battery of the tete-de-pont opened upon us that our position was untenable. The Mexicans, with artiliery and infantry strongly posted in front and flank, could and did fire from behind their walls, deliberately and without much exposure, while but few of our troops were sheltered from the storm. Yet it was gratifying to behold the obstinate courage with which these volunteers continued the fight, each one demeaning himself as if the issue of the conflict depended upon his individual efforts. The smoke was so thick that the small arms were discharged pretty much at random, and most of our balls must have fallen harmless from those solid stone walls. But the guns of the Purisima continued to sweep the streets furiously, while his Satanic Majesty, El Diabolo, blazed like a volcano. Yet our silken standard, the staff of which had been spliced since the commencement of the action, by the color-guard, still streamed like a rainbow o'er the cloud.*

The "noise and confusion" were indescribable, and the inhabitants of Monterey might well have supposed that all the embattled legions of Pandemonium were raging at their gates. Our position was just the one, it appears to me, in which any anxious candidate for popular favor, who cared

---

* At the organization of the 1st Regiment of Ohio volunteers, it was found that nearly all the companies possessed banners of various devices. These were laid aside for special occasions, and the flag of Captain Armstrong's excellent company, (E,) bearing simply the national "stars and stripes," was adopted as the regimental colors. It was attached to a Mexican lance before the close of the battle of the 21st of September, and borne on it through the campaign. Who of my fellow-soldiers is so fortunate as to possess this tattered and battle-scorched banner of our regiment? He would much gratify his comrades, I am sure, by depositing it in some public place, and I would suggest the new Capitol at Columbus, if assured that Ohio cared to count such relics among her treasures.

less for the *reports* of fire-arms than of the newspapers, less for the balls of the Devil than for the disciples of Dr. Faustus, might have ventured to express his opinions boldly and candidly on the subject of "River and Harbor Improvements," or upon any of the so-called delicate questions of the day. The loudest voice was lost in the wild uproar, and officers were often compelled to communicate orders pantomimically, even to those who were standing beside them. About noon the storm of battle was at its hight, and the scene, as described by the reserve corps at the mortar battery, was intensely exciting and grand. The devoted city seemed to blaze at every portal. General Worth's division was just then storming the Federacion and Soldada on the right; the troops of Twiggs and Quitman in the Teneria, reinforced by the howitzer battery of Captain Webster, was thundering on the left, and dashing their blows indiscriminately upon the Diabolo and the cathedral,* while our little regiment combated with the more central defenses of the town. Volumes of sulphurous smoke settled darkly and heavily over the streets, in which blazed flashes of musketry, and the ruddy flames of deep-toned artillery.

——"The swift and deafening peals
In countless echoes through the mountains ring;
Now swells the intermingling din, the jar,
Frequent and fearful, of the bursting bomb,
The falling beam, the shriek, the groan, the shout,
The ceaseless clangor, and the rush of men
Inebriate with rage!"

---

* In the cathedral, a large and massive stone edifice, occupying one side of the *plaza mayor*, (principal square,) General Pedro de Ampudia had established his head-quarters, and there remained during the battle. An immense quantity of ammunition was also deposited in the building. The Mexicans had, therefore, divested

General Butler and Colonel Mitchell having been borne wounded from the street, and the regiment being more than decimated, General Hamer decided to withdraw it to a less exposed position. Indeed there was no prudent alternative, as nothing could be gained by prolonging a contest with such odds. And since the capture of Fort Teneria, the ground was of no value to us, certainly it was not worth the lives it would have cost to maintain it.

Those persons who have read the official dispatches, are aware that General Butler at one time intended to storm Fort Diabolo with our regiment alone.* It was, however, wisely unattempted. Admitting the possibility of organizing a general assault by our scattered companies in the midst of the confusion which prevailed, it must yet have been the most hopeless of all forlorn hopes. I do not believe that

---

it of its religious character. It was most fortunate for the valiant General, who had thus hoped to sanctuarize himself, that the church was bomb-proof, for the accomplished Webster, aided by his brave and skillful Lieutenants, Donaldson and Bowen, visited it with a heavy and searching fire. The only damage it sustained, however, was in one of the towers, where a large bell was splintered into fragments.

* "A very slight reconnoissance sufficed to convince me that this (El Diabolo) was a position of no ordinary strength. Still, feeling its importance, after consulting with part of my staff as to its practicability, I had resolved to attempt carrying it by storm, and was in the act of directing the advance when I received a wound which compelled me to halt. Colonel Mitchell was at the same time wounded at the head of his regiment. The men were falling fast under the converging fires of at least three distinct batteries, that continually swept the intervening space through which it was necessary to pass. The loss of blood, too, from my wound, rendering it necessary that I should leave the field, and I had discovered at a second glance that the position was covered by a heavy fire of musketry from other works directly in its rear, that I had not seen in the first hasty examination. There is a possibility that the work might have been carried, but not without excessive loss, and if carried, I feel assured that it would have been untenable."—*Extract from Major General Butler's Report.*

thirty of the three hundred men whom we could perhaps have gathered for the charge, would have lived to reach the walls of the redoubt. The regiment must have been crushed by the weight of the converging fires of the enemy. The writer respectfully differs from the gallant General of his division, in thinking that there was even "a possibility that the work might have been carried," by so small a force as ours. Nothing less invulnerable than that celestial armor which so protected certain faithful Jews in the burning furnace of Babylon's king, that not even the smell of fire was on their garments, could have prevented the annihilation of the regiment in the rash attempt.

The battalion, now under the command of Lieutenant Colonel Weller, prepared to execute a retrograde movement under fire, the most difficult that new troops can be required to perform. From the character of the conflict, the companies had become so scattered and subdivided that it was found impossible to re-form the line with much precision. But the column retired from the town in good order, through a street several squares to the east of that by which we had entered. As we emerged from the suburbs upon the plain, we were charged by a strong corps of Lancers from the direction of the citadel. Fortunately, as the regiment had not then been instructed in the formation of the square, a brush fence happened to be near by. Behind it the men were at once drawn up, and every musket leveled upon the advancing squadrons.

The cavalry is a favorite, and very numerous corps in the army of Mexico. The infantry battalions are composed almost exclusively of pure-blooded Indians, while in the mounted regiments the greatest number are of the Spanish and mixed races. The Lancers are graceful riders, and their chief weapon one which, I am inclined to think, is generally too much underrated. Until they import a larger breed of horses, however, they will not become very formidable troops; for, with all the aid of their heavy iron spurs, they can never impart that momentum to the "mustang," which in our cavalry tactics is considered of more consequence in a charge than the arms of the rider.

The troops that so suddenly assailed us were the 3d and 7th Lancers, under General Garcia Conde. The ground was favorable to the movement, and for some distance they advanced boldly and beautifully, their long lances gleaming brightly in the sun, and their whole line decorated with bandrol and flag. A great number of our soldiers who had been wounded by the enemy's artillery, were lying where they had fallen upon the field, and various members of the medical staff were at the time engaged in attending to them. When these were reached by the Lancers, we were compelled to witness one of the most savage and shameful spectacles which ever disgraced humanity. Surely the worst fiends of hell must have filled the actors in it, "from the crown to the toe, top-full of direst cruelty!" Not content with riding over and lancing, as they did at full gallop, those of our defenseless comrades who happened to lie in their track, large parties of those base and cowardly assassins, shunning an honorable combat with us, left their ranks and murdered indiscriminately all the wounded Americans in that part of the field.* The surgeons and their assistants, flying from the fate of their patients, were hotly pursued by the enemy, from whom they made so narrow an escape, that we freely forgave their attempts to play upon our nerves by the rather unnecessary display of their tools in the morning.

The main body of the Lancers pressed on toward us in gallant style, but their speed instead of being increased was slackened as they approached. In vain did we caution our men not to fire until commanded. So excited and exasperated were they at the cruel butchery of their helpless friends, that most of them discharged their guns as they obtained a good aim, but when the enemy were too distant to secure the most satisfactory results. Had they waited but a few minutes, their vengeance would have been ample. The first volley, however, emptied several saddles, and put them to flight. A few of the Mexican officers still galloped forward in the hope of encouraging their followers to renew the charge. One of these fell mortally wounded within twenty paces of our line, and in dying threw his baleful eyes upon us, still flashing "with obdurate pride and steadfast hate." The breath had scarcely departed from his body, before Lieutenant H., of Company A, (who had lost his shoes in the ditch,) limping from the ranks, proceeded to appropriate the boots of the unfortunate Lancer. Drawing them over his own sore feet he returned to his place, remarking that "there never was a better fit." Many other little

---

* Such atrocities have often stained the annals of proud and *magnanimous* Mexico. Yet the cruelty of the Texan troops, who were perfect saints as compared with theirs, is a favorite subject of complaint and censure with the Mexican historians.

pieces of serio-comedy were played in the shifting scenes of the battle, but to rehearse which would too much delay the progress of our narrative.*

After the repulse of the Lancers, our regiment was moved to a new position near the Teneria, and within sustaining distance of Bragg's battery, where we remained for some

---

* It may be a satisfaction to the reader to peruse the subjoined Mexican account of the conflict between our regiment and the defenders of the tete-de-pont, and of the affair with the cavalry. It will be observed that the want of ammunition is again pleaded, and here, it would seem, unnecessarily. And yet, strangely enough, in almost the next sentence it is stated that the Mexican troops "increased their activity." How can we be expected to agree with an historian who does not agree with himself?

The "confounded and frantic charge," so classically described in the extract is a piece of pure romance, a fabrication more shadowy than the fabulous achievements of the deformed Tyrtæus, and to which the word "confounded," perhaps misused by the translator, might with more propriety be applied. The sortie must have been made, if at all, after the withdrawal of our regiment from the vicinity, of the Purisima. Unfortunately we knew not of it, for certainly after contending so long with concealed and inaccessible foes, there would have been no shrinking on our part from the "breast to breast, and arm to arm," conflict. They are welcome to the laurel! gained by charging the dead, and bayoneting the dying. From the passage quoted, it appears that the 3d regiment is entitled to the dishonorable distinction of lancing fifty of our wounded men.

"General Mejia was posted at the bridge of the Purisima. There revived the sanguinary contest, which was tenaciously prolonged with great carnage. When all the ammunition was exhausted, the troops asked General Mejia for the park, who answered that it was not necessary while they had bayonets. This reply was received with vivas of applause, and they increased their activity. Finally an impulse seized upon us, our soldiers leaped the parapets, and as Tyrtæus said in exhorting the Greeks, breast to breast, arm to arm, confounded and frantic ours charged, and over the ground they had gained, and over the dead bodies of the enemy, and amid the vapor of their foul reeking blood arose to heaven the victorious cry of—viva Mexico. The brave men who gained this laurel were commanded by Lieutenant Colonel Ferro.

"The Americans having fallen back, General Mejia believed a charge of cavalry proper. General Garcia Conde was ordered with the 3d and 7th, who were in the place, to charge the enemy in the rear, by the way of the citadel. Garcia Conde led the corps to the point where he should have charged, and there the 3d alone entered the action, lancing more than fifty men of various partisan enemies, and afterward withdrew to the city."—*Mexican "Notes of the War," page* 74.

hours unemployed, save as a target for the Mexican artillery. But our soldiers endured the harassing service with uncomplaining fortitude. Captain Hooker, 1st Artillery, of General Hamer's staff, and Colonel A. Sidney Johnson, of General Butler's, were constantly with our regiment, and by their professional skill and gallantry, rendered it valuable aid throughout the action.

At the approach of evening, all the troops were ordered back to camp, except Captain Ridgely's artillery, and the regular infantry of Twiggs' division, who, under the command of Lieutenant Colonel Garland, were detailed as a guard for the captured redoubt during the night. One half of the 1st Kentucky regiment, which had been all day at the mortar battery, panting for the affray, was ordered forward to reinforce this command. The battalion approached Colonel Garland's position about twilight, under a heavy cannonade from the enemy. One of its officers, a tall, thorough-bred Kentuckian, and doubtless as brave a gentleman as any in the army, supposing that they were about to be led at once against the enemy, suddenly became disgusted with the small sword with which he had imprudently armed himself. It was scarcely larger than a fencing foil, and in his strong but unpracticed hand then seemed as useless as a bodkin. Scornfully throwing it away, and seizing upon two ponderous pieces of limestone, he marched confidently forward and entered the Teneria with one in each hand, ready and anxious for the fight. This incident was related to me by the major commanding the battalion, who jocularly added, that he thought of making a requisition upon the Ordnance department for a supply of hand grenades, to be used by those of his subalterns who were not swordsmen. It will at once be presumed, by all who are familiar with the habits of American boys, that the officer thus "in league with the stones of the field," had but renewed a favorite alliance of his youthful days. How often has the writer, and you, reader, if ever a country boy, when "creeping like a snail, unwillingly to school," halted to pelt the unfortunate ground-squirrels and cat-birds encountered by the way; or, with pockets well crammed with stones, aided some truant troop in the bombardment of a hornet's nest.

Worn down by fatigue we returned slowly toward our beautiful camp at Santo Domingo. Now that the brazen throat of war had ceased to roar, the silence which had fallen with the darkness upon the valley, seemed unnatural, and was almost as appalling as the sudden thunders of the morning. Like that valorous Captain and veracious Chronicler, Bernal Diaz, after the three months' siege of Mexico, we felt "as if just released from a belfry." This quaint remark of the old Knight, reminds me that as we retired from the field, the Mexicans rang the bells of the city in merry chimes, that did not altogether harmonize with the groans of the wounded and dying. But their boastful and ill-timed rejoicing neither convinced us, nor themselves, that they were, in our Western phrase, "out of the wood." Though we had not been prepared to witness so pertinacious a spirit in the foe, yet with one of their works in our possession on the east side, and two on the west side of the town, captured the same day by Worth's division, as will be described, we knew that they could not possibly maintain the town. The most intelligent among the defenders, too, must have felt that their fate was sealed, and even while their bells were pealing so joyfully, doubtless were "sorrowfully ruminating the morning's danger." *

The Mexicans, who always greatly exaggerated our loss, while they studiously avoided (even in official reports) any allusion to their own, stated that one thousand Americans were killed or wounded during the first day's operations at Monterey. Our loss was in reality but three hundred and ninety-four, including, however, some of the most promising officers in the army. But quite enough blood had been shed to satisfy some of our people that they had not properly estimated the military efficiency of the enemy. Yet in the condition of affairs on the evening of the 21st, we saw no cause for despondency at the prospect of victory. Indeed, in the events of the day, our troops found much to cheer and encourage them. If the snake had not been killed, it was at least scotched, and could not escape ultimate destruction.

As to our own regiment, though it does not vauntingly claim to have fought "beyond the mark of others," yet may Ohio, ever more boastful of the triumphs of peace than of

* The Mexicans have a happy faculty of passing off disasters for triumphs. Their historians confess that the battle of *Molino del Rey* was celebrated with music and bells, and that Santa Anna sent a proclamation by extraordinary couriers into all parts of the nation, stating that a victory had been gained, and that he had in person led the troops of the Republic, both of which "*illusions*," as they are mildly termed, "the inhabitants generally believe to this day."

The truth is, that when with the advantage of vastly superior numbers, and a remarkably strong position, as at Monterey and the Molino, they were not routed by the first charge, they considered they had made a lucky escape, and rejoiced accordingly.

arms, be permitted to point with pride to her share in the fight; and each of her hardy sons

> "May stand a tiptoe when the day is named,
> And rouse him at the name of"—*Monterey.*

What Major General Butler says in the latter part of the following extract, from his official report, of the situation and conduct of his brigadiers—Hamer and Quitman—may, with like propriety and justice, be said of the more humble soldiers of his division:

"It is with no little pride and gratification that I bear testimony of the gallantry and general good conduct of my command. Were proof wanting, a mournful one is to be found in the subjoined return of the casualties of the day. That part of my division properly in the field, did not exceed eleven hundred, of which number full one-fifth was killed or wounded. The fact that troops for the first time under fire should have suffered such loss without shrinking, in a continuous struggle of more than two hours, and mainly against a sheltered and inaccessible foe, finds but few parallels, and is of itself an eulogium to which I need not add.

"Of my brigadiers, it is proper that I should myself speak. General Hamer was placed in a position where nothing brilliant could be achieved, but which at every moment imperatively demanded prudence, and calm, unbending courage. It is but justice to him to say that I found him equal to the emergency. General Quitman had before him a field in which military genius and skill were called into requisition, and honors could be fairly won; and I but echo the general voice in saying that he nobly availed himself of the occasion."

Dismal indeed was the night of the 21st of September. "Darkness and the shadow of death obscured it; and no joyful voice came therein." The complexion of the elements as well as the aspect of our camp was peculiarly gloomy, and pressed heavily on the spirits. Many of the soldiers sank immediately to rest upon the ground, too much exhausted to prepare supper, and needing repose more than food. To add to the discomfort of those who had no tents, a drizzling rain set in and continued to fall mournfully through the trees, while the wailing night-winds sang a requiem in their trembling boughs. Nature herself seemed to weep and moan o'er the sad scene. In the dimly-lighted hospital-tents were to be seen and heard what I shall not attempt to portray. The surgeons, unremitting in their attentions to the wounded, were engaged the whole night in dressing wounds and amputating limbs, their duties, as General Taylor remarks in his report, being rendered uncommonly arduous by the small number serving in the field. The commanding general himself, though bred to the iron trade of war, yet possessing a heart ever ready to sympathize with its unfortunate victims, visited the hospitals and the quarters of all his wounded officers before retiring to rest.

In consequence of the many melancholy duties of the night, our mess did not assemble for supper until a very late hour. When at length we approached the board used for a table, and the bright light of a couple of lanterns was allowed to fall upon it, all gazed with as much amazement and disgust upon it as if the banquet of Tereus or a feast of the Anthropophagi had been spread before them. The table was covered between the plates and cups with thin strips of human flesh and clots of gore, which the cooks, in the haste of preparation by the faint fire-light, had not perceived. Our surgeon, who evidently enjoyed the exclamations and denunciations which the spectacle elicited, stated in explanation that he had been compelled to use the mess-table at the hospital, and had "only cut off some legs and arms upon it." We insisted on having the bloody board turned upside down, and then seated ourselves around it with rather less satisfaction, as may be supposed, than we have experienced in placing our feet under the mahogany of certain friends at home. After supper, we wrapped ourselves in our wet blankets and vainly sought repose. The excitement of battle having subsided, we began to suffer from the extraordinary exertions which the body had almost unconsciously made during the day. Sinews that had been strained like bowstrings then relaxed, and the cramp racked every limb.

During the night, the fatigue parties continued to bring in the wounded, and one of them losing its way, and approaching the chain of sentinels from an unexpected direction, an alarm was spread rapidly over the camp. The "long-roll"* instantly resounded through the grove, and for a time all thought that the enemy were upon us. The weary and drowsy men flew to arms, and stumbling through the bushes, and over numberless obstacles, formed as good a line around the camp as the darkness would permit. Though the uproar was as complete as drums, bugles, and human voices could make it,

*The *long-roll* is the signal for getting under arms in case of alarm, or the sudden appearance of the enemy.

and attended by some scattering shots from a few startled soldiers of the guard, yet so great was the fatigue, and so deathlike the slumbers of some of my acquaintances, that they remained until the next morning in happy ignorance of the "stampede," when they were deeply mortified at not being at their posts. Returning to our quarters, we found the brave old surgeon of our regiment standing before his wounded colonel's tent, armed with a lance and pistols. Having, at the first sounds of alarm, hurriedly mustered the hospital attendants, servants, and other non-combatants, and placed in their hands such weapons as were within reach, he had determined to guard his patients to the death, and phlebotomize in a manner unknown to the faculty generally.

About midnight, a soldier wearing the uniform of the regular infantry, came to inform me that a wounded officer lying in the vicinity had expressed a wish to see me. I immediately desired him to lead the way, which he did, bearing a lighted candle in the socket of a bayonet, over which he held his cap to shield it from the rain. A short walk brought us to a small tent, which we entered. In the middle of it, and with only a single blanket between him and the damp turf, lay one, whom, as the light of the soldier's candle fell upon his face, I recognized as Lieutenant ——, of the 1st Infantry. I had become acquainted with him a month previous at Camargo, under circumstances that contrasted strongly with this second most painful interview. But an active military life is made up of scenes as strange and varied, as ever bard or novelist created! Though pale from the loss of blood, Lieutenant ——'s features were so calm and his voice so firm, that I did not think him severely wounded, and was quite shocked when, after remarking that "I hoped he had not fared very ill in the battle," he replied by raising the blanket and exposing to view the stump of an amputated leg. After having his foot shot off by a cannon ball, he had been placed in a wagon and jolted back to camp. The tortures endured during that rough ride, he said, were indescribable, and from which death would have been a welcome relief. Unfortunately for such sufferers, there were at that time no ambulances with the army. The Lieutenant expired a few days afterward, under, I believe, the terrible second amputation, which it was found necessary to perform in many cases in that climate.

The 22d of September, Tuesday, passed without any active operations on the north and east of the city. The citadel and other works continued to fire at parties exposed to their range, and at the Teneria. The guard left in that redoubt the preceding night, was relieved at midday by General Quitman's brigade.

On the west side of the city, however, the battle raged with unabated fury. We have already mentioned the action of San Jeronimo, by which, on the morning of the 21st, General Worth had obtained possession of the Saltillo road. Between him and the city, were yet the strong hill forts we have heretofore described. The road, following the course of the river, ran through the valley between these, and was commanded by the guns of Forts Federacion and Soldada on the south, and of the Bishop's Castle and Independencia on the north. It was obviously necessary to dislodge the

Mexicans from these exterior positions before assaulting the west side of the town.

General Worth accordingly ordered three columns, under Captain C. F. Smith, Captain Miles, and Major Scott, successively, all under the immediate direction of Brigadier General P. F. Smith,* to storm the two batteries, Federacion and Soldada, crowning the hights south of the road and river. The attack was made at 12 M., in full view of the foe, who opened a plunging fire from both works upon our men as they waded the stream, and commenced to toil slowly up the steep, rugged, and bare acclivity. The light troops of the enemy, descending to favorable points on the slope, offered a vigorous resistance. Our troops steadily advanced, firing, and the Mexicans, gradually yielding, retired slowly up the hill. In the meantime, General Smith, discovering that the ground favored the movement, with his characteristic sagacity and promptness, rapidly marched the forces under Scott and Miles obliquely up and around the hill, with the view of taking the Soldada simultaneously with the Federacion. The last named fort was gallantly carried by the

* Those who carefully noted the progress of events in Mexico, can not have failed to observe the genius and military talent uniformly displayed by General Persifor F. Smith. The commencement of the war found him, I believe, a practitioner in the courts of New Orleans. At the suggestion of General Taylor, he was selected to command the six-month volunteers of Louisiana, sent to the Rio Grande. President Polk soon afterward appointed him to the Colonelcy of the new regiment of mounted riflemen, with which corps, however, he never served, having earned promotion before its arrival in the field. At the battle of Monterey, he commanded with distinguished ability a brigade in Worth's division. He subsequently gained an enviable fame in Scott's army, especially for the splendid victory of Contreras. By his recent judicious dispositions on the Indian frontier of Texas, he has effectually secured peace and confidence to that border. I hope the President-makers will ere long discover his worth and talents.

column attacking in front, under Captain C. F. Smith, composed of four companies of the artillery battalion, and six of Texan riflemen. Captain Smith immediately moved with his main body to participate in the assault of the second fort, Soldada, about five hundred yards distant, which was stormed at nearly the same moment by the troops of Scott and Miles, 5th and 7th Infantry, and Blanchard's company of Louisiana volunteers. Lieutenant Pitcher and the color-bearer of the 5th, were the first to enter the Soldada.

The guns captured in these two works were immediately brought to bear upon the opposite hill, a valley six hundred yards wide intervening, and which was guarded by the Bishop's Castle, about midway up the slope, and the Independencia, on its crest. The possession of these works was of controlling importance; especially of the latter, which overlooked and commanded the Castle. Night, however, attended by rain, closed in soon after the capture of Forts Federacion and Soldada and operations on the west ceased for the day, the 21st. Successes had been obtained by General Worth's division almost as important as the capture of the Teneria, and, owing to the comparative weakness of the enemy in that quarter, especially in artillery, at the loss of a very small number of men. Captain McKavett, of the 8th Infantry, was the only officer killed. The troops had been thirty-six hours without food, and constantly tasked to the utmost physical exertions. They spent the night under arms in a pelting storm, and at 3 A. M., on the 22d, prepared to attack the remaining works of the Obispado.

The redoubt, the capture of which is next to be mentioned,

was perched upon the highest point of a hill, eight hundred feet in hight, and which from its steepness was almost inaccessible, save on the eastern side, where it gently descended toward the Bishop's Castle, and thence down to the street by which the Saltillo road enters the city. It was deemed by the enemy impregnable. I well remember the astonishment with which the Mexican officers, who were prisoners in our camp at San Domingo, received the intelligence that General Worth had carried the Independencia.

Lieutenant Colonel Childs was assigned to lead the storming party, which consisted of three companies of the artillery battalion, three companies 8th Infantry, and two hundred dismounted Texan Rangers. The command moved from its bivouac in the valley at 3 A. M., and was conducted to its point of ascent by Captain Sanders and Lieutenant Meade, of the Engineers. At the base of the hill, the force was divided into two parties, and silently commenced to climb the dark slopes. It required all the strength of the men to overcome the difficulties which nature had, at places, thrown in their way. Perpendicular ledges of rock and projecting crags were to be scaled, and thickets of stunted chaparral to be crept under. But "excelsior" was the motto of those invincible men who slowly and cautiously pressed up toward the lofty apex, then clothed with a thick mantle of mist. It was Night's last, still, and dark hour, always the most favorable for such enterprises.

The garrison of the work, having witnessed the mettle of our troops on the previous day, and warned by the loss of the Federacion and Soldada, were on the *qui vive;* yet such was their confidence in the difficulties of the ground, that it was supposed no assault could be successful. At dawn the storming party had reached a point within one hundred yards of the redoubt, and where among the clefts of the rocks a body of the enemy had been posted in apparent anticipation of the attack. The flash and roar which announces the coming of a summer's rain, is not more sudden and terrific than the explosion which then burst upon our stormers. The deep-set rocks around them were scarcely more firm and unyielding than were our stout-hearted men in that crashing blast. Not a shot was returned—not a cheer raised! At the thrilling word, "charge," quickly repeated by the officers, the Americans rushed forward and forced the enemy back toward the redoubt at the point of the bayonet. The summit of the hill occupied by the Mexicans, blazed like a beacon, while in the dark cloud around it, the flashes of our guns soon formed an unbroken ring of fire. Rapidly and regularly that burning circle contracted, until it mingled with the fire of the foe. Then came the deadly struggle. Those red flames were suddenly extinguished, and instead of the rattle of musketry, the shouts and groans of a fierce hand to hand encounter, floated out from the peak of that cloud-capt hill. Our men fought with unwavering courage; the enemy, for a few minutes, made an obstinate but unavailing defense; but being forced over their walls, finally fled in wild confusion toward the Bishop's Castle. Among the few Americans killed in this assault was Captain Gillespie, a popular officer of the Texan Rangers.

The next piece in Worth's brilliant programme was the

Bishop's Castle; which was below, and about four hundred yards distant from the position last carried. No artillery was found in the redoubt, and Lieutenant Roland, of Duncan's battery, aided by fifty soldiers of the line, undertook the Herculean task of dragging or rather carrying a twelve-pounder howitzer up the rugged acclivity which the troops had climbed in the early morning. In two hours the labor was successfully accomplished; and the howitzer, covered by the epaulement of the captured work, commenced to play upon the castle. Meanwhile the 5th Infantry had been brought up by its gallant Major, Martin Scott, to reinforce the hight, while the troops of Major Vinton, and the Texans under Hays and Walker, advancing to covered positions on both sides of the ridge, invested the castle with a close and constant fire, which the enemy returned from the parapets and loop-holes of that massive edifice. This contest of sharp-shooters continued for several hours, and with the fire of Roland's howitzer, produced a visible effect upon the garrison. At length the Mexicans conceived the desperate resolution of re-taking the hight, as the only means of saving the castle; and about 3 P. M., having received heavy reinforcements from the city, they made a vigorous sortie under Colonel Francisco Berra. This was a movement long anticipated, and for which the needful dispositions had been made by the accomplished strategist who commanded our troops. The enemy was allowed to advance, unmolested, for some distance up the ridge; and then, at a preconcerted signal, a general discharge from all arms was poured into his column, which caused it to reel and stagger back in dismay. Our men rising in the next instant, from the rocks, charged with a shout upon the front and flanks of the foe. The Mexicans were unable to resist this sudden and impetuous assault, and after a short but ineffectual effort to hold their ground, gave way, and, like a loosened cliff, rolled headlong down the descent. Few of the fugitives paused to re-enter the castle; but "horse and foot" fled in dire confusion past the work, and, as their own historians confess, "penetrated to the interior of the city, spreading terror."*

The Americans pursuing, entered the castle. Its guns, together with Duncan's and Mackall's field-batteries, which, the road being now open, came up from the valley at a gallop, were discharged upon the retiring and confused masses that filled the avenue leading to the city. About thirty prisoners were taken in the fortress. Lieutenant Ayres of the 3d Artillery hauled down the gaudy standard of Mexico; and in the next moment, the unpretending flag of our glorious Union floated in triumph from the battlements. As it was unfurled by the evening breeze, and the "stripes and stars" flashed in the golden rays of declining day, shouts of joy burst forth from those who, on the north side of the city, had been attentively observing the tragic scenes enacted on the hights. Thus terminated on the evening of September 22d, the second act of the drama.

---

*The enemy committed, in my poor judgment of such matters, an egregious blunder in associating some squadrons of horse with the attacking column. The practice of mixing small bodies of infantry and cavalry together, is a bad one in all places, but especially so in that. Ground more unsuitable for the operations of mounted troops, I never beheld. The proud Lancers, it may be, concluded that the disgrace and humiliation of defeat could be no greater than that of serving on foot.

That night I was again on duty. A great number of prisoners, chiefly soldiers, but among them some of the vile scum of the chaparral, were in the camp, and had hitherto been under a special guard in the center of the grove. In consequence of the paucity of our troops, and the number of our wounded, it was determined to dispense with this detail, and to place the prisoners in charge of the main-guard. It was after dark when the order for their removal reached me, and it was found necessary to exercise great vigilance to frustrate attempts at escape, during their progress through the intricate paths and gloomy shades of the wood. On arriving at the guard station, and observing a large force drawn up under arms, the Mexicans gazed at each other with anxiety and alarm; and some of them, supposing they were about to suffer the cruel fate so often inflicted upon Texan prisoners by their own troops, broke forth in prayers and lamentations.* Our assurances that no harm was intended, uttered, it is true, not in the best Castilian, and interlarded with a little dog-latin, that seemed quite as comprehensible, allayed their fears, and they all quietly obeyed the order to sit down. The jeers of some of their own number contributed to the pacification of the most timid. An old man, clad in the garb of a citizen, was greatly alarmed,

* The Mexicans—naturally sanguiniary, and debased by merciless civil wars—in their fitful efforts to subdue the revolted province of Texas, were strangely, madly, blind to the policy of humanity. They commenced the campaign of 1836, under a special act of the Mexican Congress, which provided that no prisoners should be taken. Yet they did accept prisoners of war, but only to violate the express terms of capitulation, and every sentiment of honor and justice, by murdering them in cold blood. The slaughter of Alamo, the massacre of Colonel Fanning's command at Goliad, and the decimation of the Mier captives, were act wholly unjustifiable, and which deserve to be held up to eternal execration.

and would have embraced my knees. He supplicated loudly for his release, declaring that he was not an enemy of the Americans, and had been captured while pursuing a journey of business. A promise that his case should be looked to as soon as soon as leisure permitted, and a tender of some little comforts due to his gray hairs and misfortunes, elicited from him *muchos gracias*.

Early on the morning of Wednesday, September 23d, it was discovered by General Quitman's brigade occupying the Teneria, that the enemy had, during the night, evacuated fort Diabolo, and abandoned all their exterior works on the north, except the citadel.* General Taylor immediately ordered the troops to advance cautiously, and the batteries to

* The following account of the abandonment of these works is given by the Mexican historian, in the "*Notes*:"

"This unlucky event, the loss of the Bishop's Castle, infused a silent fear which comes before defeat. With few exceptions, the officers of corps felt this; and it infected the General-in-chief himself, who was not endowed with dispatch and energy. The possessors and disseminators of these sentiments, we are acquainted with, but whose names, from shame, we hastily dismiss.

"An order was sent to concentrate the army in the interior line, by abandoning all the works more advanced at the north, east, and west; and still preserving the citadel and a few works to the south on the bank of the river. These dispositions were executed at eleven at night, in the midst of a noisy confusion arising from the troops refusing to abandon their positions without fighting. The grumbling and discontented showed themselves openly, and the military morale suffering by it in a manner beyond description. On the commencement of the 23d, it was discovered that the enemy's column, attacking from the west, had occupied the Quinta de Arista, Campo Santo, and other contiguous positions. At the points we had abandoned in the night, in the midst of frightful disorder, some drunken soldiers still remained, discharging their pieces in the air, committing excesses, and giving a clear idea of the want of concert that prevailed. General Ampudia now issued from the cathedral, where he had remained during the action, and repaired to the defenses. The azoteas were topped with sacks, and various houses pierced for musketry. At ten in the morning, the enemy occupied the posts we had deserted, and at eleven invested with firmness, generalizing their fire, which grew warm, to the very houses on the principal plaza."

open a fire upon the central parts of the town. Colonel Wood's regiment of Rangers dismounted, and joined the attacking party. They were excellent marksmen, and their equipments were most suitable for the work in hand. The Americans, no longer annoyed by the Mexican artillery, seized upon the nearest houses, and mounting to the roofs or breaking through walls, slowly forced their way toward the heart of the beleaguered city. They were soon engaged, and now upon more equal terms, in a desperate conflict with the defenders. House after house, and square after square, were wrested from them. The Mexicans fought in sullen silence, while our men, assured of victory, made the welkin ring with their cheers.

In the meantime, General Worth, supposing from the heavy fire on our side of the town, that General Taylor was conducting a main assault, and that orders for his co-operation, having to travel a circuit of several miles, had miscarried, organized two column of attack, and descending from the Obispado, launched his steady and enthusiastic battalions once more upon the foe. Bragg's and Ridgely's light artillery were brought in on the east side, and Duncan's and Mackall's on the west side of the city. Sections of these batteries thundered simultaneously through the principal streets, advancing after every discharge. The enemy thus pressed between two fires, slowly retired, defending every wall and house-top with the heroic fortitude that has characterized their race in resisting sieges. Soon after midday, as if by mutual consent, both parties took a short breathing-spell, and a deathlike stillness pervaded the streets, which a few moments before had resounded with the wild tumult of war. For about an hour the din of battle and fierce shouts of the combatants were hushed, and then were with greater violence renewed. The Mexicans, soldiers and citizens, animated with the energy of despair, boldly ascended to the *azoteas*, where, armed with heavy old English muskets, they were no match for our dextrous riflemen. If, as I am inclined to believe, our loss was greater than that of the enemy on the first day of the battle, the account was more than balanced on the third. The Americans being now as well sheltered as the Mexicans, took a more deliberate aim than when exposed in open ground to the fire of artillery. They availed themselves in this singular combat, waged as it were, in mid-air, of every possible stratagem to deceive or provoke the enemy into committing some fatal blunder or exposure. The Mexican who dared to show himself above the parapets challenged certain death. From every angle and aperture they showered their balls upon the enemy; and even the spouts, which in Mexican houses resemble the scuppers of a ship, poured forth streams of fire. Ampudia's troops continued to yield before the valor of our intrepid men. The Texans, whom the sight of a Mexican always inflamed to madness, were conspicuous and furious in their assaults. Driven back by inches, the enemy at nightfall found himself confined to the vicinity of the grand plaza, which had been barricaded for a final and desperate resistance.

In some of the newspaper narratives of the battle of the 23d, the women of Monterey are represented as actively participating in the defense, and hence the pen of fiction has already interwoven many tender love scenes in the siege. But the only account of female heroism exhibited there, which possesses any claim to authenticity, may be found in the subjoined passage from the Mexican history to which we have previously had occasion to refer.*

In the afternoon of the 23d, General Quitman's brigade was relieved by that of General Hamer. Night once more compelled the contending forces to seek a respite from their sanguinary labors, and General Taylor now prepared to concert measures with Worth for a combined attack on the Plaza the next morning. The opposing troops lay so near to each other during the night,

> "That the fixed sentinels almost received
> The secret whispers of each other's watch."

Scattered through the streets and on the house-tops were the cold and bloody corpses of those killed during the day, while the gardens of the suburbs were "reeking with the smell of death." The mangled remains of those slain on the 21st, unburied and moldering where they had fallen, tainted the night air and threatened a pestilence. A few of our men, too, who had been wounded on the first day of the battle, were, as we subsequently discovered, still lying there,

---

* "At this time, sublime as the heroines of Sparta and of Rome, and beautiful as the tutelar deities of Grecian sculpture, the Senorita Dona Maria Josefa Zozaya, in the house of Senor Garza Flores, presented herself among the soldiers who fought on the azotea, to give them food and ammunition, and to teach them how to despise danger.

"The beauty and rank of this young lady *communicated new attractions*, and it was requisite to conquer to admire her, or to perish before her eyes to be made worthy of smiles. She was a lovely personation of the country itself. She was the beau ideal of heroism in all her movements, and with all her tender fascinations."

suffering agonies, their tongues swollen with thirst, and their gashed and festering flesh devoured by worms. Among these dead bodies and helpless, wounded men, now prowled the fierce, ravening wolves of the chaparral, tearing some, limb from limb, and perhaps lapping the warm blood of others "ere life be parted."

The mortar, which had proved so inefficient on the north side of the city, had been sent around to General Worth, and now, from the vicinity of the Campo Santo, played with no trifling effect upon the enemy crowded in the plaza mayor. Many of us had never before witnessed the operation of shell-firing at night, and found it a most interesting pyrotechnic exhibition; especially upon this occasion, when the excitement it produced within the enemy's lines assured us (as a brother officer, who lay on the ground at my side, remarked) that General Don Pedro de Ampudia was about "to cave." The first few bombs that were discharged, exploded high in the air, revealing the whole shadowy outline of the city and mountains in a ghastly glare that was quickly swallowed up in darkness. A slight increase of the projecting charge deposited them in the Grand Plaza, with an explosion that shook the city, and a blaze that for an instant obscured the stars, and caused the heavens to blush upon the scene. The service of this battery during the night was admirably managed by Major Munroe, and exercised a decided influence upon the final result. It is a noticeable fact, that Ampudia's proposal to evacuate the city, is dated within an hour after the mortar opened its fire. And there can be no question but that the same proposition would have been made early on the first day of the battle had we possessed guns of sufficient weight to reach the city from any point without the enemy's lines.

Thursday morning, September 24th, we were early on foot, and waited but for the dawn to renew the assault. About 3 o'clock, A. M., a bugle sounded the parley in front of the position held by our brigade, and soon afterward a small party under cover of a flag of truce was discerned advancing down the street. It proved to be Colonel Morino, of General Ampudia's staff, whose sad countenance at once explained to all the object of his mission. He bore from his commanding-general to General Taylor a proposition to surrender the town, which, together with Taylor's reply, is subjoined.*

---

* Copies of the notes of Generals Ampudia and Taylor preliminary to the capitulation of Monterey.

"*Head-Quarters, Monterey,*
"*September* 23, 1846; 9 *o'clock at night.*

"General: As I have made all the defense of which I believe this city capable, I have fulfilled my obligation, and done all required by that military honor which, to a certain degree, is common to all the armies of the civilized world, and as a continuation of the defense would only bring upon the population distresses to which they have already been sufficiently subjected by the evils consequent upon war, and believing that the American government will appreciate these sentiments, I propose to your Excellency to evacuate the city and citadel, taking with me the personnel and material of war which is left, and under the assurance that no prosecution shall be undertaken against the citizens who have taken part in the defense. Be pleased to accept the assurance of my most distinguished consideration.

"PEDRO DE AMPUDIA.

"Senor Don Z. TAYLOR, General-in-chief of the American Army."

"*Head-Quarters, Camp before Monterey,*
"*September* 24, 1846; 7 *o'clock, A. M.*

"Sir: Your communication bearing date at 9 o'clock, P. M., on the 23d, has just been received by the hands of Colonel Morino. In answer to your proposition to evacuate the city and fort with all the personnel and material of war, I have to state that my duty compels me to to decline acceding to it. A complete surrender of the town and garrison, the latter as prisoners of war, is now demanded. But such surrender will be upon terms, and the gallant defense of the place, creditable

The Colonel was introduced to General Hamer, who immediately provided him with an escort to head-quarters at San Domingo. I was with Hamer at the reception of Marino, and was surprised as well as pleased at the assumed indifference and tranquility maintained by all who were within ear-shot when he announced his business, though we were no sooner relieved of his presence than congratulations were joyfully exchanged.

A cessation of fire was agreed upon, while commissioners arranged the terms of capitulation, and we set about getting breakfast in the captured Forts Teneria and Diabolo. We were usually pretty well provided with provisions of some sort, but it must be confessed that the table of the St. Charles, in New Orleans, was rather better than ours on that particular morning. A tin cup full of a thick liquid facetiously called coffee, and made from the berry of that name, slightly bruised with the butt of a musket, a slap-jack, weighing a quarter of a pound to the square inch, and a crawfish, which had that morning been dashed upon the wall of the Teneria by the explosion of a shell in the ditch, constituted my repast. But the stomach of the soldier is not often dainty, and the appetite, which for some days past had been scarcely

---

alike to the Mexican troops and nation, will prompt me to make those terms as liberal as possible. The garrison will be allowed, at your option, after laying down its arms, to retire to the interior, on condition of not serving again during the war, or until regularly exchanged. I need hardly say that the rights of non-combatants will be respected. An answer to this communication is required by 12 o'clock. If you assent to an accommodation, an officer will be despatched at once, under instructions to arrange the conditions. I am sir, very respectfully your obedient servant.

"Z. TAYLOR, Major-General U. S. A., commanding.

"Senor Don PEDRO AMPUDIA, General-in-chief, Monterey."

felt in the rage of stronger passions, now returned with such strength, that we could have fallen upon whatever was offered, like "a priest, a shark, an alderman, or pike." The sounds of merriment that broke from the men as they gathered around the camp-kettles for breakfast, proclaimed the joy they felt at the prospect of a termination of the siege. A remarkably happy looking mess were observed sitting on the body of a dead mule, and talking, laughing, and sipping their coffee with evident gusto; occasionally placing their cups upon the animal's bloated side, while they helped themselves to the contents of a pan that simmered over a neighboring fire. After breakfast, fatigue parties were sent out to bury the dead. While engaged in that painful duty, they happily discovered a few men who had been wounded three days previous, and who were so much reduced by hunger, suffering, and the loss of blood, that their comrades could scarcely recognize them.

A long negotiation, lasting until late in the night of the 24th, resulted in the following

"ARTICLES OF CAPITULATION."

ARTICLE 1. As the legitimate result of the operations before this place, and the present position of the contending armies, it is agreed that the city, the fortifications, cannon, the munitions of war, and all other public property, with the undermentioned exceptions, be surrendered to the commanding general of the United States forces now in Monterey.

ART. 2. That the Mexican forces be allowed to retain the following arms, to wit: the commissioned officers their side-arms, the infantry their arms and accouterments, the cavalry their arms and accouterments, the artillery one field battery, not to exceed six pieces, with twenty-one rounds of ammunition.

ART. 3. That the Mexican armed forces retire, within seven days from this date, beyond the line formed by the pass of the Rinconada, the city of Linares, and San Fernando de Presas.

ART. 4. That the citadel of Monterey be evacuated by the Mexican, and occupied by the American forces to-morrow morning at ten o'clock.

ART. 5. To avoid collisions, and for mutual convenience, that the troops of the United States will not occupy the city until the Mexican forces have withdrawn, except for hospital and storage purposes.

ART. 6. That the forces of the United States will not advance beyond the line specified in the 3d article before the expiration of eight weeks, or until the orders or instructions of the respective governments can be received.

ART. 7. That the public property to be delivered shall be turned over and received by officers appointed by the commanding generals of the two armies.

ART. 8. That all doubts as to the meaning of any of the preceding articles shall be solved by an equitable construction, and on principles of liberality to the retiring army.

ART. 9. That the Mexican flag, when struck at the citadel, may be saluted by its own battery.

Done at Monterey, September 24, 1846.

Commissioners on the part of the United States, { W. J. WORTH, J. P. HENDERSON, JEFF. DAVIS.

Commissioners on the part of Mexico, { T. RAQUENA. ORTEGA, M. M. LLANO.

Approved by { Z. TAYLOR, P. AMPUDIA.

It will be seen that the terms granted the Mexican garrison were less rigorous than those first imposed by General Taylor. But the gallant defense of the town, and the fact of a recent change of government in Mexico, (the restoration of Santa Anna,) believed to be favorable to the interests of peace, induced the commission to concur in these articles, especially that for the temporary cessation of hostilities. It was said that our straight-forward old general, vexed by the caviling and arrogant demands of Ampudia's commissioners, was more than once about to break up the conference, and "let the tongue of war again plead for our interest." The camp was full of rumors of what took place in the council-chamber; among others, that General Taylor had at first peremptorily refused to allow the Mexicans to take off any artillery, declaring that he held the town, as if it was an orange in his hand, and that he would squeeze it to a pulp if terms more in accordance with the condition of affairs were not speedily agreed upon. That thereupon the Mexican chief of artillery successfully appealed to the generosity and magnanimity of the stern old soldier, stating that arms and accouterments had been conceded to the infantry and cavalry, and declaring that he would rather die at his guns than see the artillery alone disgraced, by being compelled to march out without a single light battery. Certainly the capitulation was sufficiently honorable to our arms, and humiliating to the foe. Many mustang heroes and militia generals, both in and out of Congress, and even the Cabinet of Mr. Polk, have condemned General Taylor for acceding to it,—one of the most humane and politic strokes of war that distinguished the campaign. By its terms we gained all that could have been acquired from a further assault, save more blood, and a repetition of those horrors from which I have not attempted to raise the vail. It is one of the maxims of Napoleon, that "the keys of a fortress are well worth the retirement of the garrison, when it is resolved to yield only on those conditions. On this principle it is always wiser to grant an honorable capitulation to a garrison which has made a vigorous resistance, than to risk an assault." But no more ample and satisfactory vindication of the convention can be desired, than that contained in the following letter of General Taylor, written in reply to the strictures of the Secretary of War, and to which the attention of the reader is earnestly invited.

Head-Quarters, Army of Occupation,
Camp near Monterey, November 8, 1846.

Sir: In reply to so much of the communication of the Secretary of War, dated October 13th, as relates to the reasons which induced the convention resulting in the capitulation of Monterey, I have the honor to submit the following remarks:

The convention presents two distinct points: First. The permission granted the Mexican army to retire with their arms, etc. Second. The temporary cessation of hostilities for the term of eight weeks. I shall remark on these in order.

The force with which I advanced on Monterey was limited, by causes beyond my control, to about 6000 men. With this force, as every military man must admit who has seen the ground, it was entirely impossible to invest Monterey so closely as to prevent the escape of the garrison. Although the main communication with the interior was in our possession, yet one route was open to the Mexicans throughout the operations, and could not be closed, as were also other minor tracks and passes through the mountains. Had we, therefore, insisted on more rigorous terms than those granted, the result would have been the escape of the body of the Mexican force, with the destruction of its artillery and magazines; our only advantage being the capture of a few prisoners of war, at the expense of valuable lives, and much damage to the city. The consideration of humanity was present to my mind during the conference which led to the convention, and outweighed in my judgment the doubtful advantages to be gained by a resumption of the attack upon the town. This conclusion has been fully confirmed by an inspection of the enemy's position and means, since the surrender. It was discovered that his principal magazine, containing an immense amount of powder, was in the cathedral and completely exposed to our shells from two directions. The explosion of this mass of powder, which must have ultimately resulted from a continuance of the bombardment, would have been infinitely disastrous, involving the destruction not only of the Mexican troops, but of non-combatants, and even our own people, had we pressed the attack.

In regard to the temporary cessation of hostilities, the fact that we are not at this moment, within eleven days of the termination of the period fixed by the convention, prepared to move forward in force, is a sufficient explanation of the military reasons which dictated this suspension of arms. It paralyzed the enemy during a period when, from the want of necessary means, we could not possibly move. I desire distinctly to state, and to call the attention of the authorities to the fact, that with all diligence in breaking mules and setting up wagons, the first wagons in addition to our original trains from Corpus Christi, (and but 125 in number,) reached my head-quarters on the same day with the Secretary's communication of October 13th, viz: the 2d inst. At the date of the surrender of Monterey our force had not more than ten days' rations, and even now, with all our endeavors, we have not more than twenty-five. The task of fighting and beating the enemy is among the least difficult that we encounter; the great question of supplies necessarily controls all the operations in a country like this. At the date of the convention I could not, of course, have forseen that the department would direct an important detachment from my command without consulting me, or without waiting the result of the main operation under my orders.

I have touched the prominent military points involved in the convention of Monterey. There were other considerations which weighed with the commissioners in framing, and with myself in approving, the articles of the convention. In the conference with General Ampudia, I was distinctly told by him that he had invited it to spare the further effusion of blood, and because General Santa Anna had declared himself favorable to peace. I knew that our government had made propositions to that of Mexico to negotiate, and I deemed that the change of government in this country since my last instructions, fully warranted me in entertaining considerations of policy. My grand motive in moving forward with very limited supplies had been to increase the inducements of the Mexican government to negotiate for peace. Whatever may be the actual views of the Mexican rulers, or of General Santa Anna, *it is not unknown to the government that I had the very best reasons for believing the statement of General Ampudia to be true.* It was my opinion at the time of the convention, and it has not been changed, that the liberal treatment of the Mexican army, and the suspension of arms, would exert none but a favorable influence in our behalf.

The result of the entire operation has been to throw the Mexican army back more than 300 miles, to the city of San Luis de Potosi, and to open the country to us, if we choose to penetrate it, up to the same point.

It has been my purpose in this communication, not so much to defend the convention from the censure which I deeply regret to find implied in the Secretary's letter, as to show that it was not adopted without cogent reasons, most of which occur of themselves to the minds of all who are acquainted with the condition of things here. To that end I beg that it may be laid before the General-in-chief and the Secretary of War.

I am, sir, very respectfully your obedient servant.

Z. Taylor, Major General U. S. A., commanding.

The Adjutant General, Washington.

The fault-finders in our army were chiefly Texans. On the night of the 23d of September they had obtained possession of the highest houses in the vicinity of the great plaza, and, unsated with slaughter, they but waited for the morning to avenge signally the hoarded wrongs suffered during their long war for independenee. The capitulation on the 24th, of course, disappointed all their sweet and long cherished hopes of vengeance. Fortunately for the Mexican population the American General knew how to crown a triumph with mercy. It appears from the Mexican "History of the War," that some of the enemy were equally dissatisfied with the finale of the siege, and, it must be admitted, with better reason.* Both parties of malcontents, however, in complaining, sin against humanity.

* "The second interview resulted in the capitulation, in which the commissioners were the Generals Raquena, Conde, and Don Manuel Maria del Llano, a capitulation which, with cutting irony, was called *honorable*. This was, that the army should retain their arms and baggage, a battery of six pieces, ammunition for twenty-four rounds each, one supply of catridges for the boxes, and the rest of the material to be given to the Americans, who agreed on their part not to pass the line of the Muertos, Linares, and Victoria, for two months, in which time efforts would be diligently made to accomplish a peace.

"On the 25th, at eleven o'clock, our troops evacuated the citadel, in front of a

During the protracted conference of the 24th, and indeed until the morning of the 25th, we remained under arms. Pending the negotiation, many citizens came over to our lines, and offered themselves as prisoners of war. We declined to be troubled with them, and they joyfully scattered through the surrounding country, as glad, apparently, to leave the city as we were to enter it. Large parties of all ages passed quietly under our guns in the direction of Gaudeloupe, a picturesque village that showed its scattered roofs in the valley before the city, on the road to Victoria. Others fording the river behind the town, escaped into the rugged fastnesses of the Sierra. On the 25th, we took possession of the citadel, and became masters of the city. A large quantity of ammunition, upward of forty pieces of artillery, and a considerable amount of tobacco, clothing, and other public stores fell into our hands. Thus within a week after our arrival before Monterey, the more numerous Mexican army had been forced into a disgraceful capitulation, and driven beyond the Sierra Madre, north of which no standard now floated but that of the United States.

---

column of the enemy, commanded by General Smith. Our forces struck their flag, a salute sounded from the ordnance, and our banner fell degraded. The victors took possession of the fortress, and in hoisting their standard hailed it with hurras of delight, while we were overwhelmed with humiliation and grief. Our forces were lodged in the eastern part of the city, not having saved more than their personal effects and six pieces of artillery.

"Thus terminated the defense of Monterey. The simple relation of events will excuse us from all commentary. The judgment of the sensible part of the nation will approve this course. * * * * Our generals, with the exception of those we have honorably mentioned, suffered in the contempt of their enemies a severe chastisement, probably deserved. When the difficulties of a cotemporary description are removed, the impartial pen of the historian, referring to these transactions, will reveal some names to infamy."—*Notes for the History of the War.*

A large number of the inhabitants, including nearly all the most respectable citizens, retired with the army, scowling hatred and defiance on us as they marched out. The Mexican historian says—"When the inhabitants of Monterey saw the last of our army depart, they could not resolve to remain among the enemy, and many of them abandoning their houses and business, carrying their children, and followed by their wives, traveled on foot behind the troops. Monterey was converted into a vast cemetery. The unburied heaps, the dead and putrid mules, the silence of the streets, all gave a fearful aspect to the city." The people who lingered behind were, at first, exceedingly sullen and shy, certain "gentlemen in black," having inflamed their minds against us "outside barbarians," representing the volunteers as the scum of the United States, and destitute both of honor and courage.

And in sooth, the spectacle that some of us presented on entering the city was not very well calculated to undeceive them, though I believe we had the advantage of Falstaff's army, and could, perhaps, boast more than "a shirt and a half" to each company. But our jackets looked exceedingly shabby, and a pair of whole trowsers was a rarity. Our beards and hair too, had grown to a great length, so that our personal appearance must have been rather savage and grotesque. Some of the Monterey people, in their letters to the newspapers of the interior cities, described us as "a set of ragged vagabonds, nearly resembling the Camanche Indians, in manners, ferocity, and appearance." Complimentary, certainly! But may we not be permitted to write beneath this portrait, thus drawn by the pencils of our enemies, the words of Henry V. to the French herald on the field of Agincourt:

"We are but warriors for the working day;
Our gayness and our gilt are all besmirched
With rainy marching in the painful field;
There's not a piece of feather in our host,
(Good argument, I hope, we shall not *fly*,)
And time hath worn us into slovenry:
But, by the mass, our hearts are in the trim."

In connection with the subject of this chapter, the truly, and therefore truthless, Mexican proclamation, issued by General Ampudia, after his arrival at Saltillo, is subjoined.*

---

* "THE GENERAL COMMANDING THE ARMY OF THE NORTH, TO THE PEOPLE OF THE THREE DEPARTMENTS, TAMAULIPAS, NEW LEON, AND COAHUILA.

"*Fellow-Citizens:* Occupied, before all things, in providing for the defense of the rights and integrity of the territory of our beloved Republic against the enemy who has invaded her soil, the supreme government thought proper to intrust to me the command of the patriotic troops destined, on the northern frontier, to this holy purpose. I accepted with enthusiasm the post assigned me, (for the zeal with which I have ever defended the holy cause of the people, is notorious to every one,) and in the beginning of the month assumed the direction of such means as were within my power to repel the advance of the enemy. But fearing that the charge would prove too great for my feeble abilities, I solicited the worthy and most excellent Senor, General Don Juan Neponuceno Almonte, to come and relieve me from the command of the army, presuming that the illustrious conqueror of Panuco would, on his return to Mexico, resume the reins of our National Government.

On the 19th inst., the enemy having appeared in the vicinity of Monterey, and encamped in the San Domingo wood—*their camp being one league in length, and three leagues in circumference*—I ordered their movements to be carefully observed, and hostilities to be commenced forthwith, the generals under my command being all decided to risk a battle rather than retreat. The redoubts of the citadel opened their fires the same day upon the enemy, who were occupied, during that and the succeeding day, in reconnoitering and preparing for the attack.

On the 21st, the assault was made by a formidable body of their troops, chiefly of the regular army, upon our redoubts of the Teneria, the Rincon del Diabolo, and the bridge of the Purisima, but they were gloriously repulsed by our valiant veterans, with a positive loss to our adversaries of *fifteen hundred men*.

On the morning of the 22d, General Taylor directed his columns of attack against the Bishop's Hill, an elevation commanding the city; and although in their first advance they were repulsed in a skirmish, a full brigade of regular troops returned

That farrago of vanity, deceit, sycophancy, bombast, and falsehood, does not accord very well with his actions during the battle, or his words at the subsequent conference. The reader will not fail to remark how lightly the veracious Pedro treats his recent defeat, and how obsequiously he endeavors to propitiate "the worthy and most excellent Senor, Don Antonio Lopez de Santa Anna," whom the revolution of August had recently recalled from exile, and re-established in power. That distinguished Mexican, disappointing the hopes of those who permitted him to land at Vera Cruz, had placed himself at the head of the war party, and was then engaged in organizing a grand army at San Louis Potosi, which he proposed marching to the north. We are informed that, "irritated by the news of the fall of

---

to the charge. Unfortunately, two pieces of cannon and a mortar, which defended the position, got out of order, and became useless, and although as soon as advised of it, I sent a reinforcement, it reached the hill too late; the enemy had already succeeded in obtaining possession of the castle. This accident compelled me to concentrate my force in the Plaza, in order to present to the foe a more vigorous defense, and to repel on the 22d, as was done, the assaults made by them through the streets and houses of the city. But, as under the circumstances, I suffered great scarcity of ammunition, and in spite of the ardor with which the entire army both regulars and auxiliaries, were animated, I proposed to the American General a parley, which resulted in an understanding by which the honor of the nation and the army, the personnel, arms, and equipments were preserved.

This is a true statement of the operations of the campaign up to the 24th inst and if an inadequate supply of means, and other circumstances, have led to this result, we have not yet cause for a moment's dismay, for the Republic will now put forward all her elements of greatness, and with one single victory, which we may shall, and must obtain, will solve the problem definitely in favor of our arms.

People of the east! the event which occurred at Monterey, is of little moment The favorite general of the Mexicans, the worthy and most excellent Senor, Don Antonio Lopez de Santa Anna, will promptly take charge in person of the direction of the campaign. Let the sacred fire of patriotism continue to burn in your bosoms, and without fail we will triumph over our enemies.

PEDRO DE AMPUDIA.

Head-Quarters, Saltillo, September 29, 1846.

Monterey, he determined to chastise those who had not known how to profit by the defenses of the place and the enthusiasm of the troops." Upon the arrival of Ampudia at his head-quarters, he immediately sent that general before a court-martial. As often happens in such cases, Pedro endeavored to throw the responsibility upon subordinate officers. However, Santa Anna soon decided that there were no grounds for a prosecution, and published orders vindicating the accused. A wise conclusion this, most excellent Antonio! For if to be beaten by inferior numbers was of itself to constitute a sufficient cause for the trial of Mexican officers, none of the enemy's generals, not even "the illustrious conquerer of Panuco," would eventually have escaped the operation of the precedent.

The following congratulatory order appropriately closes the narrative of the battle of Monterey; a conflict of arms especially interesting to the country, as the first of the war in which its citizen soldiers participated. The victory of Buena Vista is commonly regarded as the most brilliant, not only of the campaign, but of the war. Yet it may well be questioned whether it reflects more luster upon American arms than that of Monterey. True, there was a more fearful array of numbers ranged under Santa Anna's banners; but were his 20,000 as formidable to volunteers, as Ampudia's 10,000 behind the walls and guns of Monterey? At Buena Vista too, be it remembered, we had a fair field for our superb batteries of horse-artillery; any one of which was an overmatch for a brigade of Mexican troops, as witness the digraceful route of General Minon's brigade by the two pieces under Lieutenants Shover and Donaldson.

Orders }
No. 123. } *Head-Quarters, Army of Occupation, Camp near Monterey, September* 27, 1846.

The commanding general has the satisfaction to congratulate the army under his command upon another signal triumph over the Mexican forces. Superior to us in numbers, strongly fortified, and with an immense preponderance of artillery, they have yet been driven from point to point, until forced to sue for terms of capitulation. Such terms have been granted as were considered due to the gallant defense of the town, and to the liberal policy of our own government.

The general begs to return his thanks to his commanders, and to all his officers and men, both of the regular and volunteer forces, for the skill, the courage, and the perseverance with which they have overcome manifold difficulties, and finally achieved a victory, shedding luster upon the American arms.

A great result has been obtained, but not without the loss of many gallant and accomplished officers, and brave men. The army and the country will deeply sympathize with the families and friends of those who have thus sealed their devotion with their lives.

By order of Major General TAYLOR,

W. W. S. BLISS,
Assistant Adjutant General.

CHAPTER VII.

The army at San Domingo.—Texan Rangers discharged.—The wounded sent home.—A new camp established —Discipline of the 1st Ohio Regiment of Volunteers.—Lights and shadows of camp life.—Our Commissariat and the Meat Biscuit.—The "spotted tiger" and "striped pig."—Savage spirit of the Mexicans.—Assassination of Father Rey.—The Sierra Silla.—Scenery hunters in a bad case.—A day in Monterey.—Condition of the battle field —Death of Brigadier General Hamer.—His character and services.—Military events of the autumn reviewed.—Saltillo and Tampico abandoned by the enemy.—The Mexican forces concentrated under General Santa Anna, at San Louis de Potosi.—Columns of Generals Kearney and Wool.—Proposition of the American government referred by Santa Anna to the Mexican Congress.—The armistice terminated.—Worth's division occupy Saltillo.—Twiggs' and Quitman's march to Victoria.

There is no situation that so severely tries the discipline of the soldier as a life of inaction in the enemy's country. The stimulus to exertion and the dangers attending the presence of a hostile force being removed, his thoughts begin to fasten themselves on pleasures and dissipations, to which the weaknesses and perhaps the manners of the conquered people offer many temptations. Especially is this the case when cantoned in a city, or in a camp, like that at San Domingo, within a short league of one. Though, as in our regiment, every effort be made, by the establishment of a strict system of police instructions, by the encouragement to manly exercises and diversions, and by the promise of extra pay for certain important labors not in the line of duty, to employ the time and attract the attention of troops, yet will the commanding officer find it extremely difficult to guard against the many troubles of a monotonous existence in camp. The lawless character and vicious habits of some men will render all orders, threats, or promises, unavailing.

A better feeling never existed in any corps, than that which prevailed in the 1st Ohio regiment after the fall of Monterey. Amid the common dangers of the recent battle, in which they had well performed their part, the men and officers formed new and strong attachments for each other, and the majority of them were disposed to be obedient and diligent in the discharge of their duties. But there were a few turbulent spirits among us, who did not seem to know that it was a greater achievement to conquer themselves than to take a city; and while they had gallantly periled their lives to accomplish the latter, unfortunately could not be prevailed upon to strive for the former more glorious victory. In consequence of the disobedience and dissipation of these, during our stay at San Domingo, the first notices of *courts-martial* were inscribed in our regimental books, while the morning reports recorded not only deaths from disease, but by assassination and rencounters not strictly military. Such sacrifices of life, unrequired by duty and therefore unrewarded by fame, did not fail to produce a beneficial effect, by demonstrating the truth of the couplet—

> "Our dangers and delights are near allies,
> From the same stem the rose and prickle rise."

After the surrender of Monterey, General Worth's division was selected to garrison the city; a well merited compliment, and which was but poorly requited by some of the over zealous friends of that officer, who boldly claimed for him the honor of the victory. The same unhappy dissensions which afterward broke out so violently in Scott's army at the city of Mexico, might have been witnessed at Monterey, had the commander-in-chief been so unwise as to breathe upon these hateful sparks of discord. Taylor possessed too frank and generous a nature, and too earnest a devotion to the cause of his country, to harbor any petty feelings of rivalry or envy in his bosom.

With the exception of the brigade of mounted troops from Texas, who, having expressed a desire to return home, were mustered out of service on the first of October, the remainder of the army remained with the head-quarters in camp. The departure of the Rangers would have caused more regret than was generally felt, had it not been for the lawless and vindictive spirit some of them had displayed in the week that elapsed between the capitulation of the city and their discharge. Such deeds as were perpetrated must have shocked the chivalric feelings of many in their own brigade, since they were calculated not only to dim the luster of our victory, but also to take from their own distinguished corps "the pith and marrow of its attribute." Gifted with the intelligence and courage of back-woods hunters, well mounted and skilled in arms, they were excellent light troops. Had they remained and given their whole attention to the guerillas, they might have been exceedingly useful. The commanding general took occasion to thank them for the efficient service they had rendered, and we saw them turn their faces toward the blood-bought State they represented, with many

10*

good wishes and the hope that all honest Mexicans were at a safe distance from their path.

Immediately after the cessation of hostilities, our wounded men were comfortably lodged in town, and those who were disabled from further service, were, as soon as convalescent, sent home to be discharged. As an evidence of the spirit that animated many of the unfortunate privates, it may be mentioned that an Infantry soldier who had lost an arm, called on General Taylor and asked permission to remain with the army. "My good fellow," said the general, "you are disabled and can do nothing more for your country in the field." "O yes," replied the gallant man, "I can work with the artillery! I can carry cartridges and fire a cannon!"

The strength of our regiment was much reduced after the operations before Monterey. Several officers had resigned and a considerable number of soldiers had been discharged on account of wounds and sickness. From one of the morning reports of November, now before me, I observe that but four hundred rank and file are returned "for duty;" and this after the remainder of the corps had arrived from Camargo, where, it may be remarked, thirteen of the number left by us, had died after our departure in September. The same report records twelve officers "absent with leave," and two "absent without leave;" the latter doubtless having remained in town, to make a night of it, at the *fonda* of "Hindoo John." Among the former were the Colonel, Lieutenant Colonel, Adjutant, and Surgeon, who had returned to the United States. The Surgeon went in attendance upon the Colonel and Adjutant, both severely wounded;

though, could the fatal diseases which prevailed in his absence, have been foreseen, it is to be supposed that both he and they would have insisted upon his remaining with the regiment. The generous argument with which General Hamer,—who, alas, too soon required for himself all of Dr. Chamberlyn's justly renowned skill,—overruled the only objection raised to the Surgeon's leave of absence, is yet fresh in my memory.

But if, when at San Domingo, the regiment was weak in numbers, it soon became much more efficient and formidable than it ever had been, even than when it landed eight hundred strong, upon the coast. Soon after the battle, we set about establishing a more permanent and orderly camp. The ground chosen was on the east side of the grove, and when marked off, was covered with an almost impervious thicket of thorns and aromatic shrubs. It was convenient to water, and most of it well shaded by wide-spreading and venerable oaks of extraordinary beauty. Some of the idlers complained of the selection in consequence of the labor required to clear out the undergrowth. But we were amply compensated for that, in possessing a most comfortable camp. Nor was it a work of much fatigue with our force. I well recollect the merry day we spent in the peaceful and pleasant labor. It was the first of October, and the weather was delicious. No "loud war-trumpet woke the morn," but the more pacific notes of the "pioneer's march" summoned the whole regiment for fatigue duty. The battalion was formed, not as usual, under arms, but under the useful tools of the husbandman. Axes and pickaxes, hatchets and spades, gleamed above the line; and the hardy men grasped the good old-fashioned weapons with many a laugh and lively sally of wit. Every officer was in his place, and throughout the day labored cheerfully with his command.

The chaparral falling rapidly beneath the heavy blows of an hundred axmen, was immediately drawn off and thrown in lofty ridges around the camp, forming thus a dense barrier that would have proved a very serious obstruction to the progress of the enemy, and which, certainly no cavalry could have crossed. The spade and pickax-men followed the choppers, leveling the surface and removing the stumps and stones from the parade-ground. Before night, the entire space was cleared and a wonderful transformation accomplished. The roving herdsman who had passed the spot in the morning, returned at evening to gaze with astonishment on the smooth and charming lawn, that but a few hours before had been a tangled thicket, through which he could scarcely force his leather-clad body. Even the gay colored birds that had reveled among the perfumed bowers just destroyed, seemed surprised and bewildered by the magical metamorphosis, and flew noisily about in quest of their favorite retreats. After subdividing the ground and assigning to each company its position, we returned to our old quarters, quite satisfied with the victory of the day; and numbering among our prisoners, sundry tarantulas and scorpions, a brace of armadillos, and a fine specimen of the genus Lacerta, which was supposed to be a genuine chameleon.

On the following morning we moved to our new position, and the tents were pitched in the beautiful and compact order prescribed by the Army Regulations. The soldiers who were without tents, constructed wigwams, by hanging the long Spanish moss gathered from the trees, upon frames of poles, which greatly enhanced the picturesque beauty of the encampment. The comfort of the men having thus been secured as far as possible, a system of instruction and discipline was at once established and energetically maintained. Experience had already taught us, that if we desired to be useful in the active operations of a campaign, we had much to learn. The company officers were urged to the fulfillment of all their responsible duties, and to encourage their men both by precept and example. But few of them failed to aid the commander of the regiment in the maintenance of subordination. It had been supposed that the practice of electing officers from the ranks, which prevailed in many, if not in all of the volunteer corps, would not be very favorable to the attainment of discipline. But whatever may be said of those who received their commissions before entering the field, the men generally made judicious selections in filling the vacancies that afterward occurred. Many of the newly elected lieutenants were exceedingly active and trust-worthy officers, and in their new position exhibited qualities which, under other circumstances, would perhaps not have been discovered. There were some, however, who took promotion simply as the means whereby they hoped to escape duty and promote their own pleasures. These so annoyed their superior officers by their pernicious practices, that they would gladly have exchanged them for the better men that remained in the ranks.

At San Domingo, particular attention was given to guard-duty, always so much neglected by young troops, and the importance of which is never so well taught as by an enterprising enemy. Pains were taken to instruct the sentinels, and to inculcate perfect vigilance, which next to fortitude and courage, I take to be the chief qualification of a soldier. The regiment was often drilled twice a day, and certain companies were exercised more frequently. But few of us had enjoyed the advantage of a military training, yet with the aid of the lucid and admirably-arranged work on Infantry Tactics, prepared by General Scott, it was an easy matter for any studious officer to acquire a correct knowledge of the evolutions announced for each day. From the period of our arrival in the country up to that date, *a surprise* would have been fruitful of disaster to our undisciplined corps; but after a few weeks of faithful application, during which the parade-ground was daily beaten to dust under the feet of the men, we dismissed all apprehensions on that score. There was no maneuver in the "school of the battalion," that they could not perform with ease, precision and rapidity. They could march in line admirably over the roughest ground; while the dispositions against cavalry, by the various formations of the square from column or line of battle, were so often practiced, that I believe we could have executed them with closed eyes or in the darkest night. These exercises gave the men confidence in themselves and in each other, by showing them of what they were capable. Before the expiration of three months, they had attained a degree of excellence that elicited gratifying encomiums from competent judges of the old line.

I trust to be excused for recalling as I do, with pleasure and satisfaction, but I believe without undue partiality, the good discipline of the 1st regiment of Ohio volunteers. Justice to many officers and soldiers demands that I should bear this testimony to the industry and perseverance by which they succeeded in elevating their corps to a condition of efficiency, certainly not excelled by any of the new battalions. The work was the more creditable to them, in view of the shortness of their term of service, and the many evil temptations incident to their position. There were some regiments that rarely left their tents for military exercises, and others that sought only to accomplish a few showy movements. The commander of one of these appeared solely intent upon teaching his men the "fire by battalion." In its acquirement, he consumed thousands of cartridges, and with his volleys terrified the peaceable people for miles around. True, the fire of his regiment was universally admitted to be perfect—there was but one flash and one explosion in his line. But, *cui bono?* He was himself an amiable man, though somewhat ambitious "to make a noise in the world," and his battalion, a capital one for a funeral escort.

In the intervals of duty, the soldiers found ample leisure for amusement, and dull indeed were the events of the day from which they could strike no sparks of fun. Their wild pranks often caused the sedate and dignified Mexicans, who happened to witness them, to make big eyes. Rarely, however, did they pass the bounds of decorum, and even upon these occasions, the commanding officer, himself no graybeard, would have preferred joining in their sports, to administering the necessary reproof. At night, the camp often presented a scene quite as enchanting as any the imagination could portray. The open and spacious parade-ground brightened by the mild radiance of an autumnal moon; the lofty arches of the grove, adorned with waving banners of moss, and illuminated by the ruddy glow of many fires; rows of tents, luminous in the dim and shadowy vistas of the wood; the silent sentinels pacing to and fro, their arms now flashing in the light, now concealed in the shade; here a group of cheerful young soldiers, whose bouyant spirits no vicissitudes can dampen, laughing over the latest joke, or hatching some harmless conspiracy against their comrades; there, seated upon a fallen tree, their bronzed and bearded faces turned toward the flames that curl and crackle around its green stump, a party of elderly men smoking their pipes and conversing with the gravity of veterans, all combine to make up a charming and interesting picture. Some of the Germans belonging to the regiment were excellent vocalists, and not unfrequently united their manly voices in the grand and beautiful songs of their Fatherland; captivating every ear with the wild melody of their choral symphonies. There were those too, in the ranks who delighted in the Ethiopean style of minstrelsy, long popular in the United States, and who awoke the echoes of the grove with the untutored, but not unpleasing, music of the banjo and the bones.

But our camp-life at this period was not all *couleur de rose*. Sickness and pain were mingled with our pleasures; and death, multiform as the clouds, flitted frequently across the checkered scene. Though the mortality was not so appalling as at Camargo, it was much greater than was anticipated in view of the season and location of the troops. It is true, many lives were lost by intemperate indulgences, assassinations, and the accidental discharge of fire-arms, yet a legion of deadly diseases lurked in the cool and delightful shades of San Domingo. Scarcely a day elapsed that the muffled drums of some regiment in the wood, did not announce the departure of one or more poor fellows to the chaparral. The Ohio regiment perhaps suffered as little as any in the camp; still our hospital-tent was never untenanted, and Dr. Heighway, the Assistant Surgeon, was kept in full practice. Nor were the poor Mexican serfs, who dwelt in the surrounding ranchos, altogether exempt from sickness. Knowing that medicine and advice would be gratuitously bestowed by our surgeons, a few of them were occasionally to be seen hanging upon the outskirts of the pale-faced party that each morning assembled at "the sick call." One old lepero, wasted to a shadow by the quartan ague, whose entire wardrobe was a dirty blanket and threadbare pantaloons, "a world too wide for his shrunk shank," and whose rags and wretchedness obtained for him the name of Lazarus, enlisted the sympathies of every beholder. Senor Lazarus received not only our pills, but with all the polite and profound acknowledgments of his race, deigned to accept the crumbs from our not overladed tables.

But we may not complain of our fare at that period of the campaign. A number of the Mexican farmers, inheriting the keen Spanish scent for gold, were soon encouraged to visit the camp, bringing green corn, pumpkins, poultry, and some fruits, with which they opened a prosperous traffic. At no time indeed did our people want for the common necessaries of life; and there was no one in our regiment who will not remember and appreciate the indefatigable exertions of its commissary, Captain Stevens. He was always prepared to feed the hungry, and at the right time and place, no matter how hurried or long the march.

While in the wood of San Domingo, most of our companies built bake-ovens and succeeded in making excellent bread, which we found an agreeable substitute for *pan-de-maiz*, slapjacks and ship-biscuit. The last named ration, by the way, had also begun to disclose a very suspicious meaty flavor, and caused the coffee or liquid in which it was usually soaked by those whose teeth were otherwise unequal to its mastication, to assimilate vermicelli soup. It will be observed therefore that the famous "meat-biscuit," which was exhibited by a Texan gentleman at the Wold's Fair in London, is nothing so very new under the sun; and my belief is that the invention was suggested to him by a specimen of our army bread.

As the troops were regularly paid, and with those almighty dollars whose talismanic influence is acknowledged in all quarters of the globe, it was within their power to obtain many little comforts. To many, however, "the shining mischief" but furnished the means of indulging the passion for gaming, to which soldiers seem peculiarly addicted, and the greatest portion of their pay soon found its way into the pockets of the gamblers and adventurers who swarmed, like famished harpies, in the track of the army. Every effort was made by a few vigilant officers to break up these ambulatory "hells," but with indifferent success; as even the soldiers who had been bitten made it a point of honor not to reveal the haunts of "the Tigers." Though they changed their spots frequently to avoid detection, yet our patrols occasionally surprised them in the sequestered recesses of the chaparral, and captured considerable sums of money, together with blankets, stools, tables, etc; all of which were confiscated for the benefit of the hospital.

It was even more difficult to combat the parent of vices, drunkenness; and the "striped pig"* proved to be a more formidable beast than the "spotted tiger." No Maine Liquor Law, no military authority, or moral suasion, could restrain the appetite of some old Bacchanalians in the regiment. A few of them were always taken with fits of piety on Sunday, and seldom failed to solicit permission to attend divine service at the cathedral in Monterey. Of course, being in town, they must needs "go the whole pig;" and on these occasions they generally returned to camp in such a state of uproarious excitement, that the officers on duty were fain to offer them an asylum with the usual restoratives in the guard-tent. Many Americans suffered a severe penalty for their indulgences, from the knife or lasso of the Mexican bravos. These murders were too often followed by the tacit

---

* This singular sobriquet, (the meaning of which it is unnecessary to explain to an American reader,) is even more applicable in Mexico than in Massachusetts, where, I believe, it originated; for in the former country, *pulque* and other intoxicating liquors are actually kept in hogs' skins. And since the time our Saviour caused the swine on the shores of Galilee to be possessed by the devils of Legion, we venture to assert that those valuable domestic animals have never been filled with more filthy and disgusting spirits.

enactment of the *lex talionis*, under which the innocent probably suffered equally with the guilty. These scandalous affairs seem to be inseparable from war, and are to be universally deplored and condemned. But considering the facts, that no contributions were levied upon the natives, and that many sacrifices were made to secure their confidence and good-will, it is not strange that these bloody deeds should have irritated to retaliation. Indeed, it may be considered somewhat remarkable, in view of the relative position and character of the two races, that these unfortunate occurrences were not more frequent. Though the ears of General Taylor, ever open to the complaints of the people, were often assailed with accusations of the volunteers, yet I can recall but one outrage of that foul dye, which was not provoked by similar conduct on the part of Mexicans. To the lasting honor of my own regiment be it recorded, that while several of its number were treacherously murdered, it never sought fcr blood save upon the battle-field.

The assassination of the learned and pious Father Rey, which occurred about this time, illustrates the indiscriminate and implacable hatred of our enemies. One of the soldiers of the 1st Ohio regiment, who, at the request of the worthy priest, had been relieved from military duty for temporary service with him, was killed at the same time. Of course, the heathen who could thus "give the flesh of a saint to the beasts of the field," would have no mercy for a layman. The murderers, perpetrating the deed in the face of open day, and on the high road, certainly knew the holy calling of their principal victim; but to be an American was a crime that admitted no benefit of clergy. Doubtless also, the ruffians were confident of obtaining plenary absolution for "the deep damnation of his taking off." Father Rey was, I understand, a member of the society of Jesuits,—an unpopular order in Mexico,—and whether his presence with our army was designed to promote the objects of certain statesmen or churchmen, or both, is part of the secret history of the war. It was hinted by some, that while his ostensible mission was to counteract the influence of the Mexican priests and their insidious attempts to cause disaffection among our Catholic soldiers, his object was to secure, in the progress of events, the interests of his order, whose vast estates and possessions had been confiscated upon their banishment.

During the two months we remained in camp near Monterey, the weather was perfectly dry, and generally of a mean and pleasant temperature; though we occasionally suffered from the *Northers* which prevail in that latitude between the autumnal and spring equinox. To protect ourselves against those chilling tempests, which however rarely lasted more than two or three days, and to procure timber for the construction of bomb-proof magazines in the citadel, we were compelled to consume a goodly portion of the grove of San Domingo, the pride of the province. Beyond that necessary destruction, I am not aware that the country in the vicinity of our army suffered much from its presence. The probability is that it was considerably enriched. Never having entertained the mercenary motives so recklessly imputed to them by some opponents of the war, our troops were content with the barren laurels of victory. The spoliation of private property is an odious feature of ocean warfare; and for the abolition of which, it is to be hoped that all civilized nations will hasten to unite. It has recently been justly denounced as "the vicious relic of a barbarous age," and is fostered by a spirit but little better than that of the old Flibustiers of Barrataria. The only public property, other than munitions of war, captured at Monterey, consisted of cigars, which were distributed among the troops. Tobacco, it is known to most of our readers, is one of the articles monopolized by the Mexican government, and is a source of very large revenue. Its culture is prohibited, except in certain districts, and even in those, is restricted to a limited number of farmers. The tobacco produced is purchased by the government at a price barely sufficient to compensate the planter, and after being manufactured by public agents is re-sold at enormous profits.

There are some interesting and notable sights in the neighborhood of Monterey, but which the claims of duty never allowed me time to examine. I was particularly anxious to obtain a view of the landscape from the summit of the Sierra Silla, and which for extent, beauty, and sublimity, was represented as being unsurpassed in the observation of those of our people who accomplished the ascent. That lofty mountain is seen far and wide over the plains, and in all the long array of giant peaks, is the first to challenge the rising sun and the last to witness his departure. It wears the usual conical form of volcanic mountains, and the curious saddle-shaped depression in its top, may have been caused by the falling in of the ancient crater. A geological reconnoissance would perhaps confirm the belief that it is ignigenous, so forcibly suggested by its appearance. Standing on the east side of Monterey and a short distance in advance of the Sierra Madre chain, it was scarcely a league from San Domingo. Yet, though probably not over five thousand feet in hight, so steep and rugged are its sides, that the persons who essayed to climb it, were usually absent two days from camp. Some officers of our brigade who had made the ascent in a sweltering day in November, determined to pass the night among the bare rocks, on the very pommel of the Saddle; and from that lofty perch, to behold the whole gorgeous panorama of the dawn. Before they had been many hours in that situation, one of those sudden and not unfrequent commotions in the atmosphere occurred, changing its temperature almost immediately from "India's fire to Zembla's frost." A freezing Norther swept across the plains and howling up the dark ravines of the mountain, broke with the fury of a hurricane upon our unprotected adventurers. With its first breath, all the loose articles in their bivouac were carried away; and it was only by prostrating themselves upon the rocks, that the heaviest men avoided being borne off by the tempest. It is needless to add that the unlucky party, now chilled to the bone, awaited the god of day with increased impatience; not, however, that they might see him in the brightness of glory, glancing from mountain to mountain, from valley to valley, and causing the whole earth to glow with a thousand hues in his dazzling flight, but that they might take the "wings of the morning," and fly from that bad eminence to our more genial camp below.

In company with a friend, (who, alas, like many other young companions of that period, is now among the dead,) I spent a day in riding through Monterey and in examining such places as were thought worthy of attention. A brief sketch of that visit may not be unacceptable to the reader, especially as he has obtained, in the preceding chapter, but a distant bird's-eye view of the city. It was more than a month after the battle, and the unburied carcasses of horses and mules yet remained in the suburbs. Around these still lazily stalked many of the voracious and insatiable vultures, which, in anticipation of the banquet, had been observed to descend from their mountain eyries to the field of carnage, as soon as the last echoes of the combat had died away. We entered the city by the road which passes under the eastern wall of the citadel. That fortress, and indeed all the minor Mexican works, were said to be constructed on scientific principles; and so admirably arranged as a whole system of defense, as to strengthen and protect each other. During the battle, the citadel was commanded by Colonel Uraga, who, I am forced to believe, tacitly permitted, if he did not actually authorize, the slaughter of several volunteers captured near his position on the 21st of September. This Colonel is probably the present General Uraga, the military leader of the late successful revolution; I mean that based upon "the plan of Guadalajara," by which President Arista's government was overthrown in January, 1853.

From the citadel, we rode first to the western suburbs, and gratified our curiosity with a view of the hights and works captured by General Worth's division. At the base of the castle hill, we saw a giant cactus, more than twenty feet high, and which, when in bloom, must be a magnificent floral spectacle. We next directed our course to Arista's palace, and its adjacent gardens, then filled with luscious and tempting fruits. The building possesses little architectural beauty, but its lofty and spacious rooms and breezy corridors formed agreeable quarters for the sick and wounded soldiers who occupied them. The massive edifice inclosed three sides of a smoothly-paved *patio* or court, which was filled with vases of flowers and fountains of crystal water, that shed a grateful coolness over the atmosphere. The fourth side of the square opened upon an extensive garden, which, in its arrangement, displayed a degree of horticultural taste and knowledge not often surpassed in our own country. Parterres of flowers, hedges of pomegranates, alleys of limes, clumps of orange trees, bowers formed by the grape, the broad-leafed fig and the golden shaddock, the air filled with perfumes and the melody of birds; altogether formed a scene that Shenstone might have envied, and that Downing might have been pleased to contemplate.

From that delightful spot we turned to examine a widely different place, the *Campo Santo*, or cemetery, situated between Arista's palace and the town. It was surrounded by a high wall, and, like almost everything else built by Spanish hands, strong enough to withstand an ordinary siege or earthquake. A large body of Mexican troops had occupied it at the commencement of the battle, but, after the fall of the Bishop's Castle, it was evacuated, a few balls skillfully thrown from Duncan's battery having caused them "to bile over the walls," as an old artillerist expressively remarked. The walls served the double purpose of enclosing the "holy ground," and as a place to deposit the dead. Rows of tombs were built in it, some of which being open, exposed to view "dead men's bones, and all uncleanness." Leaving that gloomy receptacle of poor mortality, we entered the city by one of the streets which Worth's division had fought through, to the *Plaza de la Carne*, in the center of which is a rudely constructed *jet d'eau*. Thence we proceeded by the way of the *Plaza Mercado*, or market square, to the great Plaza, around which are clustered the public buildings of the city.

The streets of Monterey are all well paved with round stones, and sloped to a gutter in the middle. They are uncommonly narrow, which, however, causes no inconvenience, since the people possess but few vehicles, and it seldom or never happens that

> "Laden carts with thundering wagons meet,
> Wheels clash with wheels and bar the narrow street."

The dreamy and dignified old Hidalgos would probably prefer the roar and crash of Paixhan-guns, to the rattle and clatter of omnibus and cab in their idle and quiet city. Beside scaling off a little of the everlasting stucco from the walls, and sundering some of the scarcely more durable iron bars that protect the windows, our light artillery had not damaged the town. The houses, nearly without an exception, are built of stone, and in the square, massive style well suited to that sultry and *revolutionary* country; combining comfort with a solid strength that makes them as defensive as so many fortresses. The floors as well as roofs, the latter being supported by beams of imperishable mountain-cedar, are covered with a hard and beautiful cement, in the manufacture of which the Mexicans have excelled for many centuries. But few of the mansions are more than one story high, though the great elevation of that, being eighteen or twenty feet with its crowning parapet walls, give to the exterior of the buildings a hight quite proportional to the breadth of the streets. The best establishments cover a wide extent of ground and are generally arranged in a quadrangular form, the stables and offices occupying one side of the square, with a court or small garden in the center. This, as well as the building, is reached from the street by a single large *porte-cochere*, in which a small door is inserted for the convenience of pedestrians. These huge barn-like doors and the few closely-barred windows,—so unlike our inviting porticoes and bright venetians,—give an exceedingly cheerless and inhospitable aspect to the streets. The interior of the dwellings, however, excite very different impressions. In their internal arrangement, elegance and comfort are often judiciously combined. From the wide entrance just described, the visitor passes to the right and left, into spacious reception-rooms; the polished floors, lofty ceilings and solid walls of which inclose a refreshing atmosphere even in mid-summer. These front rooms generally communicate with the more private apartments of the family, situated in the wings of the building, all of which open upon a pleasant arcade, that surrounds the *patio*, or space in the center. This comfortable appendage to the dwelling, affords the inmates a secluded place for exercise or amusement. And while it protects the inner walls from the sun, is itself generally sheltered by the overhanging branches of fruit trees and rare flowering vines, that breathe a delicious fragrance through its cool arches. These colonnades, as we afterward discovered when stationed in the city, were just the places in which to enjoy a siesta or a bottle of *vinto tino* and cigar, after a fatiguing drill in the *Plaza mayor.*

After visiting the churches and other public buildings, which presented nothing remarkable either in design or embellishment, we entered a restaurant, where a very poor dinner was obtainable for sixteen rials, including the luxury of a table-cloth. The Mexicans are much more temperate than the Americans, both in eating and drinking ; and their cafes consequently are not as flourishing as those in our towns and villages. Their favorite beverages now, as at the princely feasts of the Aztec nobles in the days of their barbaric splendor, are the pulque, distilled from the aloe, and the chocolate, prepared from the cacao. A very good red wine is grown in parts of the *tierra templada*, the quality of which might be much improved by the careful and cleanly process of manufacture pursued in our Ohio vineyards.

Nearly all the shops of Monterey were open, and some of them contained assortments of rare and valuable goods, particularly of Chinese fabrics. The market also seemed to be well attended by the country people. Relying on the friendly assurance contained in the proclamation of the military governor of the city, the citizens had gradually returned to their homes. But they evidently avoided any familiar intercourse with the Americans. Naturally taciturn and serious, the countenances of the better classes seemed to be yet more darkened with scowls of mingled hatred and sadness; doubtless attributable to wounded pride and disappointed hopes. I do not recollect ever to have heard a hearty laugh from Mexican lips; and rarely indeed could they be induced to smile, "though Nestor swear the jest be laughable." The miserable leperos, however, who bask in the sunny plazas and hang around the huts of the suburbs, appeared perfectly indifferent to the fortunes of the city and even to their own fate. No spark of true patriotism, religion, or virtue, ever warmed their hearts. They seem incapable of the least intellectual effort; and in their present ignorance and wretchedness, no proof of the influence of Christianity and civilization in purifying and elevating the Indian race, can be recognized. The Indians of Mexico, comprising, it is said, at least two-thirds of its population, seem to have exchanged the rude virtues of their warlike ancestors for the vices of their conquerors. Ages of slavery under Spanish masters, commencing with the *repartimiento* system, so justly denounced at its inception by the renowned Las Casas,* have rendered them incapable of appreciating or enjoying liberty; even as the fish, long confined in the dark lakes of the Mam-

* Fray Bartolome de la Casas, bishop of Chiapa, was born at Seville, in 1474; and was the first person admitted to priest's orders in the New World. A benevolent missionary and devoted friend of the aborigines, he was honored with the title of "Protector-General of the Indians." He was the first to propose, as the means of ameliorating the condition of the conquered natives of Cuba, that negro slaves should be introduced into that island. It would seem then, that the most enlarged philanthropy of the 16th, as of the 19th century, extended to but one favorite color. In the former the *black* was enslaved for the benefit of the *red* race; and now the meek Chinaman is being substituted for the African.

moth Cave, have lost the organs of vision from the absence of light.

On the way to camp, after the visit to Monterey just mentioned, I rode over the battle-field, and was shocked to perceive that the dogs and wolves had opened many of the shallow graves. The glacis, thrown across the gorge of the Teneria after its capture, and in which many of the enemy had been buried, was a promiscuous mass of bones and rags. The remains of our own soldiers were afterward more carefully interred. The officers who fell in the battle, were buried together in a little cemetery on the border of the wood of San Domingo, over which a cross was erected in the hope that it would protect the hallowed spot from desecration. Many Mexicans have as little regard for the sanctity of the grave of an heretical Yankee, as the hyena itself; and there have been instances in which dying foreigners have been compelled to profess the Catholic religion in order to secure even the privilege of burial.

Among the gallant officers whom death released from the service in the autumn of 1846, were Captain Randolph Ridgely, of the Artillery, and Brigadier General Thomas L. Hamer. The former possessed one of those dauntless spirits that revel in danger as if it were their natural element; and by his conspicuous courage and skill in battle had already gained a brilliant reputation. After the death of Major Ringgold at Palo Alto, he had succeeded to the command of the "Flying Artillery,"—a post for which he was eminently fitted. In battle, he seemed to bear a charmed life; but though shielded in the midst of so many perils, it was not proof against the accidents of fortune. He was the most accomplished horseman in the army, and yet by one of those inscrutable and most unexpected dispensations of Providence, met death by the slipping of his horse while riding in the streets of Monterey.

General Hamer, commander of our brigade, died in camp at San Domingo, on the night of the 2d of December, after a very brief illness. The writer, who became acquainted with him at the commencement of the war, and enjoyed much of his society during the campaign, is conscious that his rude and unpracticed pen can not portray his character, or render more than a feeble tribute to his many excellent qualities of head and heart. Never was a general more beloved by his troops; and indeed, his frank and popular manners gained him friends in every society in which he was thrown. Throughout his sickness, his tent was besieged by the men with sorrowful faces and anxious inquiries. The devotion of his own brigade was evinced in one of those sad scenes, which I was often called to witness,—the death of a soldier. Early in the night of General Hamer's decease, private Collins of our regiment breathed his last; and with his dying words expressed the most affectionate interest for his General. A few hours afterward that loved superior suddenly expired, in the presence of his physician, Dr. Caldwell, and a few officers of the brigade, exhibiting in his last moments his usual serenity and fortitude:

> "—— So calm his exit!
> Night dews fall not more gently to the ground,
> Nor weary, worn-out winds expire so soft."

The whole camp, from the commander-in-chief down to the

roughest soldier in the ranks, esteemed him and lamented his death.* General Hamer was well known as an able lawyer, and the most popular and eloquent orator of the Democratic party in Ohio. The complexion of his politics was not, perhaps, quite *red* enough to suit his party in the times in which he lived; yet was he universally esteemed as a true patriot and a sound statesman. He had represented his district in the councils of the nation, where his excellency of speech and wisdom commanded the admiration and confidence of his peers. But lately re-elected to Congress, and with a brillant position in the army, a dazzling career of

---

* When General Taylor was informed of Hamer's death, he exclaimed, "I have lost the balance-wheel of my volunteer army!" The following communications manifest to some extent, the regard entertained for the deceased General at head-quarters:

Head-Quarters, Army of Occupation,
Camp near Monterey, December 3, 1846.

"Sir: It becomes my melancholy duty to report the death of Brigadier General Hamer, of the volunteer service, who expired last evening, after a short illness. The order to the army announcing this sudden dispensation, expresses but feebly the high estimation in which the deceased was held by all who knew him. In council, I found him clear and judicious; and in the administration of his command, though kind, yet always impartial and just. He was an active participant in the operations before Monterey, and since had commanded the volunteer division. His loss to the army at this time can not be supplied, and the experience which he daily acquired in a new profession rendered his services continually more valuable. I had looked forward with confidence to the benefit of his abilities and judgment in the service which yet lies before us, and feel most sensibly the privation of them

"I am, sir, very respectfully, your obedient servant,

Z. TAYLOR, Major General U. S. A., commanding.

The Adjutant General, Washington, D. C."

Orders No. 150. — *Head-Quarters, Army of Occupation,*
Camp near Monterey, December 3, 1846.

"With feelings of profound sorrow, the commanding general announces to the troops the decease of Brigadier General T. L. Hamer, of the volunteer service, who expired last evening, after a short but violent illness. The ability and judgment displayed by the deceased general in the exercise of his military command, and the sterling qualities which marked his private character, endeared him justly to the

earthly honors was opening before him, and had he lived, he would probably have "touched the highest point of mortal greatness." His manners were natural, graceful and winning; his person robust and manly; and his features, though not handsome, exceedingly prepossessing and intellectual. He was one of those men, whose souls appear to be ever beaming through their faces. His conversation was cheerful and interesting, and the wit and anecdote with which he pointed and adorned it, was always brilliant and charming. It has never been my fortune to know one who understood better than Hamer, when and how to use "the word fitly spoken," which, "is like apples of gold in pictures of silver." His cool head, ripe judgment, enlightened spirit and comprehensive genius would have made him eminent in any position. During the campaign he had shown a practical good sense and talent for military affairs, not often displayed by those suddenly elevated by political influence from civil life to high rank in the army.

The funeral ceremonies on the 4th of December were solemn and touching, and there were not many dry eyes at

---

army and to his many personal friends. By the army in the field, and by the citizens of his own state, his loss will be severely felt; to those connected with him by closer ties it will be irreparable. The deceased will be interred at 10 o'clock, A. M., to-morrow, with the honors due to his rank. Brigadier General Quitman, commanding the volunteer division, will conduct the funeral ceremonies, and will command the escort, to be composed of one regiment of volunteer infantry, one company of cavalry, and two pieces of artillery. The cavalry and artillery of the escort will be designated by Brigadier General Twiggs from his division, and will report to General Quitman at 9 o'clock to-morrow.

"All officers off duty are respectfully invited to attend the funeral, from the head-quarters of the Ohio and Kentucky brigade.

"By order of Major General TAYLOR:

W. W. S. BLISS,
Assistant Adjutant General."

the grave. The remains of the venerated General were subsequently conveyed,—in accordance with a resolution of the Legislature of Ohio,—to his former home in Brown county, where a vast concourse of his old friends and neighbors united in his final obsequies. His name and fame will never be forgotten by the brave and patriotic people of the great State he served and honored. So long as purity of purpose, wisdom, eloquence and courage are esteemed, they will treasure his memory in affectionate rememberance. I trust the day is not far distant, when Ohio (emulating the generous example of her sister States) will testify her appreciation of such services and sacrifices by rearing a monument in honor of her own lamented dead; and inscribe high upon its marble muster-roll the deathless name of "Hamer,"—statesman and soldier,—*in utroque fidelis.*

Before concluding this chapter, I desire to review briefly the military movements of the autumn: And first, those of the Mexican forces. We have seen that the army of General Ampudia after the battle of Monterey, had retreated not only beyond the line agreed upon by the convention of September 24th; but to the city of San Luis de Potosi, situated hundreds of miles in the interior. The pass of the *Rinconada* or *Los Muertos*, is the gate to the broad table-lands of Northern Mexico. It is two marches from Monterey and is the strongest natural position for defense I ever saw, or read of, save Thermopylæ. Nature scarcely needed the assistance of art in defending the pass; yet on the brow of the mountain and commanding the narrow and steep ascent, strong intrenchments had been thrown up, and preparations made for a serious resistance. By its abandonment, the State of Coahuila, with its rich capital, Saltillo, was left open to our arms.

A month later, on the 27th of October, the garrison of Tampico under General Parrodi, after dismantling their batteries and throwing their heavy guns into the sea, also retreated to San Luis through the pass of Tula. The people of the frontier States of Mexico witnessed these movements with surprise and alarm; and complained loudly of the central government for having thus left them to the tender mercies of the enemy. But these dispositions attest the sagacity and military talent of General Santa Anna, who having recently been restored to power, had entered the bloody arena as proudly and boldly as one of his own favorite game-cocks. He foresaw the impossibility of making head against the American arms, with even the preponderant force his country had heretofore set in the field. To prevent the Mexican divisions from being beaten in detail, he wisely determined to concentrate the entire military strength of the Republic; and then by one heavy and sudden blow upon a weak point of his adversary, restore the *morale* of his troops and the sinking fortunes of his country. The point too (San Luis de Potosi) which he had selected for the re-organization of his grand army, being nearly equi-distant from all parts of our widely extended line, favored his designs; and at the same time would enable him to meet promptly invasions from any quarter or *pronunciamientos* at the capital. Keeping a strong division of Infantry and Lancers in observations at Tula, and throwing his numerous Cavalry forward on the road to Saltillo, he remained quietly at San Luis until the 28th of January, 1847; during which time many and exaggerated accounts of his forces and designs reached our camp. There were some among us, who saw in every fire that blazed upon the mountains, the signal for an insurrection; and who magnified every plump of partisan Lancers seen in the valley, into the van-guard of an approaching army. But General Taylor, from his time-worn tent at San Domingo, calmly watched the gathering storm; and when told that Santa Anna would finally advance with thirty thousand men of all arms, is said to have replied, "In that event, I shall want ten thousand."

Let us now examine the position and strength of the American forces at this period. It will be remembered that at the commencement of hostilities, our government determined to invade Mexico with three columns. The first or "Army of the West" under General Kearney, marching from the frontier of Missouri across the Indian territory, was ordered to conquer the State of New Mexico; and, with the co-operation of our Pacific fleet, the State of Alta California. This column performed the task assigned it before the close of the year 1846. Those distant departments of Mexico were virtually annexed to the United States, and supplied with constitutions of the most approved pattern, and laws of the latest fashion. It must be confessed that the establishment of these civil governments, was not calculated to convince the world, that the object of the Cabinet at Washington was different from that which had been previously disclosed with such amiable *naviete* by our minister to

Mexico, a plain-spoken Buckeye, who had not studied diplomacy in the schools of Metternich and Talleyrand.

The second column, or "Army of the Center," under General Wool, marched about the same time from San Antonio, Texas, in the direction of the enemy's State of Chihuahua, with orders to capture and hold it subject to a definitive treaty of peace. General Wool, finding no practicable route to Chihuahua, except one by way of the towns Monclova and Parras, which brought him within a few leagues of Saltillo, was fortunately ordered by General Taylor to abandon his original purpose, and await further orders at Parras. Though this expedition had thus been defeated in its object, the long and weary march of Wool's command had been favorable to the training of the volunteers composing it; and who soon afterward exhibited their discipline and constancy on the field of Buena Vista.

With the progress and condition of the third column or "Army of Occupation," as it continued to be designated, the reader is already familiar. He has seen it dislodge the enemy from Monterey, and then quietly encamp in and around the city, to await the progress of diplomacy during the armistice. Our government had sent to that of Mexico a proposition to open negotiations for peace immediately after the return of Santa Anna from exile; and had been briefly informed, in reply, that the question would be laid before the new Mexican Congress, which was to assemble in December. Now if that Congress should consent to treat for a termination of the existing war, and a peace upon the basis of the *uti possidetis* should be established, it was clearly desirable that we should be found in possession of the the whole country north of the Sierra Madre. And if the Mexican Congress should refuse, as it did, to enter into negotiations, the possession of Tampico and the establishment of a new basis of operations on the East would facilitate the conquest of a peace. Our Cabinet therefore very wisely determined to prosecute the war in the interval that must elapse before the assembling of the Mexican Congress, with the utmost vigor, and issued orders for a combined attack upon Tampico by land and sea. The movement was arrested by the news of the capitulation of Monterey, at the date of which General Taylor was not apprized of the changes that had occurred in the views of his government. The enemy, however, as we have seen, hastened to abandon the threatened port, Tampico, and it was soon afterward occupied by the naval force under Commodore Perry.

On the 3d of November, General Taylor was instructed by his government to terminate the armistice. All the hopes of peace which he had reasonably entertained were dissipated. On the 6th of November, he sent Major Graham to notify the Mexican general-in-chief, that the temporary suspension of arms would cease on the 13th, the date at which the notice was expected to reach San Luis de Potosi. Major Graham proceeded no further than Saltillo, whence his dispatches were forwarded to Santa Anna by the governor of Coahuila. The Mexican general in his acknowledgment of their arrival, thoughtlessly or maliciously insinuated that the notice was not warranted by the terms of the convention of Monterey; but added that Taylor might commence hostilities when he pleased, and that he would duly correspond to them. This note met General Taylor at Saltillo, which city he had entered without opposition on the 16th of November, at the head of Worth's division. He at once, in a second communication, vindicated his government from the imputation of a want of faith, and concluded by expressing the hope that the august Mexican Congress would find it for the interest and honor of the nation, to enter upon an amicable negotiation for the settlement of existing difficulties. General Santa Anna, in reply, courteously submitted to General Taylor's better judgment of the armistice; but assured the American General, that neither the Congress *nor any Mexican* (the words in italics were probably intended to clear his own garments from the smell of treason) could ever listen to any proposition for peace, until the forces of the United States had withdrawn from the national territory.

General Taylor leaving Worth and twelve hundred regular troops at Saltillo, now our advance post, with Wool at the head of twenty-four hundred men, on his flank at Parras, returned to Monterey and prepared next to occupy Victoria, the capital of Tamaulipas. That city was not only an important point, politically, but being situated at the debouchee of the Tula pass, a strong force there would threaten the flank of the Mexican army should it attempt to advance upon Saltillo. Accordingly on the 13th of December, the commander-in-chief, having previously ordered Patterson's division which had been left in reserve upon the Rio Grande, to meet him at Victoria, marched eastward with the brigades of

Twiggs and Quitman, leaving General Butler in command at Monterey, with a small battalion of Regulars, the 4th Infantry, in the city, and our brigade still in camp at San Domingo.

CHAPTER VIII.

FALSE reports.—Why and how we went to Saltillo.—The loan of a donkey.—Forced march across the Sierra Madre.—Mountain scenery.—La Rinconada.—The aloe plant.—Los Muertos.—The *tierra templada.*—Bivouac at the Palomas pass.—Conduct of the natives.—A cotton factory.—Scarcity of fuel.—Sufferings of the troops.—Rabbit hunts.—A visit to Saltillo.—Christmas-eve.—Another stampede.—Christmas-day in Saltillo.—Lassoing a team.—Return to Monterey.

THE reader who traces on the map of Mexico, the long line occupied by our troops in the winter of 1846, in distant and small detachments, and then looks at the position of the united Mexican forces at San Luis de Potosi, might perhaps suppose that General Taylor had committed a palpable fault in so dividing his army as to prevent its timely concentration at any threatened point. But when he is informed that there are no practicable passes through the rocky barrier of the Sierra Madre, save at Tula and Rinconada, and that it is impossible to transport artillery through the former; that between San Luis and Saltillo, there is a vast desert, which is of all natural obstacles the most difficult for an army to overcome; he will perceive how the rules of war are governed by the country in which it is waged, and admit that the American arms were in no way compromited by the dispositions which followed the termination of the armistice. Our greatest difficulty was in obtaining reliable information of the enemy's designs, and we were consequently annoyed by many false and vexatious alarms. On the other

12

hand, General Santa Anna was correctly advised of all our movements by the citizens in our vicinity; and unfortunately by the sad capture and death of Lieutenant Richey at Villa Grande, obtained possession of dispatches which revealed to him Scott's proposed descent upon Vera Cruz, to be preceded by the withdrawal from our line, of the *elite* of Taylor's victorious army. Every one remembers how he profited by this knowledge; how despite the clamors of his own countrymen concerning his inactivity, he remained at San Luis drilling his troops and collecting the necessary material for the campaign, until all our regular and many of our volunteer regiments had joined General Scott upon the coast; and how, when the long anticipated moment arrived, his mighty host rapidly crossed the desert and rolled, like the swelling tide of Fundy, up through the valley of Angostura.

It has been stated in the preceding chapter, that General Taylor marched for Victoria on the 13th of December, leaving the 1st Ohio and the 1st Kentucky regiments, formerly Hamer's brigade, and which after his death had been broken up, in camp near Monterey. The departure of so considerable a portion of our force, and especially of the commander-in-chief, whose presence always seemed sufficient to inspire the weakest corps with confidence, gave room to many vague surmises concerning the enemy, and which soon attained a threatening magnitude. The most important of these, generally known as "Worth's big stampede," caused a commotion that was felt from Saltillo to the Brazos, and brought every battalion several marches up the line. On the night of the 16th of December, General Butler commanding at

Monterey, received a message from General Worth to the effect that Santa Anna designed to take advantage of the diversion of force toward Victoria, to strike a heavy blow at Saltillo; and if successful, then at General Wool's force at Parras. This rumor, caused by some unimportant movement in the enemy's camp which was reported by our spies, obtained color from the advantage it was supposed to promise the Mexicans. General Butler immediately commanded the 1st Ohio and 1st Kentucky regiments, with Captain Webster's howitzer battery, to move by forced marches on Saltillo; and dispatched orders to hasten up troops from the rear. The intelligence also overtook General Taylor at Montemorelos, who immediately turned back with Twiggs' divisions, leaving Quitman's brigade to continue its march eastward. But on his return to Monterey, learning that the expected movement of Mexican troops had not taken place; and that in addition to our brigade, General Wool's column was also hastening to reinforce Worth at Saltillo, he made a rapid countermarch on Victoria.

General Butler's order reached our camp at San Domingo at 2 A. M. on the 17th of December; and as we were expected to be in Monterey at dawn, but few hours were allowed for preparation. We however, "took the instant by the forward top." The men set fire to their huts, hurriedly packed their knapsacks by the light their flames afforded, and then cooked breakfast upon the glowing embers. As there was not a wagon or pack-mule in the camp, and the march was to be a rapid one, the soldiers were required to reduce their baggage to the smallest possible compass. Many articles of comfort, that had been collected during our long stay at San Domingo, were therefore necessarily abandoned. Yet when the battalion was formed, I was surprised to observe heavy and rudely-constructed bird-cages hanging upon the backs of a few men. These contained birds of the parrot tribe, caught in the grove, and which their owners preferred to carry rather than more useful articles. Though somewhat enervated from long inaction, the troops shrank not from the fatigues in prospect. More tranquil than before the battle of Monterey, they were yet as ready for the encounter, and animated by as good a spirit as could be wished. The reflection too, that the regiment had now attained a degree of discipline which rendered it doubly as formidable as it had previously been, was a source of no little satisfaction to its commanding officer.

Leaving a small guard to attend the sick, and follow with the tents as soon as the means of transportation were supplied, the column cheerfully set forward. Long, and tedious to many, as was our sojourn at San Domingo, yet will its grateful shades resting now upon the graves of many brave comrades, ever be remembered with associations of mingled pleasure and sorrow. It was quite dark when we moved from the grove, but before we reached the city, the sun emerged from the golden portals of the East, shedding a glorious effulgence over the mountain-tops, and which gradually descended upon the trembling shadows of the valley, until the whole scene at length rejoiced in the perfect day. We entered the town without beat of drum, and stacked arms in the plaza, just as a group of priests were hastening to matins. They paused upon the steps of the cathedral in evident surprise at the sudden appearance of our brigade in marching trim; and their manner went far to satisfy me that General Santa Anna was at that moment calmly reposing at San Luis de Potosi. The conduct of the intelligent and well-informed natives, was a tolerably good index to such matters.

After making such an early start, it would have been possible to reach the Rinconada in one march; but we were unfortunately detained in Monterey several hours in obtaining a supply of ammunition, shoes, etc. It was not until 11 o'clock, and when a thermometer in one of the cool mansions of the city indicated a temperature of ninety degrees, that the column composed of our brigade and Webster's battery, attended by General Butler in person, was ordered to move. In the meanwhile, some of the men in addition to the weight of their equipments, had succeded in getting "bricks in their caps." Those we would have left as being overladed, but they insisted that they "could march the better, since their knapsacks were now balanced." Judging from the replies that were generally encountered by officers on such occasions, one might reasonably infer that the Mexican *aguadiente*, like the Falstaffian beverage, sherris sack, had a "two-fold virtue in it," making men witty as well as "very hot and valiant." Passing round the hill of the Obispado, we bade adieu to the beautiful and balmy region in which we had long lingered, and entered the gorge so often noticed in previous pages of this narrative; on our right, the Miter mountain, on our left, the Sierra Madre, soaring to the skies. The road for several miles, is closely flanked by mountains, and the scenery most grand and picturesque. The river, which we were often compelled to wade in the course of the day, meanders through the narrow valley and embraces in its graceful arms some spots of rich verdure. The shades of evening closed around us at Santa Catalina; and as many of the men were lagging from fatigue, we determined to halt in the hamlet. An hour afterward, the rear-guard with the stragglers, came up in high glee, driving before them what, from its great size and singular motion, appeared to be a camel or bunch-backed dromedary. On approaching the camp-fires, it was discovered to be a moving mass of knapsacks: but it was not until they were unbuckled and removed one by one, that the motive power was disclosed to the amused spectators, in a diminutive donkey, much jaded and looking quite woe-begone. Had it been one of Ericson's caloric engines, I could scarcely have been more surprised; so utterly disproportionate were the weight and bulk of the burden, to that of the animal.

General Taylor had published an order prohibiting the men from owning riding animals; but the soldiers often *borrowed* them on emergencies like the present. They were always cheerfully restored to the Mexican claimants after a a few hours' use. It may be needless to add that the double-jointed and iron-ribbed donkey that brought such a mountain of baggage into Santa Catalina was—*a forced loan.* The ass,—one of the things specially mentioned in the commandment against covetousness,—is almost the commonest species of property among the Mexicans, as among the Israelites. So common and cheap indeed, that no divine or human injunction concerning it was ever much regarded. It was always,—"nothing but a d——d jackass any how;" and generally received more curses than corn. On the hurried march to Saltillo a number of them were at various times and places pressed into the service. I recollect one occasion when, having ridden unexpectedly to the rear, I surprised a party of soldiers engaged in lifting a donkey bodily over a stone wall that separated his pasture from the road. Though it never displeased me to know that the animals of the enemy were sometimes required to assist our men in bearing "the burden and heat of the day;" yet it was impossible to overlook this singular highway operation, lest the offense, once countenanced by an officer, should be changed "to virtue and to worthiness." The party being caught *flagrante delicto*, at once took up their arms and resumed the march, leaving the patient and stupid ass dangling across the wall. Calling them back to relieve the animal from that ludicrous attitude, I rode rapidly off, not doubting however, but that they would find it much more convenient to pull him into the road, than to push him back into the field.

With the first glimmering of dawn on the 18th, we left Santa Catalina, and soon afterward began to climb the broad mountain which lies between that village and La Rinconada. It is eight leagues across that dreary and voiceless Sierra; and not one human habitation or drop of water in the whole distance. Though the ascent is gradual, yet so rough was the road and so warm the day, that many of the men enfeebled by sickness or relaxed by previous inaction, suffered greatly from exertion and thirst. No one seemed to bear the fatigue better than a Mexican boy, about twelve years of age.

who (his father having been killed in the battle of Resaca) had attached himself to Captain Hamilton of our regiment.* It was nearly noon when we arrived, thirsty and panting, at the top of the mountain, where we halted for those who had loitered behind, unable to keep up with the march. The view from the lofty ridge we had gained, was grand beyond example. No trace of verdure could be seen; but in every direction bare and bristling peaks, flashing in the hot sun, met the astonished eye. A single glance, and we were ready to exclaim with the poet,—

> "A scene so wide, so wild as this
> Yet so sublime in barrenness,
> Ne'er did my wandering footsteps press."

It was many a weary step from the summit of the mountain to the water at Rinconada; and over a more rocky and precipitous road. Soon after commencing the descent, we met a Mexican driving a few mules, which were laded with apples for the Monterey market. A very poor variety of that fruit is imperfectly grown on the high land around Saltillo; sufficiently hard and knotty to bear transportation in rough hampers lashed upon the backs of mules. The oranges and other fruits of the *tierra caliente*, are brought back in exchange, to the inhabitants of the mountain regions. The startled *arriero* was much rejoiced to find that he would be allowed to pass unmolested; and politely offered us water from a large gourd which he carried; a generous sacrifice,

* The boy's name was, I understood, Carlos de la Cruz. He was a sprightly youth, a great favorite with the soldiers, and after he had acquired our language was often a useful interpreter. After enduring all the hardships of the campaign, he was brought to Ohio by his excellent patron, Captain Edward Hamilton; and is yet enjoying the favor and protection of that gallant gentleman.

nardly to be expected from one who had such a dry and toilsome path before him. The traveler in Mexico soon learns to estimate highly the precious element with which the Creator has so bountifully blessed our own land, and to appreciate fully the many beautiful allusions to floods, and wells and water-brooks contained in the Bible.

At *La Rinconada*, which is, as its name signifies, "a little corner" or nook, we found a rapid stream of warm water, strongly impregnated with sulphur. It issued from a narrow glen, so gloomy and forbidding in its aspect, that, with the hot brimstone flavor of the water on his tongue, the spectator might readily suppose it the entrance to Hades. In this sequestered spot and hemmed in on three sides by towering mountains, is a single large rancho, built of adobes, and designed, I presume, chiefly for the accommodation of travelers. Scattered over the few acres of arable ground around the house, we saw, for the first time in perfection, that miracle of the vegetable kingdom, the aloe, (*agave Americana;*) and which was to the Aztecs, all that the reindeer is to the Laplanders.* Though the officers and men generally were active and cheerful, and untiring, throughout the march, in efforts to encourage and assist the

---

* The distinguished historian, Prescott, in his "Conquest of Mexico," gives the following account of the various and important uses to which the maguey was applied by the aborigines. To these, the modern Mexicans have added another, by converting it into a hedge plant, for which it is very valuable in the great scarcity of wood for fencing.

"Its bruised leaves afforded a paste from which paper was manufactured; its juice was fermented into an intoxicating beverage, pulque; of which the natives to this day, are exceedingly fond; its leaves further supplied an impenetrable thatch for the more humble dwellings; thread, of which coarse stuffs were made, and strong cords, were drawn from its tough and twisted fibres; pins and needles were made of the thorns at the extremity of its leaves; and the root when properly

weak, it was late in the afternoon before the last feeble and foot-sore soldier limped down to the stream at La Rinconada. Some of the foremost troops had already kindled fires, expecting to pass the night there; but when the rear-guard came in, General Butler determined to push across the next sierra by the famous pass of Los Muertos, and encamp at Agua Caliente. The men were cramped and stiffened by the toilsome march they had already performed; but they at once shouldered their arms and fell into ranks. A few, utterly exhausted, were unable to proceed, and did not overtake the column until the next day.

The road at the Rinconada turns abruptly to the left, and winds for a league up through a narrow gorge, at the head of which the enemy had erected a strong field-work. About half way up, it turns a bold shoulder of the mountain; and for the rest of the distance sweeps round a deep hollow in its bare sides, every foot of which might be commanded by a battery on the summit. The sun had left the valley before us, and the mountains, obscured by the gathering shades of night, loomed up in black and shapeless masses against the sky. The faint light which remained, revealed to us a number of rude crosses that studded the steep ascent.*

---

cooked, was converted into a palatable and nutritious food. The agave, in short, was meat, drink, clothing and writing-materials for the Aztec! Surely, never did nature inclose in so compact a form so many of the elements of human comfort and civilization."

* Los Muertos or "the dead men's" pass, obtains its name from the number of murders committed in that wild and dismal spot. It is customary to mark those scenes of violence with the symbol of the Christian faith. In consequence, as I suppose, of the difficulty of planting crosses in the hard mountain road, those in the pass of Los Muertos were supported by large piles of stones, beneath which, many of our people believed, were the bones of the dead.

Before getting through the pass, we experienced a most unwelcome change of temperature; often so sudden and perceptible when *altitude* regulates the climate, as in Mexico. The cold night-wind flowing through the gorge from the table-lands above, to the warm valleys we had left, was keenly felt; and after our halt benumbed us all. It was quite dark when the weary stragglers reached the bald crest of the mountain; but they were there stimulated to exertion by the blaze of the bivouac fires in advance, and around which were assembled their comrades preparing the evening meal.

We encamped near some hot-springs, of which there are many possessing various mineral properties along the Sierra Madre range. After the cravings of hunger and thirst were appeased, cheerfulness returned even to those who were compelled to undergo the additional fatigue of guard-duty. So true it is, that the soldier in active service is alike heedless of past suffering and indifferent to the future. Thirst was his greatest tormentor in Mexico, but every stream from which he drank seemed to possess the quality of Lethe's waves. Though the day thus spent in crossing the Sierra Madre was one of the most fatiguing of the campaign, it was yet full of interest and excitement; inspired both by the cause of our forced march, and the grand marvellous exhibitions of nature around us.

On the 19th, we had an early *reveille*, and marched before dawn, determined to reach Saltillo in the afternoon, though some of us were far from believing that Santa Anna was hastening, as reported, toward the same point. The road, now by an easy grade, led us to the table-land of Coahuila, and we soon found ourselves in a vast and elevated plain, which was encompassed by a lofty mountain rampart. At the south-western extremity of the plateau, near the point at which the rocky ranges converge to form the valley of Angostura—(in which is the pass of Buena Vista) is the capital of the State, Saltillo. About midday, we met Lieutenant Colonel May with his Dragoons, *en route* for Monterey. He informed us that the report of Santa Anna's advance, had not been confirmed; that there was no necessity for haste; and that General Worth desired us to encamp on a stream two leagues this side of Saltillo, near Canon of Palomas (pass of Pigeons,) by which, it was rumored, a division of the enemy designed to get in rear of the town and cut off our communication with Monterey.* At this intelligence, we slackened our pace and proceeded leisurely to the spot designated.

The face of the country, over which we marched, was bare, even of chaparral, and was in appearance exceedingly sterile. But the many ranchos and numerous fields gave evidence of a more settled and industrious population than any we had yet seen; the austerity of the climate, unlike the genial temperature of the lower country, rendering systematic labor necessary. In the summer season, the rough aspect of that region is probably much softened, by the green and attractive garniture with which it is decked by Ceres and Pomona.

* It was through this same "Pigeon Pass," that Minon's cavalry brigade *did* cross two months afterward, viz—on the day preceding the battle of Buena Vista. It is rather remarkable that the rumor should have floated to our ears so long before the movement was executed.

The soil though dry, is generous, and by the simple application of water is made productive. Irrigation therefore, is extensively practiced on those elevated and thirsty plateaus. In the neighborhood in which we encamped, were numerous canals, which, gathering water from the only stream in that part of the country, assisted in fertilizing many a broad acre of the parching plains. As the soil would be utterly worthless for agricultural purposes without the application of water, the poor husbandmen are compelled to pay high rents to the proprietors of the canals as well as to the landlords. We were informed that two crops were gathered from the same land every twelve months, as in the *tierra caliente*; but here one of them was a crop of small grain. Wheat sowed in November, is ready for the sickle in April; and corn is planted immediately after the wheat harvest.

Soon after encamping, we observed that the inhabitants of some *ranchos* not far off, alarmed at the vicinity of the dreaded *voluntarios*, were preparing to abandon their homes. To these we immediately sent assurances of good treatment, and offered a guard for their property if desired. This tranquilized them, and they were soon induced to enter our lines; bringing chickens, eggs, and what was most acceptable, some dried fruit. Some of them were intelligent people, and conversed freely about their government, with which they expressed much discontent.

Between our camp and Saltillo, and located upon the stream before mentioned, was a cotton factory; the only establishment of the kind, I believe, in Northern Mexico. Indeed, notwithstanding the adaptation of large tracts of

Mexican territory to the growth of cotton, and the high tariff policy of the government, there are but few manufactories in any part of the country.* The most extensive are at Puebla; but none of them are said to be prosperous, though the price of coarse cotton goods (not smuggled) is from thirty to forty cents per yard. The owners of the factory did not appear to be particularly friendly to the United States, whose traders they said were following our armies and filling the Mexican markets with cheap cottons. One of them informed me that the Mexican editors were all for war to the bitter end; and based many hopes upon the peace party in the United States, which was soon expected to *pronounce* against President Polk.

---

* I am tempted to quote in this connection,—as explanatory of the causes that have operated against the development of the industrial interests of the country,—part of an excellent article that appeared in the number for May, 1847, of that valuable periodical, "Hunt's Merchants' Magazine." The difficulties encountered in the recent Tehuantepec negotiations, confirm what the writer says concerning the jealousy and opposition of the natives to the enterprise of foreigners.

"Whoever contemplates the map of the world, and reflects upon the course of commerce in relation to the East, from the discoveries of the Portuguese, down to the present day, will naturally fix upon Mexico as that nation of all others best calculated from its frontier to take the lead in commerce. Her geographical position is good; and the eyes of all nations have, since the abandonment of a north-west passage to India, been fastened on the Isthmus, as the great future road for commerce between the Atlantic and Pacific oceans. Mexico labors, however, under many disadvantages. On the Gulf coast she has not a single good harbor; and the cities are not habitable for foreigners during many months in the year. The land ascends rapidly from the coast to the interior, making the transportation of goods difficult and expensive. But Mexico enjoys also many great advantages. Nature has blessed it with every possible description of mineral and agricultural wealth in profuse abundance: and an industrious people, with an efficient government, would not fail to place it foremost among the nations of the earth. Unfortunately, however, the natives passed under the dominion of proud, indolent, and rapacious Spaniards,—a people essentially anti-industrial and anti-commercial. Down to 1789, Spain continued its barbarian prohibitive policy, allowing only one galleon of 1400 tons to enter Mexico annually with Chinese merchandise; and one, once in three years, from Seville or Cadiz, was chartered by government with

The manufactory was a very substantial structure, two stories high, and built of *adobes*. Its machinery (about forty looms and twelve hundred spindles,) was made in New Jersey. The native operatives seemed sufficiently active and intelligent. A small chapel was erected for their accommodation near the mill, in order, perhaps, that they might lose but little time in paying their devoirs to the many inferior divinities of the Mexican church, every saint's day prompting to idleness.

European merchandise. In 1790, the trade was thrown open; and private capitalists engaging in it, it soon reached from $11,000,000 to $19,000,000. This trade was, however, still burdened with most onerous impositions under four general heads: *first*, on articles of Spanish produce in the markets of Seville or Cadiz; *second*, on shipments for Mexico; *third*, at Vera Cruz; *fourth*, transfer duties at every step from merchant to consumer. Under such arrangements, the trade did not prosper much; but on the breaking out of the civil war, the new government opened the leading ports of commerce. The Spanish merchants withdrew to Cuba and Cadiz, and their places were supplied by British and Americans, who, settling in the interior, supplied the people with goods in exchange for dollars. The jealousy of the natives, who, themselves exceedingly indolent, are instantly enraged at contemplating the prosperity of a diligent foreigner among them, caused an imbecile government to make absurb threats against foreign artificers and traders; and thereby prevented the growth of enterprise in the country. These circumstances conspired to leave Mexico, at the era of the war of independence, in 1822, entirely without those great conservative commercial and industrial interests, without which the military inevitably obtain the mastery and control of affairs. The long war of independence turned all the energy the nation possessed, into a military direction. From 1808 to 1821, the history of the revolution is only that of a sanguinary guerrilla warfare, leading to no results other than destruction to trade and insecurity to property. In 1821, the sudden secession of Iturbide from the royal cause, in favor of liberalism, resulted in his ascending the throne as Emperor Augustin I. From that time down to the present day, the political history of Mexico, has been one rude scene of violence and military anarchy. A turbulent banditti, as faithless in their foreign dealings as they were rapacious, cruel and treacherous in their domestic affairs, have, for twenty-six years, held possession of that unhappy country. Room for enterprise, encouragement to industry, or security for property, there were none. The roads, particularly the splendid way constructed by the merchants of Vera Cruz from that city to the upper county, were suffered to go to decay; not even the injuries they sustained during the war have been repaired. Their antipathy to carriages, and means of transport and communica-

We lay in our position near Saltillo, from the 19th of December until the 1st of January, 1847, suffering much from the inclemency of the season. In the hurry of our departure from San Domingo, much of our camp equipage had been lost, and some of our troops were compelled to dig holes in the ground, in which to shelter themselves from the piercing blasts that nightly swept across the open plain. Fuel was more scarce, in that region, than water; a single wagon-load of wood, brought from a distance of twenty miles, being distributed each day for cooking purposes, among the companies in camp. Many poor inhabitants of that country obtain their subsistence by daily carrying small faggots on their backs to the Saltillo market.

The soldiers off duty, often engaged in such athletic sports, as aided them in resisting the severity of the climate. A

---

tion, is even more strong than that of the Spaniards. While the government in its enactments and practice, has shown itself far more hostile to commerce than to crime, traffic has been more oppressed than vice, and merchants more rigidly fined than murderers. The repeated revolutions have left those who gain power, no other prospect than to get rich by peculation; and it has become a seemingly well understood system, that those going out of power should empty the treasury, and leave their successors to fill theirs by the most approved system of plunder. The readiest mode of replenishing the treasury and feeding the cupidity of the officers, has been found in the prohibitive tariff system; because, while under pretense of encouraging home manufactures, by keeping foreign goods scarce and high, it made the sale of special privileges to import goods more profitable to the dictator. The higher were the profits to be realized by the merchant, the better price could he pay for the privilege. Hence, although a dishonest government had pledged the custom's revenue to discharge the interest on its debt; by this device of the special privileges, they could still be made available to the officer. A system of low duties would not have admitted such an operation.

"All these causes have operated powerfully against the development of those great conservative industrial and commercial interests, without which there can be no stability of government, no efficient execution of the laws, nor any means of keeping in check those military adventurers, whose turbulence has torn that ill-fated country in internal brawls; and whose non-observance of treaties and plighted faith has involved two nations in the horrors of war."

favorite diversion was rabbit-catching by a circular hunt or "surround." Those animals were neither rare nor shy in that vicinity; and from their unusual size and the extraordinary length of their ears, were designated by the specific term "jackass-rabbits." Some of them are nearly as large as the red fox of the North. Their hair is very long and fine, and it is known that the ancient Mexicans possessed the art of weaving it into a soft and delicate web. Three or four hundred of the men, unarmed, generally united in the hunt, the scene of which was a plain adjoining our camp, covered with sedge and bushes not much higher than the knee. By skillfully and rapidly forming a large circle, the men always inclosed one or more rabbits. Then marching with loud shouts toward the center, and closing the intervals between them as they advanced, no means of escape were left to the terrified and bewildered animals, save by jumping over the heads of the soldiers, which was sometimes successfully attempted.

The day after our arrival, I visited Saltillo on military business and to see the town. It contains some handsome and extensive buildings, and the streets are tolerably well paved. The principal plaza is embellished with shade trees and a fountain, and the whole city is abundantly supplied with good water. The church is a vast and irregular edifice, nearly two hundred and fifty feet in length, and elaborately ornamented within and without. The wall behind the grand altar is about fifty feet high, and all covered with a mass of gilding in raised figures, that dazzled and wearied the eye. A profusion of paintings, statues and wax figures, were displayed upon the sides of the building, or grouped around the various shrines, representing the Virgin, our Saviour, and sundry saints, both native and foreign, "our Lady of Guadaloupe" having as usual a conspicuous place. To all of these, the artists had given the the dark complexion of the Mexicans, and which pious fraud, it has been remarked, "is intended to flatter the race for the good of their souls." There are no pews in their churches, and an American, even an American Catholic, as he strolls through them, finds it difficult to divest himself of the idea that he is examining a museum or picture-gallery. But when in the performance of some religious ceremony, the priests, in their flowing and picturesque habits, are gathered around the altar, and the broad floor is covered with kneeling worshippers, while the deep tones of the organ fill the ear with sacred melody, the effect is impressive and solemn.

Bleak and comfortless as was our bivouac, I can yet recall some cheerful hours spent there. And what position or circumstance could damp the exuberant spirits of youth, engaged in an exciting campaign in a country so full of curious and novel scenes! We had determined that nothing but the approach of the Mexican army, (in which event, I ween, birds of a stronger wing and fiercer spirit than *doves* would have wheeled in the "canon de Palomas") should prevent us from observing with customary honors the "hallow'd and gracious time" of Christmas. On its sacred eve, the country around us assumed a more cheerful aspect. The people were abroad with songs and music; bonfires and rockets blazed in every direction; the little chapel at the mill was illuminated, and the sound of bells floated far over the plain. In our camp too, there were some merry little parties. Some of my readers will *perchance* recollect a certain company of jovial friends that assembled at our Assistant Surgeon's tent to discuss a bucket of foaming egg-nog, mixed according to the Old School prescription and administered in no Homeopathic doses; they will remember too, that when in the full enjoyment of their "flowing *tin*-cups," a courier, who had come in hot haste from Saltillo, entered with the intelligence that the Mexican troops were rapidly advancing, and an order for the brigade to be held in readiness to march at a moment's warning;—and how, in the midst of the song and toast, those "merry, merry men" buckled on their swords and hastened to their posts, with the white froth yet upon their mustaches and the red blood bounding gladly in their hearts.

An old Mexican residing in the neighborhood, and whom, for certain reasons, I was inclined to believe, had on that day assured me with many solemn protestations, that Santa Anna's forces were still at San Luis de Potosi. But with the brightening prospect of another glorious "stampede" at least, the men were directed to sleep on their arms. Toward morning as we lay "'twixt sleeping and waking" on the hard ground, the faint but unmistakable sound of many distant hoofs was heard; and after the lapse of a few anxious moments we saw advancing across the arid plain, what, in the uncertain light appeared to be a large body of cavalry. They approached slowly and cautiously as if hoping to surprise the camp; and we were just indulging in a little quiet mirth at the disappointment which awaited them, when the enemy at a closer view were transformed into pack-mules, about five or six hundred in number.

But the excitement caused by the report received on the previous night, was not allowed thus tamely to subside. Early in the forenoon of Christmas-day, a dragoon galloped into camp with a communication from General Butler, who had now assumed command at Saltillo, ordering us to repair to town forthwith. The messenger stated that the game was now afoot beyond doubt; that General Wool's column, which had arrived within a few miles of town, had actually seen and skirmished with the enemy.

We started immediately at a rattling pace and reached Saltillo in an hour. After halting a few moments in the suburbs to dress the ranks, we entered the town with the cadenced step and flying colors. On every side were evidences of excitement and alarm. The garrison (General Worth's division) was under arms; while groups of frightened citizens, whom the appearance of our volunteers was not calculated to pacify, were hurrying to and fro. For several hours we remained in the plaza, awaiting orders. In the meanwhile, a hundred contradictory rumors floated around. Plans of battle there were many; but of retreat, not one. All reports agreed in estimating Santa Anna's army at more than twenty thousand. With General Wool's force, we could have mustered about four thousand effectives, and sixteen pieces of artillery. But a resolute courage animated every breast and each felt that,—"the fewer the men the greater share of honor." We had expected to pass the night under arms in the open country toward Buena Vista, a position not then selected for a battle-ground, but at dark, scouts coming in with the intelligence that no enemy was within fifty miles of us at least; we were provided with filthy quarters in town and slept on Christmas-night,—for the first time since leaving the United States,—under a roof.

The next morning, it was satisfactorily ascertained that the Mexican army was still at San Luis, and we marched back to our old position near the Palomas pass. About a week afterward, some regiments long kept in the rear, (the 2d and 3d Indiana and 2d Kentucky,) having arrived to claim places in front, we were ordered to return and garrison Monterey. The men, finding themselves deceived in the prospect of a battle, and disgusted with the privations of their dreary and miserable bivouacs among the mountains, contemplated their return to the cheerful and smiling valleys of Nueva Leon with much pleasure. On New-Year's day, 1847, we set out, attended by a large train of empty wagons going down the line for provisions. At the moment of starting, one of the teams took fright, and dashed off at full speed into the plain skirting the wood. A Mexican who happened to be near, with a *lariat* as usual hanging to his saddle-bow, immediately gave chase. Overtaking the runaways he dexterously threw his lasso over the head of the leading mule, (there were five in the team;) and then by gradually checking and turning his prize in easy circles, as a skillful angler would play a strong fish, finally succeeded in bringing the fugitives back to the starting point, panting and quite subdued. I have never seen the lasso thrown more gracefully or to so good a purpose.

We reached Monterey on the 4th of January, in excellent health, after our forced marches; but sadly deficient in clothing and camp equipage.

CHAPTER IX.

MONTEREY garrisoned by our regiment.—The battalion of San Patricio.—How the monks of San Francisco diddled us.—A few words about volunteer troops.—Expedition against Vera Cruz.—Arrival of General Scott in Mexico.—His letter to General Taylor.—Its bearer, Lieutenant Richey, killed.—The divisions of Worth, Twiggs and Patterson sent back to the coast.—General Taylor returns to Monterey.—His letter to General Scott.—Scouting parties captured by the enemy.—Taylor joins Wool at Saltillo.—Changes his head-quarters to Agua Nueva.—Reasons for taking that position.—Advance of Santa Anna.—Taylor falls back to Buena Vista.—Sights and sounds at Monterey.—General Urrea moves from Tula upon our line.—He captures Lieutenant Barbour's train.—Besieges Lieutenant Colonel Irvin at Marin.—Attacks Colonel Morgan's battalion.—Glorious news from Buena Vista.

THE months of January and February passed rapidly away. We were comfortably quartered in town, and our old friends of the 1st Kentucky regiment held the citadel. The weather was temperate and serene, and the gardens and environs of the city rejoiced in the gay flowers and blossoms of spring. The citizens, beginning to appreciate the mild and respectful treatment they experienced, evinced a more friendly disposition; and the soldiers preserved a commendable deportment, although their position was not remarkably favorable to discipline. It had been supposed by many, that the volunteers were unfit for garrison duty; and that a life of comparative ease in a populous city would foster and strengthen the spirit of lawlessness and insubordination some of them had displayed. Hence the regular troops had generally occupied the towns, while the volunteers were compelled to "rough it" in the chaparral. By this procedure, of which no experienced volunteer officer will ever complain, the enemy gained rather more than was expected, namely, the notorious battalion of *San Patricio*, made up of deserters from our regular army, who availed themselves of opportunities presented while in garrison, to abandon the service of "the model republic." More than fifty deserted at Monterey, during the period it was occupied by the regulars. These the enemy joyfully received and speedily enrolled in their ranks, where they served with a courage and fidelity they had never exhibited in ours. Doubtless, the humblest soldier of the battalion of Saint Patrick, was honored with much consideration by the Mexicans; and we may imagine that those distinctions were not lavished in vain upon the warm and enthusiastic nature of the Hibernian.

So far as I am informed not a single volunteer, either among the native or adopted citizens, went over to the enemy. There were some who, volunteering in haste and repenting at leisure, deserted their flag before leaving the United States and returned to their "anxious mammas." But was there one so faithless to his country, as to take up arms in the cause of faithless Mexico?* Nearly a third of our regiment were Catholics; and among them were seventy or eighty gallant Irishmen, some of whom, I have reason to know, were proof against the fascinating lures of an insidious foe. When stationed in Monterey, they more than once

* Since writing the above, I have been reminded that a lieutenant of a certain volunteer corps resigned with a view of joining the enemy. He left Monterey with the words of Cataline upon his lips,—"I held some slack allegiance till this hour, but now my sword's my own."

informed their officers of the presence of Mexican emissaries and were unusually active in their detection. According to a preconcerted arrangement, a noted partisan was arrested by the very men to whom he had made liberal and flattering offers of money and rank. They were all Irishmen and never did ferrets pursue a rat more indefatigably, than did they their pretended friend. He was a wily rascal and scenting his danger, had, after many windings and turnings ensconced himself in a bake-oven, in one of the back yards of the city, whence he was finally dragged by the heels and lodged in the guard-house.

There can be no doubt but that the Mexican ecclesiastics,—monopolizing the wealth and intelligence of the country, fattening on the traffic in "indulgences," and many of them "wanton, more than well beseems men of their profession and degree,"—knowing that even the presence of an American army would be unfavorable to their interests, were our most bitter enemies. There are not wanting among them, especially in the obscure villages, truly pious priests whose unblemished lives aptly illustrate their holy teachings. But the greatest number are pampered and frantic friars,

> "Such as do build their faith upon
> The holy text of pike and gun."

They unblushingly announced to their people, that our object was to make war upon their religion; and spared no efforts to weaken our ranks or strengthen their own. They even availed themselves of the protection we always extended to their churches and other religious houses, to convert them into secret magazines for arming our enemies. A lieutenant of our regiment, strolling on a pleasant morning in February, under the walls of the Franciscan convent in Monterey, was astonished at observing some gunpowder sprinkled upon one of the window-sills next the river-bank. The guard was immediately called and the building searched,—but too late. A few scattered cartridges alone were found. But the number of empty boxes which remained, satisfied us that a considerable quantity of arms and ammunition had been recently removed; perhaps to equip the guerrillas then assembling in the vicinity. The heavy tread of the guard in the corridors of the monastery, startled from their cells, some drowsy-looking individuals in flowing robes and skull-caps of silk; whose thoughts however, just then very conveniently, happened to be so intent upon the bliss or brimstone of another world, as to prevent them from accounting for the mysterious presence of the sublunary *saltpeter*.

In consequence of the limited number of the garrison, and the large details often required for escorts, and daily for guard, fatigue and patrol duty, the men were kept sufficiently busy. Yet would our position at Monterey have been more pleasant, had it not been for the unnecessary labors and petty annoyances imposed upon the troops by certain individuals in authority, who did not know how to wear very becomingly the greatness thrust upon them. Fortunately they were not in supreme command, and could do no great harm to the cause of their country. But the soldiers and subaltern-officers, whom they vexed and wearied by their thoughtless and ill-timed orders, were often induced thereby, to recall the more prudent conduct and bearing of the wise and modest Hamer. Had the conceited and ambitious plotters at Washington, succeeded at that time in their ungenerous and shameful efforts to foist a political lieutenant-general upon the army, the spirit of discontent, already rife in consequence of the conduct of certain favorites of the President, would have been so inflamed as to threaten the efficiency, if not the very organization and existence of some divisions in the field. They err greatly, who suppose that the volunteers were anxious to hail any civilian as their general-in-chief. They valued the experience of their veteran leaders too highly to sigh for the authority of new men ; and least of all, for that of those in whose selection they could have no voice. Political topics were rarely discussed in the army ;—certainly I never heard the terms Whig and Democrat uttered by the rank and file ; and notwithstanding recent political events, I do not doubt but that, if our government was now to call out a hundred thousand volunteers for a war with any European nation, at least ninety-nine thousand of them would prefer Winfield Scott as their leader to any living man.

When men stake their lives and reputations in war, they want a general of acknowledged military genius and capacity,—one who combines experience with patriotism, prudence with resolution, and wisdom with valor. They prefer a military to a political strategist, and look for proof of ability on hard-fought battle-fields rather than in long-winded Congregressional debates. But while it will readily be admitted that the chief even of a volunteer army, should be a man trained to the profession of arms ; it is questionable whether West Point officers would make the most successful regimental or company commanders of citizen troops. This however would depend upon the amount of good sense, tact, and temper they might happen to possess. With the benefit of their experience and example, there can be no doubt but that our volunteers would soon be found superior to the best drilled automaton armies of Europe. *That* benefit may be obtained to some extent, by a union of our regular and citizen troops in the same armies, and causing them to march, encamp, and fight together. The American volunteer is a thinking, feeling, and often a capricious being. He is not and never intends to become a mere moving and musket-holding *machine;* and something more than the Tactics and Army Regulations is required for his instruction and government. His patriotism, pride, ambition, and enthusiasm, may be so controlled and directed, as to be rendered auxiliary to his arms. These, united with his native courage and intelligence and a proper degree of discipline, make him the most formidable soldier in the world.

The position of an officer of volunteers, elected from the ranks, as the majority of us were, is one of peculiar delicacy. While he should not allow himself to forget that he owes his rank and power to the kindness of those he commands, he must yet know now to maintain discipline and exact obedience. He should not be eager to assert his authority on light occasions ; but be as ready to encourage as to find fault, and as mindful of the comforts as of the delinquencies of his men. He should know how to temper severity with indulgence, and mingle affability with authority, so as to retain a personal as well as an official influence over subalterns ; and thus govern as much through the affections as the fears. He should not attempt to enforce all the minutiæ of military etiquette, but insist upon a complete observance of all the essentials of discipline. Above all things, he should know how to govern himself; and though mild and forbearing, yet be prompt and resolute, when occasion demands. He must set an example of submission, vigilance, and zeal, in his own person, if he would be respected and cheerfully obeyed. Volunteers are ever ready to regulate and justify their conduct by that of their officers; among them "a choleric word" is as "flat blasphemy" in the captain as in the soldier. Most men like a tranquil and even-minded officer; stern and severe if necessary, but firm and unchanging. Indeed, a respectable dog's life, would be preferable to that of a soldier who is continually subjected to the caprices of an insolent, ignorant and irascible officer, puffed up with a power he knows not how to exercise. Volunteers in taking the field, are apt to suppose that *courage* is the only essential quality to be desired in their leaders. Let them beware how they place themselves under the command of brainless bullies, whose vanity, arrogance, and overweening conceit, may be as fatal to their success and welfare as cowardice itself.

While we garrisoned Monterey, certain important military events transpired, which demand a passing notice in this rambling narrative. Our government at length perceived, from the hostile tone and attitude of Santa Anna and the Mexican Congress, that it would be necessary to carry the war to the gates of the enemy's capital ere a peace could be obtained: "*Jamais on ne vaincra les Romains que dans*

Rome!" That grand achievement was reserved for the commanding genius of Scott. It was accordingly determined to transfer the war from the northern to the eastern part of Mexico, and make Vera Cruz the *point d'appui* for future operations, to be directed by the masterly mind of the general-in-chief of the American army. As the request of that officer to be allowed to put his sword into the harvest of Mexican laurels, had previously been peremptorily refused by the President, some explanation of his employment at this period, may perhaps be found in the difficulty that had recently sprung up between General Taylor and the Secretary of War, and which resulted in a sharp controversy, now included in the documentary history of the times.

General Scott, hastening to execute the orders of the government, arrived at Brazos San Iago in the latter part of December. Being anxious to invest the city of Vera Cruz before the season of the deadly *vomito* should again occur; and finding that the ten additional regiments of regulars and new volunteer levies, which Congress had lately called into service, would not reach the scene of action in time to enable him to accomplish that object, he determined to supply himself with troops from the northern line. He accordingly wrote to General Taylor, revealing his plan of operations and requesting him to send at once to the coast, the regulars (Worth's and Twiggs' divisions) and enough volunteer troops to swell the force to 10,000. "With these forces," he concludes, "and adding three or five regiments of new volunteers, Providence may defeat me, but I do not believe the Mexicans can." Before this dispatch arrived at Monterey,

General Taylor had marched, as previously stated, to Victoria. It was immediately sent after that general; but its bearer, Lieutenant Richey of the 5th Infantry, a gallant and meritorious young officer, was unfortunately killed in discharging the hazardous duty, and the letter found its way to the hands of Santa Anna. General Scott however, had taken the precaution to communicate his wishes to General Butler also: and that officer, who, since the great *stampede* of December had remained in command at Saltillo, lost no time in the absence of Taylor, in putting Worth's division in motion for the rear. The regulars marched through Monterey about the middle of January *en rout*e for the Brazos, much to the satisfaction of the Mexican citizens, some of whom but ill concealed the pleasure caused by their departure. General Taylor, soon after his arrival at Victoria, having been advised of the orders of the general-in-chief, sent forward to Tampico the regulars of Twiggs and the volunteer brigades of Quitman and Pillow. Thus the entire force intended for the descent upon Vera Cruz was enabled to reach the general rendevous behind the island of Lobos, before the end of February. General Taylor now, for the want of troops, was compelled to abandon his design of occupying the line of the Sierra Madre. He was not able to leave a garrison at that important point, Victoria; of which circumstance the Mexican corps of observation at the pass of Tula soon availed itself.*

* In a Mexican field-report, (for Febuary) of Santa Anna's forces, the strength of this division of observation is given as follows,—

Infantry—of General Vasquez;	11	chiefs,	117	officers, and	1655	privates.
Cavalry—of General Urrea;	8	do.	95	do.	2121	do.
Total of Division	19	do.	212	do.	3776	do.

On the 24th of January, General Taylor returned to Monterey, bringing with him the light artillery companies of Captains Bragg and Sherman, which he had fortunately reserved. Washington's and Webster's batteries had also been retained with General Wool's brigade at Saltillo. Without these, Buena Vista would not occupy the proud eminence it now does, in the column of American victories. Taylor encamped as usual in the grove of San Domingo, with a small quarter-guard. His presence again restored confidence; and all the uncomfortable apprehensions aroused by the departure of so large a portion of the army from our line, disappeared at his coming. Stripped of his veteran infantry, and left with a little band of volunteers to struggle with the twenty thousand Mexican troops, soon to be precipitated upon him; he was yet as calm and undismayed as if threatened only by a summer shower. He says in a letter to Major General Scott, written about this time,—"I feel that I have lost the confidence of the government, or it would not have suffered me to remain up to this time ignorant of its intentions, when so vitally affecting the interests committed to my charge. But however much I may feel, personally, mortified and outraged at the course pursued, unprecedented at least in our own history, I will carry out in good faith, while I remain in Mexico, the views of the government, though I may be sacrificed in the effort."

There is no period in the history of General Taylor more interesting than this, replete, as his whole career is, with honorable deeds, and instructive examples of patriotic and self-sacrificing magnanimity. View him in his tent at San

Domingo, patiently bearing the burden of neglect and injustice, calmly submitting to the behests of his *official* superiors; and with a placid courage, and unshaken loyalty, preparing to take his place, "in the forefront of the hottest battle,"—and his character assumes a grandeur, which all his victories alone could not bestow. It was expected that he would now abandon his advanced post, Saltillo, and concentrate his few and scattered regiments within the strong walls of Monterey. But to have done so would neither have contributed to the honor of his arms or the interests of his country. A retreat generally proclaims weakness or timidity; and does not fail to encourage the enemy, while it disheartens the troops who are compelled to give ground.* General Taylor wisely decided to meet Santa Anna on the edge of the desert that stretches between San Luis de Potosi and the Angostura; and fight his exhausted troops before they could reach the granaries of Saltillo. Had the Mexicans been permitted to pass the mountains, the fruits of our victory at Monterey would have been lost. With their large cavalry force, and by the extraordinary rapidity of their infantry marches, they would have swept all the feeble posts on our line back to the Brazos.

General Taylor remained but a week at Monterey, after his return from Victoria, namely, from the 24th to the 31st of January. On the day last named, he changed his head-

* "At the commencement of a campaign, *to advancc* or *not to advance*, is a matter for grave consideration; but when once the offensive has been assumed, it must be sustained to the last extremity. However skillful the maneuvers in a retreat, it will always weaken the *morale* of an army, because in losing the chances of success, these last are transferred to the enemy."—*Napoleon's* "*Maxims of War.*"

quarters to Saltillo, in consequence of the startling intelligence received from General Wool, that two reconnoitering parties of the Kentucky and Arkansas cavalry under Majors Gaines and Borland, had been captured by the enemy. Soon afterward, on the 5th of February, in order to restore confidence among the troops, which had been a little shaken by the disasters just mentioned, he established his camp at Agua Nueva, a position eighteen miles in front of Saltillo. From that camp he wrote as follows to the government: "Although advised by Major General Scott to evacuate Saltillo, I am confirmed in my purpose of holding not only that point, but this position in its front. Not to speak of the pernicious moral effect upon volunteer troops of falling back from points which we have gained, there are powerful military reasons for occupying this extremity of the pass rather than the other. The scarcity of water and supplies for a long distance in front, compels the enemy either to risk an engagement in the field, or to hold himself aloof from us; while, if we fell back upon Monterey, he could establish himself strong at Saltillo, and be in position to annoy more effectually our flanks and our communications." The American army assembled at Agua Nueva consisted of the 1st and 2d regiments of Illinois, the 1st Mississippi, the 2d Kentucky, the 2d and 3d Indiana, *of Infantry;* two squadrons of regular Dragoons and the Kentucky and Arkansas *Horse;* together with four batteries of light artillery; comprising in all about 5000 men. Of these, but few had ever been in action; some too were undrilled, and many of the cavalry companies wretchedly mounted.

In garrison at Monterey, under General Marshall, were the 1st Kentucky and 1st Ohio regiments, mustering together an effective force of 800 men. Below Monterey, at the posts of Marin, Cerralvo, and Punta Aguada, was the 2d Ohio regiment, in detachments under its three field-officers. At Mier and Camargo, were the 3d Ohio and 1st Indiana regiments.

Such were the positions of our troops on the 21st of February, 1847, when General Taylor was induced, by the information brought him by that trusty and accomplished scout, Captain McCulloch, to change his ground from Agua Nueva to the gorge of *Buena Vista.* As my object is not to write a history of the war, but simply to relate a few incidents of the campaign concerning which I have some personal knowledge,—introducing such others, as may be well authenticated and necessary to form a connected narrative;—I shall not presumptuously attempt to describe how 20,000 troops, the flower of the Mexican nation and assembled under the banner of their most popular chief, were disgracefully routed by the handful of men whom General Taylor set in battle array on that memorable field. The story has been often told at length, by the graphic and graceful pens of eye-witnesses and is yet fresh in the minds of American readers. I propose here, to give some account of minor cotemporary events, with which I claim to be more familiar.

General Santa Anna, well informed by his numerous spies, and the intercepted dispatches, of all the movements that had taken place on our line, did not, as many predicted he would, hasten to succor the menaced city of Vera Cruz; but anticipating an easy victory over Taylor, he issued a stirring proclamation to his soldiers, and on the 28th of January marched from San Luis de Potosi toward Saltillo.* About the same time, the Mexican corps of observation was ordered to debouch from the pass of Tula, and at the proper moment fall upon our flanks, prevent the passage of supplies and reinforcements to the front, and be in position to cut off Taylor's *beaten and retreating battalions.* This division, as we have already shown from a field report, consisted of about

---

* I append the document, as a fair sample of the military papers of "the Napoleon" of Mexico. It is translated from a copy found in Monterey.

"*Companions in Arms:* The operations of the enemy require us to move precipitately on their principal line, and we are about to do it. The independence, the honor and the destinies of the nation depend on this movement and your decision. *Soldiers!* the entire world is observing us, and it is obligatory on you that your deeds should be as heroic as they are necessary. From the neglect with which you have been treated by those whose duty it is to aid you, privations of all kinds await you; but when has want weakened your spirits or debilitated your enthusiasm! The Mexican soldier is well known for his frugality and capability of sufferance. Never does he need magazines or provisions, when about to pass the deserts; but he has always an eye to the resources of his enemy to supply his wants. To-morrow you commence your march through a thinly settled country, without provisions; but you may be assured that very quickly you will be in possession of those of your enemy, and his riches; and with them all your wants will be superabundantly gratified. *My friends!* we are about to open the campaign, and who can tell how many days of glory await us! What a perspective, so full of hope for our country! What satisfaction you will feel when you have saved our independence; when you shall be the objects of admiration for the whole world, and our own country shall shower blessings on your heads! When again in the bosoms of your families, you shall relate your dangers, your combats, and your triumphs over your daring presumptuous foe; when you tell your children that you have given them their country a second time, your jubilee will be complete. *Soldiers!* the cause we sustain is holy; our honor, our religion, our wives, our children! What sacrifices are too great for objects so dear? Let us conquer or die! Let us swear before the Eternal, that we will not rest one instant until we completely wipe away from our soil the vainglorious foreigner who has dared to pollute it with his presence. No terms with him. Nothing for us but heroism and grandeur!"

ANTONIO LOPEZ DE SANTA ANNA,
General-in-chief of the "Army of the North."

Head-Quarters, San Luis de Potosi,
January 27, 1847.

two thousand cavalry under General Urrea and sixteen hundred infantry under General Vasquez.* It was soon rumored at Monterey, that a large force had entered the valley, and was moving upon our line; but being unprovided with cavalry, we were unable to learn anything definite concerning its strength, position, or designs. The citizens, whose conduct at once underwent a change, could not be prevailed upon to disclose any particulars, and in their dealings with us, they assumed a less gracious air and bearing, as if preparing for our defeat. At one time it was rumored that Santa Anna's whole army had come through the Tula pass and were in rapid march upon Monterey. Our suspicions that some hostile movement was about to be executed, were confirmed by the continued departure of families from the town; the few schools it contained were broken up and the children removed to distant villages. Before the 22d of February, Monterey was like a city of the dead. I do not believe that there were ten Mexicans who remained within its walls. Not one was to be seen abroad in any quarter. Never was a city so rapidly and completely evacuated by its inhabitants of all classes. Every house was closed and the intense silence that reigned day and night over its empty streets and vacant plazas, was alone broken at intervals by

* I have never been able to ascertain with certainty, whether the infantry of Vasquez entered the *tierra caliente* with Urrea's brigade of cavalry. It was never displayed before any of our posts, and the probability is that it joined Santa Anna in his march to Buena Vista. An intercepted letter however, from a Mexican officer to his wife in Monterey, requesting her to leave the city, as it would soon be attacked by a column of 5000 men, caused some to infer that the entire division of observation, swelled to the number stated by rancheros, was at Montemorelas about the middle of February.

the firm tread of its determined little garrison. Beacon fires were nightly flaming on the lofty peaks of the Sierra Madre; a primitive mode of telegraphing for which the country is well adapted. The gloom of approaching danger was the more oppressive, because its position and extent were unknown. Every possible precaution was taken against surprise. A careful watch was maintained upon all the roads leading to the city, and the highest officers relieved each other in mounting guard at night. All the public stores were removed to the citadel, which fortress, under the superintendence of Captain Frazier of the Engineers, had been much strengthened since it fell into our hands. The 1st Kentucky regiment lay in the work, while ours remained in the town. For more than a week preceding the battle of Buena Vista, (23d of February,) and indeed for several days succeeding it, we did not take off our boots or clothes, but remained under arms day and night. Such restless vigilance was more harassing than bodily fatigue. *Stampedes* were of frequent occurrence; and at the first sound of the "long-roll," every man hastened to the post assigned him, either upon the house-tops or at the barricades of the *Plaza Mayor*, which quarter of the town alone, our force was sufficient to hold.

Up to the 24th of February, no very satisfactory information was received at Monterey, of the movements of the enemy. It was evident however, from the non-arrival of couriers, that our line of communication had been cut both above and below us. On the 23d, a lieutenant of our regiment who had gone to the summit of the mountain behind the city, to reconnoiter the surrounding country, returned with the intelligence, that while in that elevated position he had heard two faint reports of artillery in the direction of Saltillo. As a sharp-eared sentinel at the citadel had also heard the same sounds, we were convinced that a battle was progressing in front. But General Taylor's position, at the last account, being distant at least eighty miles by the road, and perhaps fifty in an air line, many were disposed to entertain the painful belief, that he was retiring before the enemy toward La Rinconada.

About the same time, General Urrea, doubtless informed that Santa Anna had commenced operations in front, presented himself upon our line, with all his regular cavalry and a large body of rancheros under General Canales. He invested Marin, garrisoned by a part of the 2d Ohio regiment under Lieutenant-Colonel Irvin, with eight hundred horse: with as many more he fell upon one of our trains near Ramas, killing about fifty of the wagoners and capturing the escort, which consisted of thirty soldiers of the 1st Kentucky regiment under Lieutenant Barbour. A part of his force was also thrown between Colonel Morgan's detachment at Cerralvo and Major Wall's at Punta Aguada.

On the morning of the 24th of February, the painful uncertainty and suspense which had so long prevailed at Monterey were partially dispelled. A messenger arrived from Lieutenant-Colonel Irvin, stating that the enemy had been for some time in force around Marin; that the little garrison was much harassed by the close siege and desultory attacks of the foe; that their ammunition was failing rapidly and that assistance would be acceptable. Colonel Ormsby of the 1st Kentucky regiment, who had recently assumed command at Monterey, promptly dispatched Major Shepherd of his regiment, with a mixed command of five companies and two field-pieces, to Irvin's relief.* Major Shepherd marched at noon, and reached Marin at 9 P. M., the enemy suffering him to enter the place without opposition. The next day (25th) the Mexican cavalry were withdrawn from the vicinity of the town, and the now united commands of Irvin and Shepherd started to return to Monterey. General Urrea, instead of opposing, would I suppose, cheerfully have hastened their departure; since he must have been advised of the advance of a smaller detachment under Colonel Morgan, which he could attack advantageously, only before it formed a junction with the American troops at Marin. Colonel Morgan, having been ordered to concentrate the 2d Ohio regiment, and march to Monterey, had called up Major Wall's command from Punta Aguada and set out from Cerralvo on the 24th of February. He marched that day and the following night with but few brief halts, and arrived at Marin soon after the departure of Lieutenant-Colonel Irvin, who, it seems, was unapprised of his approach.

Early on the 25th, a solitary Kentucky volunteer staggered into Monterey, nearly dead with fatigue and hunger. He brought us the first account of the capture of Lieutenant Barbour's train; stating that he believed he was the only soldier

* This detachment was composed of the following companies:—Captains Triplett's, Bullen's and Kearn's of the 1st Kentucky regiment; Captains Bradley's and Vandever's of the 1st Ohio regiment; a few files of Kentucky cavalry under Lieutenant Patterson; two four-pounders, with squads of volunteer artillerists.

of the escort who had escaped, and that all the drivers had been massacred and horribly mutilated by the enemy. Shortly afterward a few teamsters came straggling in, breathless with terror and covered with wounds. They had been hunted far and hotly through the chaparral, by Urrea's men, and had escaped by avoiding the road and ranchos, and making a detour around Marin. In addition to these, it was afterward ascertained that twenty-five drivers and wagon-masters had succeeded in joining Colonel Morgan's advancing command. Among the fugitives was a negro-boy, who, with eyes protruding and wool almost "on end at his own wonders," narrated his hair-breadth escape. The Lancers had gashed him severely, or, to use his own very expressive words, "Dem Lanceers plugged into me, jes as if I was a green water-million."

Before dark on the 25th, Major Shepherd, attended by a score of officers and men, returned with the information that he had relieved Irvin, and that the remainder of the detachment were *en route* and would probably reach Monterey early that night. Fortunately, Lieutenant Colonel Irvin did not make such rapid progress as was anticipated, but bivouacked eight miles from town, not far from San Francisco; for scarcely had he resumed his march on the morning of the 26th, when he was overtaken by Lieutenant Stewart of his own regiment, who being well mounted had gallantly and successfully dashed through the enemy's line, with the information that Colonel Morgan with the remainder of the 2d Ohio regiment, was surrounded by Urrea's troops a short distance from Agua Frio. Irvin's command immediately turned back, and with the aid of the artillery soon succeeded in extricating his Colonel (Morgan,) who in the course of his march from Marin had been repeatedly assaulted by the enemy. The intelligence was also forwarded to Monterey, and in less than ten minutes after its arrival, two hundred men of the 1st Ohio regiment set out for the scene of action. Being unincumbered with aught save their arms, and stimulated by the perilous condition of their friends of the 2d regiment, the men strode lightly and quickly forward; and marched to San Francisco (four leagues) in two hours. At that village, we met Colonel Morgan's regiment, and those of our own corps who had aided him in shaking off the pertinacious foe; among whom were distinguished Captain Bradley and Sergeant Howell,—the latter commanding one of the volunteer gun-squads. After exchanging hearty congratulations with our gallant friends of the 2d Ohio regiment, whom we had not seen for more than six months, we fell into the rear of the weary column and slowly retraced our steps to Monterey. The garrisons having been thus, with much peril and some loss, withdrawn from the three posts of Marin, Cerralvo and Punta Aguada, the enemy obtained temporary possession of the country between Monterey and Camargo.

It was not until after these affairs, just described, that we received the glad tidings of the battle and victory of Buena Vista; and over which we rejoiced and lamented by turns, as the messenger described each charge and repulse; and told how, for so many long hours the fortunes of our countrymen, who had been compelled to fight with the desperation of men, " whose only safety was in the despair of safety," had trembled in the balance. Every allusion to "Old Rough and Ready,"—from his heroic reply to Santa Anna's summons at the commencement of the action, to his memorable order, "A little more grape Captain Bragg," at its close, was received with shouts and tears of joy. We immediately fired salutes and rang the long silent bells of the city in honor of the glorious achievement. In a few days the citizens began to return to their homes and property, looking—much to our amusement—quite disappointed and crest-fallen.

After one of the most lamentable retreats recorded in history,—and in which the Mexican writers confess that he lost from desertion and death in every horrible form, ten thousand five hundred men,—General Santa Anna re-entered San Luis de Potosi on the 9th of March. We were soon afterward informed, by a person who traveled from San Luis to Monterey, that the dead were strewed along the road for sixty leagues. But while we may well exult in the heroism of our troops and skill of our officers, the impartial observer of these events, must also respect and admire the valor and patriotism with which our enemies, undismayed by a series of disastrous defeats, prepared to continue the war. Look for example at the alacrity and fortitude with which Santa Anna's shattered battalions, yet bleeding from the wounds of Buena Vista, hastened to meet the army of General Scott and to incur new disasters at Cerro Gorda.

CHAPTER X.

Bearers of dispatches from head-quarters arrive.—We prepare to escort them to Camargo.—A train tacked on.—Description of the convoy.—Appearance of the country and villages.—The Massacre near Ramas.—The affair with the Mexican cavalry at Cerralvo.—General Urrea retreats to Tamaulipas.—Friendly reception by the citizens of Cerralvo.—Pronunciamiento of the teamsters.—Arrival of Colonel Curtis' command.—We resume our march to Camargo.—Fortifications of that town.—Another march to Monterey.—Mustang Gray.—Wholesale slaughter of rancheros near Marin.

The long suspension of communication between Head-Quarters and the coast, caused much apprehension in the United States for the safety of General Taylor's army. Reports of the capture of the Arkansas and Kentucky scouting parties in the vicinity of Encarnacion, the advance of Santa Anna's host, and the assembling of the rancheros with Urrea's corps in the lower country, had spread through the Union and awakened the most painful solicitude, which in those days of *mail-coaches* and *pony-expresses*, was not dispelled for many weeks. Colonel Curtis of the 3d Ohio regiment, being the senior officer on the Rio Grande, considering the perilous position of our troops, thought it advisable in the emergency to call upon the adjacent states for volunteers. Each anxious day deepened the gloom that rested upon the public mind. But thanks to an all-wise Providence who guided and guarded our arms, the sun of victory arose at last, and with a radiance the more brilliant and dazzling from the preceding darkness.

On the 3d of March, Mr. Crittenden, volunteer aidde-camp, and Major Coffee of the pay department, arrived at Monterey on their way to Washington. They were the bearers of those dispatches from Buena Vista, which, while they excited the admiration and called forth the gratitude of the nation, carried desolation and mourning to many a home and heart. That night, an order was received by the Major commanding the 1st Ohio regiment, to march on the following day to Camargo, with five companies of infantry and two light pieces, as an escort to the bearers of dispatches. Wearied by inaction and the monotony of garrison life, that officer had long desired such an opportunity for employing his men; and for that and other reasons, he prepared to execute his commission with no ordinary zeal and pleasure. Knowing that his march would be opposed by General Urrea—perhaps daily harassed by the attacks of the light squadrons of the enemy—and that much would depend on celerity of movement, he had determined not to encumber his troops with more than their blankets, and provisions barely sufficient for the journey. With this compact little escort, he felt assured that the merely mounted force of the Mexicans, could not compel him even to halt or change the order in which he proposed to march. The companies—who had all now acquired the discipline and weather-beaten aspect of veterans—burned for another fight before their term of service should expire, and pleasantly contended with each other for places in the expedition. But as two companies of our regiment had been detailed for the previous enterprise under Major Shepherd, the Kentucky regiment reasonably claimed that two of theirs should be attached to this command. The detachment therefore was organized as follows: three companies of the 1st Ohio regiment under Captains Bradley, Armstrong, and Keneally; two companies of the 1st Kentucky regiment under Captains Howe and Fuller; and two gun-squads, each with a four-pounder, commanded by Lieutenant McCarter and Sergeant William Howell of the 1st Ohio regiment, both of whom were skilled in the exercise of artillery. Our assistant surgeon, Dr. Heighway, also accompanied the party, which comprised in all, about two hundred and fifty fighting men, whose strength was augmented by the resolute spirit with which they sought the hazardous service. It was a well-appointed escort; and its commander,—knowing his men and confidently relying upon their endurance and courage,—had assured Messrs. Crittenden and Coffee that they would reach Camargo in five days. But unfortunately, just as we were about to start from Monterey on the 4th of March, an immense number of wagons were descried approaching the city on the Saltillo road. It proved to be a train, made up chiefly of wagons which had accompanied General Wool's column in its long march from San Antonio,—now going to the rear for supplies. Much to our dissatisfaction, the escort was immediately ordered to delay its march until the following day in order to convoy the train. This at once changed the aspect of affairs, and gave a different character to the detachment. Its commanding officer, though impressed with the belief that his force was entirely inadequate for the protection of so large a train, was not disposed to avoid the additional responsibility so unexpectedly thrust upon him;

and contented himself with replying that this new arrangement would probably result in the detention of important dispatches on the route, longer than was expected, and that he hoped his force would not be held accountable for the safety of the entire train. It was supposed however, by the officer commanding at Monterey, that General Urrea, learning the result of the battle of Buena Vista had withdrawn from the line; or that remaining, he would not be tempted by empty wagons to make an attack which promised more blows than booty. The number of the detachment therefore, was not increased,—except by the addition of a dozen Arkansas horsemen under Lieutenant Thompson. But the companies composing the escort or *convoy*, were made up of men who would stand by their officers to the death; and we left Monterey with the determination, that, though some public property might be lost on the way, honor should be saved, and if possible, some glory won.

In surveying the apparently interminable string of wagons which, on the 5th of March, followed us from the city and stretched for miles over the plain, I must confess that, much as General Taylor had complained of their scarcity, I heartily wished them all with Pharaoh's chariots,—at the bottom of the Red Sea. It was the largest train that ever passed over the road; and consisted of at least one hundred and fifty wagons, with perhaps seven hundred animals in harness,—many of them wild and stubborn Mexican mules. The ordinary difficulties attending the movement of such a train, even through a friendly country and under the most favorable circumstances, would vex a Job-like temper and patience.

But when it is remembered that there were more than a thousand active enemies upon the route; that the train when extended and in motion, must be nearly or quite two miles in length; that there was no military organization and but little subordination among the drivers; that the road for much of the distance was closely hedged in by dense thickets, most suitable and convenient for ambuscading, while it was only at rare and distant intervals in the chaparral that the wagons could be parked; the disadvantages under which the escort labored will be apparent. With the prospect of an action with a strong cavalry force, to have scattered a small body of infantry around so large a mass would have endangered the whole. The detachment was therefore divided into but two parties;—three companies marching in front and two in the rear of the train, each having a piece of artillery, which, had the country been more open, would have afforded prompt and efficient protection to the flanks. It was evident however, that a vigorous assault on judiciously selected ground, by an enemy numerically so superior would result in the destruction of some portion of the train. The drivers who had escaped the massacre at Ramas, had already by their accounts of it, so terrified their fellows, that most of them were prepared to desert their teams at the first sign of danger. A number of clerks, camp-followers, and other Americans not connected with the army, alarmed at the threatening aspect of affairs in Mexico, availed themselves of the protection of our escort to leave the country. These being poorly armed and undisciplined would have embarrassed, rather than have aided the detachment, had not Mr.

Crittenden undertaken the difficult task of making them march at least, in some order. He so far succeeded, that an enemy reconnoitering us from afar, would perhaps have supposed them to be a formidable body of Rangers. Among those who solicited permission to accompany the train was a Mr. R***, a genuine Yankee, who had long resided at Durango, where he had been engaged in some manufacturing enterprise. His party consisted of his wife, two or three children, and a friend who had been employed in the same business with himself. It was represented to him that the Mexican troops were on the road, and would probably fight a small force; and that he had better remain until the line was re-opened. But as he had been detained at Saltillo during the battle of Buena Vista,—much to the terror of his family,—he was determined not to make another halt south of "the little town of Bosting;" and accepting the risk, concluded to march with us.

A poor account of the poor country between Monterey and Camargo has been given in a previous chapter. Its appearance was now rather less attractive, if possible, from the absence of water. During the six months that had elapsed since we first marched over it, scarcely a cloud had floated in the sky. Parched by the hot suns, the shrub-covered hills and plains had assumed a brown and fading hue, the gaudy flowers of the cactus and variegated convolvuli had disappeared from the valleys, and many of the streams which at the period of our upward march had been both broad and deep, were now "consumed out of their places." But unlike "the troops of Tema" and "the companies of Sheba," we neither looked nor waited for "the deceitful brooks;" and sometimes traveled an entire day without water.

In consequence of the usual delays in starting from Monterey, it was late on the 5th when we reached Agua Frio, where we established ourselves for the night. The train was securely parked in the bend of a deep *barranca* or ravine; and every arrangement made to guard against any meditated surprise or sudden assault, from which alone any serious danger was apprehended. The wagons, when halted around our camp, instead of requiring protection rather afforded it to us, while, at the same time, they were in a position to be effectually sheltered by our arms. It was only when in motion and winding its slow length over the rough hilly road, and but a small part of the train could be seen from any one point of view, that it invited attack. The village of Agua Frio was deserted by its inhabitants; and we were somewhat surprised to find in one of the vacant houses, four mustangs, bridled and saddled for the road; and which probably belonged to some of Urrea's spies lurking in the neighborhood.

Many articles, of but little value however, plundered from Lieutenant Barbour's train, were discovered in the hamlet; which circumstance, some persons with the detachment (not soldiers) would have made the pretext for the commission of excesses, but being promptly arrested they were careful not to betray any lawless designs during the remainder of the march. With our own men, the commander, had every reason to be satisfied. They were obedient, patient and courageous; and too deeply impressed with the responsibility and dangers of the expedition, to indulge in the usual levities and petty maraudings.

The second day, notwithstanding the many breakings of harness and wagons, and indeed many of the villainous mules had to be broken afresh every morniug, we traveled with uncommon swiftness, and passing through Marin and Ramas, at nightfall bivouacked at Papagallos. Towns and ranchos were all deserted, and not a Mexican was seen in the course of the day's march. A suspicious silence reigned over the whole country; and but few now doubted that the enemy was prepared at some point to dispute our progress. The complete abandonment of the villages was partly explained by the shocking spectacle that met our gaze as we descended into a deep and narrow valley near Ramas. It was the scene of the massacre ten days previous, (24th of February,) and the inhabitants of that region had doubtless fled from the retribution which they feared it would provoke. The ground for the attack on Lieutenant Barbour's little command, had been well selected by the enemy. The valley is inclosed by lofty ridges, over which, on either side, the road passes by a rough and abrupt ascent. It is so intersected by ravines, cut by the rains in their passage from the hills, as to make the progress of a train through it slow and difficult. The unfortunate party had been permitted to enter the valley, and when involved among the ravines and thickets, were suddenly and furiously assailed by the Mexicans who had been stationed in ambush. The startled escort, taken by surprise, was almost immediately surrounded by ten times its number and forced to capitulate without firing a shot. But no quarter had been given to the drivers,—the bodies of more than fifty of whom still lay festering there; naked, bloated and blackened by sun and fire. Some of them, after being smeared with tar, had been burnt to a crisp upon the wagons. Others, frightfully mangled with wounds, had been placed in an erect position with pieces of their own flesh thrust into their mouths. The hearts of some had been torn from their breasts, and suspended upon the bushes or left to roast upon the rocks, reminding us of the revolting sacrifices of the Aztecs to the Sun. Indeed such barbarous atrocities could only have been perpetrated by the progeny of those cannibals and the cruel torturers of Gautemozin.* The effluvia arising

---

* It has been supposed by many persons that these barbarities were committed by the semi-savage rancheros of Canales alone. In the Mexican "Notes of the War,"—a work to which I have often heretofore referred,—a chapter is devoted to the guerrilla operations both on the lines of Scott and Taylor; from which I quote the subjoined extract to show that officers of rank and troops of the line were present at, if not actual participators in this merciless butchery. Let it be remembered that the enemy commenced this sort of warfare. Their historian does not deny it; but after remarking that,—"this kind of hostilities the Americans called barbarous,"—he hastens lamely to justify them by adding,—"but they soon established the same on their side." General Urrea was undoubtedly the commander-in-chief of all the Mexican troops north of the Sierra Madre at the time. He, I believe, is generally known as the executioner of Fanning's Texans. The Iturbide mentioned in the following extract is a son of the ill-star'd Emperor of that name, and is also well known in the cities of the United States. It is believed that the name of Lambert is a misprint, and should be "Langberg;" at least it is so written by that officer himself in a certain *considerate and modest billet* now in my possession. He is probably a German, and takes pains to announce himself "a foreign officer," in the note which will be given to the reader on a subsequent page of these Memoirs. After describing the guerrillas on the Vera Cruz line, under the famous Padre Jaurauta and Robolledo, the Mexican historian writes as follows:—

"The guerillas of Tamaulipas were recruited from the rancheros of the villas and were commanded by Canales; along with the squadrons of Guanajuato, of Allende and Fieles de Guanajuato, commanded by Generals Urrea and Romaro. They had under them likewise, several officers of the army of the line, such as Emelio Lambert, Augustin Ricoy, Augustin Iturbide, Pantaleon Gutierrez, and

from the mass of putrefaction tainted the atmosphere to the summits of the hills bordering the valley. The road was marked for a considerable distance with the dead bodies of men, the carcases of mules and pieces of the wagons, which had been broken up and partly burned to avoid detection and recovery. The fugitives had evidently been hotly pursued and some of them were slain far from the train. At one place even beyond the valley, I saw the half of a human head, which had been cleft from the crown downward, lying in the road at a great distance from any corpse. The face was upturned to the sun, and the shrunken and ghastly features, caused some stanch old horses of the passing escort to snort and tremble with fright.

Altogether the scene was one of the wildest savagery; and the terrible bloodshed it provoked, of which the reader will be informed at the close of this chapter, may perhaps, to some minds, "prove but a jest," when "exampled by this heinous spectacle."

It has been stated that we bivouacked the second night of the march at Papagallos. As at Agua Frio, the ground was carefully selected, and the camp a strong one,—the wagons being parked around a low but steep conical hill, to the commanding summit of which the artillery was dragged by hand.

---

others. They passed from Tula to the State of New Leon, making marches and countermarches to surprise detachments of the enemy. On the 24th of February, 1847, they attacked a convoy and captured 121 wagons loaded with clothes and provisions; and 137 mules also loaded with clothes, besides leaving many killed, wounded, dispersed and prisoners taken; breaking up the force that accompanied the train which exceeded 300 men. War made systematically by guerrillas, appears to us would in the long run have ruined the enemy and given success to the Republic."

The dreadful objects passed during the day, and the prospect of a conflict before reaching Camargo, afforded topics for conversation to the men who sat around their fires cooking, or cleaning the dust from their arms. It was late in the night before silence stole over the camp; and toward dawn it was again broken by the clatter of hoofs on the road in advance of our position; which sounds, the officer of the guard reasonably supposed, proceeded from a scouting party of the enemy. These increasing signs of danger, caused uneasiness for the safety of the wagons alone. The troops were abundantly able to protect themselves from many times their number of Mexican cavalry; but the experience and observation of the two past days had convinced us that the train when in motion, was never in any other than a bad position and only perfectly safe when closed in mass. But the interminable thickets which skirted the road,—while they were intersected by many paths and little glades favorable to the operations of an attacking party,—presented but few openings spacious enough to contain our wagons. Especially is this the case between Papagallos and Cerralvo, a distance of twenty-eight miles, which we marched on the third day, 7th of March. The solitary rivulet with which nature occasionally gladdens the first twenty miles of that journey, was dried up. But at the "Robbers' Rancho,"—eight miles from Cerralvo,—which we reached early in the afternoon, a supply of water was obtained. The scorching heat and rough road had so jaded both men and animals, that the commanding officer had concluded to encamp there; but on learning from the wagon-masters that they were short of forage, he determined to push forward to Cerralvo. The "Robbers' Rancho" was also deserted, but, as it was Sunday, an officer of the detachment sportively remarked that "the forty thieves had probably gone to church." Some new brogans, several packs of playing cards and other sutler's goods were found in that *very respectable establishment.*

After leaving the Rancho, the teams began to lag, as usual toward the end of a day's march. When the head of the train was about a mile from Cerralvo, a small party of horsemen who had been kept in advance galloped back with the information that, just as they were cautiously entering the suburbs of the town, the Mexican troops began to pour out, through many streets, upon the plain. So sudden indeed was the appearance of the enemy that one of our people, being poorly mounted, was overtaken and killed in the retreat. Before hearing this report, the long array of Lancers, then rapidly approaching, had admonished us to prepare for action. Fortunately there was a slight elevation in the plain, rather bare of chaparral, about 200 yards in front of the spot we occupied when first advised of the enemy's presence. This, the commander of the escort determined to gain as a favorable position for his artillery, while the open ground about it would afford ample space to park the train, for which orders were immediately given. Our four-pounder and the three companies of infantry were at once rushed forward to the desired position; and formed upon it just as the leading squadrons of Lancers had arrived within good range for canister shot, with which they were promptly greeted. They continued to advance, but in a slower pace and evidently much confused and disconcerted by their unexpected reception. Before our cannon was re-loaded, we were enabled to open a lively fire of musketry upon their line ; at which they broke and fled in disorder, many of them throwing themselves upon the necks of their horses the better to avoid our balls. A rapid glance from the point we occupied had revealed a heavy force between us and the town ; and large bodies of men, moving rapidly through the chaparral upon our flanks and rear. There seemed to be quite enough of them to overwhelm us by the mere weight of numbers. At the moment of the attack, the rear-guard,—composed of Howe's and Keneally's companies with Lieutenant McCarter's gun-guard, was more than two miles behind us ; while the wagons were strung out in the intervening road, which was for the most part hemmed in by thickets. The sudden volleys and shouts of the combatants, conveyed to those in the rear, the first intimation of the affair on hand. Captain Howe then marched his company to the front, leaving Keneally's (Company A, 1st Ohio regiment) alone in the rear ; which unaccountable movement,—had the latter company been composed of less resolute material,—might have seriously endangered the whole command. But the commander of the escort, was not apprehensive that the rear-gun would be captured so long as one gallant Irish heart was left to bleed in its defense.* At the sound of the first shot, the drivers in the center of the train abandoned their teams

* Captain Keneally's company was composed of Irishmen ; and was for many years well known in Cincinnati as—"the Montgomery Guards." The gallant Captain lost his life on the Vera Cruz line, a few months after the events here narrated.

and ran either to the advance or rear-guard. But few of those men deserve censure, for the road was so narrow that the stopping of a single wagon necessarily detained all others behind it. And even at those rare places where the track was wide enough to admit of passing, many of the brainless native mules, being accustomed only *to follow*, refused to pass those halted in advance of them; thus, by their provoking obstinacy, defeating the efforts of the most diligent and courageous drivers to bring up their wagons. To remain with such brutes was certain death; and indeed, so sudden was the onset of the cavalry at all points, that more than a dozen of the teamsters were lanced in their saddles; while others, unable to join either division of our force escaped in the chaparral, and wandered off toward Monterey or Camargo.

Meantime the wagons were being gathered as rapidly as possible around the advance and rear-guards, and by prompt and unceasing exertions,—in which some of the wagon-masters and drivers fearlessly discharged their duty,—we succeeded in saving about one hundred and twenty of them. The remainder, probably forty in number, were lost chiefly by the mules taking fright, and dashing through the openings of the thickets into the enemy's hands. Had we fifty or a hundred good dragoons, even those should have been recovered. The ranchero portion of Urrea's force, under General Canales, after unhitching the animals immediately set fire to the wagons. Among those burned was our ammunition wagon, which, though placed in charge of two drivers recommended as trusty men, had been lost in the first alarm. They excused themselves by asserting that their horses became unmanageable at the noise of the affray, and that they did not leave their saddles until in danger of being carried over to the enemy. The sad story of its loss was first communicated to us by the sound of its explosion, which was followed by an unearthly yell of pain. It seemed that a party of Mexicans, perhaps engaged in wrangling for the horses, an unusual and much coveted booty, were assembled around it while it was burning; when, as we afterward learned from one of the sufferers who was captured, three of the number were instantly killed and several wounded by an explosion that shattered the wagon to fragments. This unlucky event, a more persevering foe than General Urrea would have turned to good account, assured as he must have been by the slackening of our fire, that we had no cartridges to waste upon a distant mark. It was no easy matter to prevent the loss from having a depressing effect upon our troops; but the circumstances of our position when fully understood, strengthened every heart and arm.

The enemy, foiled in his first and most serious attack in front, after re-forming, continued to menace us with a charge; but was as often driven back by the unflinching steadiness of our men, and a few round shot from the piece of artillery under Sergeant Howell, some of whose balls rebounded into the town, creating no little consternation among the citizens. Our first object being to collect and park the wagons, the men were directed to husband their ammunition, and content themslves with keeping the enemy at a respectful distance. While engaged in these skirmishes, altogether defensive on our part, we could not refrain from again lamenting that it had not been our fortune to march from Monterey with the escort alone, as at first designed. Arrested in our progress more by the train in our rear, than by the foe in front, we could, if unembarrassed with the former, have thrown the latter from our path as easily as a buoyant ship casts the billows from her prow. Encouraged by our apparent inactivity, a party of the enemy dismounted, approached under cover of the chaparral and opened a rattling fire of escopetts upon our left flank. Their balls pattered among the mass of wagons then collected, but beside wounding a few mules did no damage. Our four-pounder was moved in that direction, and with a few raking discharges swept the skulking gentry from the bushes. While the fight was in progress, a game-cock, that courageous and vigilant bird, which the ancients, with their nice perception of the fitness of such things, dedicated to Mars, belonging to a soldier, flew upon a bow of the wagon in which he had been confined, and crowed in a style that would have caused the whole tribe of overgrown and loutish Shanghaes to hide their diminished heads. His clarion notes were greeted by the men with cheers and shouts of applause.

Among the laughable little incidents was the following, to which my attention was called by a gentleman near me. In one of the foremost wagons of the park was a beardless youngster,—perhaps a clerk,—whose only weapon was a little brass pocket-pistol. But he fought with that, as if victory depended upon his single efforts ; discharging it with the most astonishing rapidity,—now disappearing in the wagon to load, and the next instant rising to fire at any Mexican in sight, no matter how distant. Much excited, he continued his animated *fusillade* long after the troops had ceased firing. Whenever he dropped to charge his pistol, the driver of his war-chariot, who sat upon his mule, shaking with laughter, was engaged in selecting the next *victim*, and at which the *terrible piece of ordnance* was leveled as soon as loaded.

Another amusing scene occurred about this time. A teamster who had escaped from the massacre at Ramas,—and who was a driver in our train also,—had been suddenly set upon by a couple of Lancers; and failing in his attempt to give "leg-bail," he had darted head foremost into a cluster of chaparral about twenty feet in diameter. Into this the enemy were unable to force their horses; and being afraid to dismount, contented themselves with riding around the thicket and thrusting their long lances at the fugitive. Our driver, now on his hands and knees, and dodging from side to side like a wounded partridge in a brush-heap, succeeded by dint of hard scratching, in eluding all the blows aimed at him. The Lancers, alarmed at the proximity of some of our troops, finally rode off; when the teamster, venturing cautiously from his friendly cover, fled to the escort, with clothes torn to shreds and hands and face badly lacerated by the thorns. Overjoyed at his narrow escape and regarding himself as one returned almost from the dead, he gave utterance to his delight and attracted attention by some lusty cheers *for himself*. Jumping into the air and swinging the remnant of an old straw-hat exultingly around his head, he shouted,—

"Hurrah for Bill Robbins! Hurrah for Bill Robbins! run over by Lancers two times, and a living agin!"

But there were some incidents connected with the affair at Cerralvo of a different character, that interested more seriously the hearts of those present, and with one of which I propose to detain the reader. The Mr. R——, of whom mention is made at the beginning of this chapter, happened, at the commencement of the fight to be near the front of the train, while his friend and family were riding in a wagon far away toward the rear. He at once made a desperate effort to join them, but after a fierce hand to hand conflict in which he killed one of the enemy, was forced to abandon the attempt and unite with our force in front, then hotly engaged. Covered with blood and bathed in tears, the gray-haired old man approached the commanding officer, and in a voice tremulous with wild excitement stated the position of his family and implored assistance. It was not the moment for a consolatory conversation, yet sympathizing deeply with his sudden and great grief, the commander briefly assured him that he should have our arms, as he already had our sympathies, at the earliest possible moment; that in order to be able to aid him effectually we must first secure ourselves; and suggested that his wife and children were probably safe with the rear-guard. And so it proved. Their wagon had been attacked with others, and R——'s friend had been killed before the eyes of the family. But the women and children, supplicating mercy in the Spanish language, with which from their long residence in Durango, they were familiar, had been spared and suffered to join Captain Keneally's party in the rear. The old man,—husband and father,—being agitated with a thousand fears for his loved ones, could think of nothing but their fate; and throughout the action stood by the commanding officer, occasionally taking hold of his stirrup and looking mutely and imploringly up into his face, as if to remind him of his promise. Doubtless each moment seemed an age to the one. I know that duty and the tenderest feelings of our nature were making wild war in the breast of the other.

The enemy, it will be observed, being all mounted and acquainted with the ground, had been enabled with their superior numbers to dash almost simultaneously upon all parts of the train. A heavy column had briskly charged the rear-guard, but meeting with a determined resistance had been compelled to retire with loss and in disorder. They then formed in force, between the two divisions of our detachment with the view of preventing a junction. From the time of the arrival of Captain Howe's company in front, we had been greatly concerned for the safety of the company and artillery left in the rear. Lieutenants Fyffe and Moore, acting staff-officers, had both gallantly volunteered to bear any communication to Captain Keneally. But the commander, believing from the mutual confidence which existed between that officer and himself, that the Captain needed no encouragement to do his duty; and would count with certainty upon our aid when the proper moment arrived,—declined to risk the lives of his staff unnecessarily. He did not believe that there was a company in the 1st Ohio regiment, which, under the circumstances could be induced to lay down their arms and surrender that piece of artillery, contrary to his orders and the interests of the whole detachment. Company A, certainly was not one to withdraw from danger and thereby involve their comrades in greater peril.

The Mexican force in our front having been repulsed, and now disposed to content themselves with random volleys of escopetts from a distance, Captain Bradley was ordered to march with eighty men, to the rear; unite his force with Captain Keneally's and bring up the wagons collected there. Just as Captain Bradley was about to set out, Captain Keneally himself—cheerful and sprightly as usual—rode up on a gaily caparisoned Mexican horse. He stated that his company was surrounded, and that he had received under cover of a flag the following communication, which was written with a lead pencil on a mammoth sheet of foolscap.

" The Colonel Langberg, offers to all the *soldiers*, life and security, if you surrender yourself.

(Signed) " EMELIO LANGBERG, *Foreign Officer*."

Captain Keneally also stated that upon receiving the note he had requested an interview with Colonel Langberg; that he had found him with a large force under General Romaro, occupying an intermediate point of the road; and that Langberg, who spoke our language fluently, had remarked to him that further resistance would be useless as the Mexican force amounted to sixteen hundred men *and three generals*.* Keneally next inquired, if the remainder of the detachment

* I have no doubt but that this statement of the strength of the Mexican force at Cerralvo is nearly correct. We were afterward informed by citizens of the town, that all Urrea's troops, both regulars and rancheros, had been concentrated there, as a suitable point for their operations; it being about equi-distant from our posts

had been captured? To this interrogatory, Langberg truthfully replied in the negative; a circumstance from which I am disposed to infer that he is a soldier of more honor than many of those with whom he has associated himself. Captain Keneally then demanded permission to consult his commander, which was immediately granted and a horse placed at his disposal. The enemy also cheerfully agreed to a truce of *one hour*, during which time he had proposed, doubtless, to practice some of his perfidious arts. The men, who seemed to guess at once, the purport of Captain Keneally's message and the contents of the paper he delivered, swelled with silent indignation at the bare idea of a capitulation. But one however, ventured to make a remark, and that *sotto voce*. "Boys,"—said he to those next him in the line,—"boys, how would we look cracking *pandy-mice* in Urrea's camp to-night?" *

The commander of the escort, not intending to be duped by the wily foe, became, after hearing Keneally's report, doubly solicitous to concentrate his force without further loss of time. The captain was forthwith sent back with a suitable reply to the enemy, and a word of encouragement to his own company. Immediately upon the heels of Keneally was dispatched Captain Bradley with the force previously designated: so that if the Mexicans had calculated upon

---

at Monterey and Camargo. The generals so vauntingly alluded to, were Urrea, the commander-in-chief, Romaro and Canales. But generals are as plentiful in Mexico, as Colonels in the snaky counties of Virginia.

* The reader will perceive the *kernel* of this remark, when he is informed that the Mexican soldiers, who are their own commissaries, subsist chiefly on "*pan-de-maiz*,"—corn bread,—which they make from corn coarsely bruised or *cracked* upon flat stones.

having an hour's truce in which to spread their nets, "they reckoned without their host." Captain Bradley possessed an intrepid spirit, united with a rare combination of prudence and promptness, which, I take occasion to remark, rendered him eminently worthy of this dangerous and honorable distinction. Captain Keneally having notified Colonel Langberg of the termination of the truce, courteously advised him to move his troops, as they were in a dangerous position and might get hurt if they persisted in remaining. Upon rejoining his company, he was informed by Lieutenant McCarter commanding the artillery, that during his absence some squadrons of the enemy had moved to a new position within short range of the piece. These were immediately fired upon. Bradley, who had advanced rapidly on the main road, was enabled at almost the same moment to pour the whole weight of his fire upon other bodies of cavalry, who, taken by surprise at these sudden offensive movements on our part, gave way on all sides and suffered the rear-guard to be re-inforced. Among the foremost in Captain Bradley's command, marched the gallant old New Englander,—R***, who had learned from Keneally the melancholy fate of his friend, and the joyful tidings of the safety of his wife and children. His meeting with these, after such sanguinary scenes as all of them had witnessed, I leave to the imagination of the kindly affectioned reader. The now united commands of Captains Keneally and Bradley, had but little difficulty in bringing up the remainder of the train: and thus, in less than two hours after the first attack, we had the satisfaction of seeing our little force again concentrated, and with a loss of but two soldiers, fifteen drivers and about forty wagons. The Mexican loss we had no means of ascertaining, but the people of Cerralvo, subsequently informed us that it amounted to between forty and fifty killed and wounded. It was General Urrea's last appearance in that theater, from which we argue that he at least, did not think attacking trains a very profitable business *in the long run;* or agree with the Mexican historian that—"a guerrilla war would have ruined the enemy and given success to the Republic."

It should be stated that before the junction of our troops was effected,—indeed but a few minutes after the departure of Captain Bradley,—General Urrea commanding in our front, sent a flag toward us, which Major Coffee volunteered to meet midway, as it was not desirable that any of the enemy should be allowed to inspect closely our force and position. Its bearer, who did not speak English very intelligibly, was understood to inquire why we had violated a truce by firing on the general-in-chief. This strange inquiry, *strange*, because the truce was construed by us as extending only to the rear-guard, served to show that General Urrea, though more distant from the scene of contract than ourselves, was cognizant of it before we were; and strengthened our suspicion that some preconcerted scheme was about to be put in execution; and which was thwarted by our promptness in reinforcing the rear-guard. The demand for a surrender was also iterated, but the envoy was given to understand that General Urrea had failed to convince us of its necessity; and that as his object in these parleys was evidently to gain time and information, we would not regard or hesitate to fire upon the next flag he presumed to send.

After the arrival of the rear-guard, a few more shots were exchanged with the enemy, but he finally gave up the contest and withdrew from the field. It was beginning to get dusk, but the commander of the escort determined to make an effort to reach the town, in the direction of which the Mexicans had retired. The wagons closed in mass, covered several acres of ground, and though empty of aught save curses, with which they had been pretty heavily laded, especially since the attack, embarrassed our operations greatly. On the four sides of the park, were posted in as many divisions all our available force, including the miscellaneous command of Mr. Crittenden. In this order we resumed our march. But the bushes skirting the road so impeded the progress of the train, that, after many short detentions, we were compelled by the darkness to halt outside the town. It was supposed, too, from the sounding of bugles in advance, and the movements of the enemy, dimly discerned in the faint starlight, that preparations were being made to dispute our entrance; and it was therefore deemed best to await the morning before making the attack. Strong picket-guards were thrown out, and the men were ordered to lie down in their places and sleep on their arms. Many of the poor fellows were too much fatigued with the exertions of the day, either to eat or sleep; but a feeling of contentment and a sober joy pervaded the whole command, arising from the consciousness that they had done their duty and were an overmatch for the enemy. During the night General Urrea evacuated the town and marched southward into Tamaulipas; nor was our line of communication afterward interrupted, save by the *indigenous* robber bands.

Early the next morning, 8th of March, we took possesion of Cerralvo; after having been met in the suburbs by some deputies of the citizens, who, governed by their fears rather than their inclinations, greeted us cordially and proffered every service needful. These humble characters on the previous day had doubtless been cheek-by-jowl with Urrea. But the *ayuntamiento* of Cerralvo are not singular in the amiable faculty of accomodating themselves to the power that happens to be in the ascendant. Learning from two wounded Americans whom we found in the town, that they had been kindly treated by the citizens,—the Alcalde was notified that in return for his humanity, and a liberal supply of beef and corn during our stay, we would extend to himself and people our protection and "distinguished consideration." Notwithstanding these friendly demonstrations at Cerralvo, we did not relax our usual vigilance, and took up a strong position in the town. The same day, the commanding officer dispatched a Mexican courier to General Urrea, with some details of the battle of Buena Vista; and requesting him him to release Lieutenant Barbour's party and other Americans then in his hands, upon the assurance that General Taylor would promptly reciprocate the act by giving liberty to an equal number of prisoners. The messenger returned on the following day, with the intelligence that Urrea had retreated toward Victoria; and that despairing of success in any effort to overtake him with his poor *mustang*, he had abandoned the chase. Though the man had been promised, in the event of his success, that his brother, then our prisoner, should be released; yet there were many who placed no confidence in his report. Among those whose minds were filled with the belief that the enemy yet lingered in the vicinity with some ulterior designs upon our train, were the teamsters. On the 9th, the commander of the detachment issued an order for the companies and wagons to be got ready for resuming the march in the direction of Camargo. He was soon informed by the chief wagon-master, that the teamsters positively and unanimously refused to drive. This unexpected *ne exeat* of Jehu involved us in a dilemna, for which, so far as I am informed, neither Mars nor Marcy had made any special provision: the oracles of the god and Secretary of War, being alike ominously silent concerning teamsters. They were not enlisted men, or considered subject to martial law. Beholding in perspective a fate as dreadful as that already encountered by some of their comrades, the little subordination that had heretofore prevailed among them was now lost in an appalling sense of danger.

The commanding officer, not being altogether satisfied himself, that the enemy had abandoned the road; and knowing that in the event of another sudden attack by such a force, more lives and wagons must be lost, was not disposed to resort to any extreme measures to compel obedience. He was free to admit too, that the unarmed drivers had some reason to dread an enemy who had proved so unsparing to them: and in this connection it may be remarked that in Langberg's note, life and security were offered to the *soldiers* alone.

But being anxious that the important dispatches from Buena Vista should not be delayed, he next concluded to divide his force,—to leave one-half at Cerralvo in charge of the train, and march with the other to Camargo. He stated to Major Coffee and Mr. Crittenden the embarrassments of our position, arising from the temper and conduct of the drivers; and informed his officers of the plan proposed. To this it was replied among other things, that there was a scarcity of cartridges,—but ten or twelve rounds remaining for the muskets and a less number for the artillery;—and that if the enemy had not retreated toward Victoria, and should be tempted by a division of our force to invest Cerralvo, as he had besieged Marin; a failure of ammunition or of supplies from the surrounding country would be fatal to the party left with the wagons. After calmly weighing all the difficulties that surrounded him, the commanding officer finally decided to await the arrival of a force under Colonel Curtis, supposed to be on the march from Camargo; and in the meantime dispatched a messenger to Major Crossman, the quarter-master at that post, requesting the provision of supplies on the route. The messenger who was a Mexican smuggler, familiar with the frontier, returned in a few hours and stated that he had encountered some of Canales' men; but as he had fortunately refused to take a written message, they had released him after searching his clothes and saddle for papers. He however, stated his belief that it was possible to get through by making a circuit to the north-west, crossing the Rio Grande and descending to Camargo on the Texan bank. This he immediately undertook to do, in company with a volunteer; whom he shaved, painted and disguised as a Mexican with a skill that proved him an adept in such matters. The second attempt was successful, and we afterward found our march greatly facilitated by the satisfactory arrangements that Major Crossman had promptly made for supplying the train on the road.

We were detained at Cerralvo four days, at the end of which time Colonel Curtis arrived with a column of more than twelve hundred men; comprising his own, the 3d Ohio, regiment, four companies of the new Virginia regiment under Lieutenant-Colonel Randolph,—a squadron of regular dragoons under Lieutenant-Colonel Fauntleroy,—four pieces of artillery; and a corps of Texan Horse, lately called into service. Some of the fugitives from our train had met him at Mier, with the usual report in such cases, that our detachment was cut to pieces. On receiving this intelligence, Lieutenant-Colonel McCook of the 3d Ohio regiment, had proposed a rapid advance to Cerralvo with the cavalry alone. But his wishes were not acceded to, and the whole force in hourly expectation of an attack continued to advance by slow marches. The same misrepresentations of our fate reached General Taylor,—then at Monterey;—who, in the absence of any official report of the circumstances, though fresh from his glorious victory over Santa Anna, immediately started on a bush-whacking hunt after such small game as Urrea. That wily gentleman however, hastened to burrow in the Tula pass, from which he did not again emerge during the campaign.

After obtaining from Curtis' command some needful supplies; and thirty Texan Rangers, to be employed as scouts and flankers, we continued our march, and arrived at Camargo without further interruption on the 15th of the month. At that post we met Colonel Mitchell, Lieutenant-Colonel Weller, Surgeon Chamberlyn and other officers of our regiment who had just arrived from the United States. The town of Camargo we found much changed since our former visit in August of the previous year. It had been *fortified* too,—(as the reader, *peradventure*, knows,) but in such a bungling manner, as to expose a certain one of Mr. Polk's generals to the *suspicion* of incompetency. An extensive and well-constructed field-work had been built on the west bank of the Rio San Juan (opposite the town) by the 2d Ohio regiment, and named in honor of the officer who superintended it—"Fort Major Wall."

On the 20th of March, five days after our arrival at Camargo, we again entered upon the dry and weary road to Monterey; with a train of one hundred loaded wagons, and a force augmented to five hundred men, by the addition of some companies of the Virginia regiment; a company of United States Dragoons; and a company of Texan Rangers under the famous "*Mustang*" Gray;—the whole column commanded by Colonel Mitchell, whose wound was sufficiently healed to enable him to take the saddle. Nothing worthy of notice occurred during our journey until our arrival, on Sunday, the 28th of March, at the scene of the massacre between Ramas and Marin, already described. There Captain Gray and his Rangers separated from the command, for the purpose, as was said, of obtaining forage.

The column pursued its march a few miles farther, and encamped for the night at the stream near Marin. I was informed that one of the Texans had recognized a brother among the decaying remains of mortality in the valley, and with tears of grief and rage, had insisted upon avenging his death in the blood of the first Mexicans they encountered. The departure of the Rangers therefore, seemed to bode evil to the neighboring rancheros; for human vengeance,—especially Texan vengeance of the *Gray species*,—armed with power, is seldom over nice in the exercise of it.

We saw nothing more of them until dark, when they rode into camp laded with forage, and driving a couple of terrified old Mexicans before them; both so covered and hung about with flapping and complaining fowls, as to resemble in no small degree their ferocious ancestors, when clad in their gorgeous panoplies of "plumage" or feather-mail. The fright which evidently possessed the old men, was most lamentable; and they hastened in anxious silence to leave the camp as soon as relieved of their burdens. Little did we suppose that they were going home to weep over the dead bodies of relatives and friends. Nor was it until after our arrival at Monterey that we learned that twenty-four men, comprising nearly the entire male population of a village, about eight miles from our camp, had been put to death.*

---

* This massacre gave rise to an interesting correspondence between General Mora Y. Villamil (commanding the nearest Mexican garrison, at San Luis de Potosi) and General Taylor, in which the latter displayed his usual candor and ability; as will be perceived in the following extract from his letter:

"But as you have thought proper, in communicating the instructions of your government, to address me somewhat at length on the manner in which the war has been prosecuted on my part, I embrace this opportunity to make a few remarks

Various opinions were expressed at Monterey, about this sanguinary and merciless transaction. Many justified it by the wanton cruelties inflicted upon our countrymen near Ramas, in which some of these same Mexicans were probably engaged; and for which outrages the rancheros certainly had no apology whatever. Others thought it necessary as a warning and example to the people, whom we had so long in vain endeavored to conciliate, and whom we could only intimidate by some such sudden and heavy blow. Some excused it as the result of a wild storm of passion; by the long rankling injuries of the Texans, or by the border code of "blood for blood." It forms one of the darkest passages in the history of the campaign; and in fact, can not be justified on the score of necessity of any kind. I would fain blot it out from these memoirs; and it is alluded to here chiefly because as an officer of that detachment, I desire to exculpate my own regiment from any participation in the atrocious

on that subject. The outrages to which you have specifically referred became known to me soon after their occurrence, and I can assure you that neither yourself nor the president of the republic could have felt deeper regret than myself on those occasions. Every means in my power, within the operation of our laws, were employed, but in most cases in vain, to identify and punish the delinquents. I can not suppose you so badly informed as to believe that such atrocities were committed with my connivance or consent; or that they furnish a fair example of the mode in which the war has been conducted in this part of Mexico. They were in truth unfortunate exceptions, caused by circumstances beyond my control. It is proper to inform you that, from the moment the American army first entered the territory of Mexico, it has sustained losses of individual officers and soldiers, who have been murdered by Mexicans, sometimes almost within sight of its own camp. I do not recall these facts for the purpose of justifying, in any degree, the practice of retaliation; for my government is at any rate "civilized enough" to draw the distinction between the lowest acts of individuals and the general policy which governs the operations of an army; but you have chosen to institute a comparison between our respective governments in their mode of waging war, which can not pass unnoticed. In this connection let it be remembered that Mexican troops have given to the world the example of killing wounded men upon the field of battle."

deed; which future historians, in the absence of all evidence to the contrary, might perhaps charge to the entire escort. Let the perpetrators, whoever they may be, vindicate their own conduct. The Rangers denied plumply having been concerned in it; but of that, the reader can now judge as well as myself. General Taylor made every effort to discover the offenders, but without success,—the Mexican witnesses failing to come forward to identify them; being afraid that they might incur a similar fate. The whole truth of the case will probably remain locked up in the cells of flinty and guilty hearts, until that day when the omniscient God who witnessed it, "shall come with righteousness to judge the world and the people with equity."

CHAPTER XI.

Condition of General Taylor's army after the battle of Buena Vista.—Tranquility restored.—Courts established.—Glance at General Scott's campaign.—The homeward march.

With the battle of Buena Vista, and the guerilla affairs already described, the campaign in Northern Mexico may be said to have closed. The attention and power of the enemy were concentrated on General Scott's army, and the defense of their now seriously threatened capital. Active operations were necessarily suspended by General Taylor, in consequence of the nearly approaching expiration of the term of service for which the old volunteers had been enrolled. The new levies, destined for the northern line were late to arrive; and neither their numbers nor discipline would justify the immediate execution of any hazardous forward movements. A march to San Luis de Potosi, it was thought, too, would be attended with peculiar difficulties, chiefly from the absence of water. In that barren region which intervened, Santa Anna had lost the greater part of his army, made up of men accustomed to all the fatigues and privations of the country. Many of our new troops were already suffering much from disease, and the unusual hardships they had been compelled to endure. The Virginia regiment appeared sadly worn and reduced in health on reaching Monterey. The new Mississippi (2d) regiment, was almost immediately wasted to two-thirds its original strength by the small-pox. The North Carolina and Massachusetts troops were in rather better plight; but still the force was entirely inadequate to the enterprise of penetrating to the heart of the republic, even if it had been in condition to encounter the melting suns and incredible toils of the desert march. No great number of the old volunteers could be induced to re-enter the service until they had once more seen those homes to which amid all the various changes and chances of the war, their hearts had been fondly turned.

In this condition of affairs, events began to stagnate north of the Sierra Madre; and the eyes of both nations, so long fixed upon the fascinating drama which concluded amid shouts and tears at Buena Vista, were turned to the more gorgeously appointed spectacle upon which the curtain was rising at Vera Cruz. Even the robbers, awed by the rapid and searching patrols of the few companies of Texan Rangers, again in the field, were perfectly quiescent; and our trains were permitted to pass unmolested with even smaller escorts than at any previous time. Such protection was given to the conquered States as they had never before enjoyed, and the people returning everywhere to their homes, embarked in their various pursuits with a prospect of greater rewards than they had derived under their own rulers. There is no lack of the material for general comfort and prosperity in Mexico. The mere assurance that property will be secure from the rapacity of officials and the numerous professed banditti, would of itself give a great impulse to the country. The protection afforded by our military occupation of the Republic, had it continued a little longer, would have planted commerce and the useful arts upon her soil in a manner calculated to insure their growth.

Up to the period of the withdrawal of the Mexican troops from the Northern States, the *jus gladii* had been the only authority acknowledged and respected within their borders. In the clash of contending arms, the laws of the country (at all times speaking in a feeble tone and often to the perversion of justice) had remained perfectly silent. General Taylor's *dictum* settled many disputes, and the enemy never had cause to complain of the prompt decrees and stirrup verdicts he often enunciated. From Palo Alto to Buena Vista he had prohibited all wanton injuries to the Mexicans in person or property, and never failed to punish the perpetrators of them when detected. And indeed, as we have before had occasion to remark, his scrupulous sense of justice and generous leaning to the side of the vanquished, sometimes caused the scale of his own soldiers "to kick the beam," when the complaints of the natives were light and false. With the ill-fated King Henry VI., General Taylor might truly have said—

"I have not stopp'd mine ears to their demands,
Nor posted off their suits with slow delays;
My pity hath been balm to heal their wounds,
My mildness hath allay'd their swelling griefs,
My mercy dry'd their water-flowing tears:
I have not been desirous of their wealth,
Nor much oppress'd them with great subsidies,
Nor forward of revenge, though they much err'd."

Though fully authorized to levy contributions for the support of his army, the only pecuniary burden he ever imposed upon the Mexican people, was a tax to indemnify his government for the loss of the train near Ramas on the 24th of February; and even the collection of that was suspended, and its final decision made to depend on the future good conduct of the rancheros.

With the restoration of tranquility in the conquered States came the necessity for the establishment of tribunals for its preservation and the administration of justice. Unfortunately for the Mexicans, the American government did not think proper to bless the States of Tamaulipas, New Leon and Coahuila with such permanent governments as it had bestowed upon New Mexico and California. That work, in the rapid march of events on this continent, it will be called upon to perform at no distant day, to the great benefit of Liberty and Christianity. Our armies, however, assumed temporarily supreme civil as well as military jurisdiction; and boards of officers—"courts of military commission"—were organized for the adjudication of all cases, not falling within the cognizance of courts-martial. By these all disputes between Americans and Mexicans were adjusted. Their jurisdiction extended to the whole catalogue of crime, and the punishments were awarded in accordance with the laws of the particular State which the officers composing the court happened to represent. The citadel at Monterey was converted into a quasi-penitentiary, and scarcely a day passed after the establishment of the "commission" at Monterey, in which some *chevalier d'industrie* was not sentenced to hard beans and labor at the fort. That court was organized soon after our return from Camargo, and I can safely affirm that, during the two months in which I was familiar with its proceedings, a patient hearing was given to every party interested; and justice administered without fear or favor. As might be supposed, there were many cases on its docket between Mexicans and Texans. The latter too, were generally if not always the defendants; and their answers to the complaints (the pleadings were *oral*) almost invariable began, continued and ended with the Alamo, or Goliad or Mier; and wrongs or injuries long since suffered thus attempted to be set up in justification of present conduct.

The great *beauty* of these military tribunals was in the *promptness* with which they dispatched business. In this respect they were model courts. There were no ridiculous or barbarous forms of pleading to dodge an issue or raise a false one; no learned counsel with heads full of *sesquipedalia verba* and bags full of precedents to obstruct or turn away the stream of justice. Hence there was at least, none of that tedious, heart-breaking and mind-destroying litigation against which Dickens has recently turned his powerful pen. Certes, but our court at Monterey would have decided even the tough case of "Jarndyce and Jarndyce" at a single sitting.

About the middle of April an account of the fall of Vera Cruz reached Monterey; and about a month later news was received of the wonderful battle of Cerro Gorda. The first reports of both came from Mexican tongues and the facts were greatly misrepresented. They acknowledged however to a shameful defeat at Cerro Gorda, and stated that Generals Scott and Santa Anna were both killed. The arrival of our own couriers from the coast with authentic reports, was followed by official announcements of the victories, by salutes and rejoicings in which every American heartily united. The exploits of General Scott's army, rivaling upon the same theater those of Cortes, even when viewed through the clear medium of the present, before Time has thrown its magnifying mist around them, seem more like the highly-colored pictures of romance than the sober truths of history. The nineteenth century, so fruitful of great and remarkable events, furnishes few more striking to the imagination than the second conquest of Mexico. What American can contemplate that campaign without feeling his heart swell and glow within him! Commenced with a force of ten thousand men, who, after pouring out their blood as freely as the clouds drop rain, upon the thirsty sands of the coast, the rough slopes of the mountains, the fertile valley of the capital; after warring against every unpropitious circumstance, finally succeeded in capturing a city of two hundred thousand people, splendidly fortified, and prostrating the last standard the enemy dared spread to the breeze, on the very spot where, more than five centuries ago, its device of "the eagle, serpent and cactus" had originated.*

* The city of Mexico was founded in the year 1325, by one of those migratory tribes of aborigines which entered the valley from the remote regions of the North. Prescott gives the following account of the humble beginnings of this splendid capital.—

"After a series of wanderings and adventures, which do not shrink from a comparison with the most extravagant legends of the heroic ages of antiquity, the Aztecs at length halted on the south-western borders of the principal lake, in the year 1325. They there beheld, perched on the stem of a prickly-pear, which shot out from the crevice of a rock that was washed by the waves, a royal eagle of extraordinary size and beauty, with a serpent in his talons, and his broad wings opened to the rising sun. They hailed the auspicious omen, announced by the oracle, as indicating the site of their future city, and laid its foundation by sinking

The brilliant campaign of General Taylor, crowned though it be with the splendors of Buena Vista, may not be considered more glorious to American arms than the series of operations conducted by General Scott in Eastern and Central Mexico; planned with consummate genius, and executed with a courage, daring and skill that have never been surpassed. He who undertakes to institute a comparison between the characters and actions of that noble pair of American Generals, will engage in a difficult and thankless task. In Mexico, both led small armies against an enemy vastly superior in numbers, and always overcame him whenever and wherever he offered battle—in the walled city, mountain defile or open plain—and accomplished with the means at command, all and more than their government could reasonably expect. And to the permanent honor of both it will be recorded, that their campaigns were graced alike by the milder virtues of a compassionate forbearance and magnanimity. Both loved peace more than war; and prizing the *Olive* more than the *Laurel* wreath, were conquerors only to become pacificators. The honor and interests of their country were dearer to them than their own. May that country ever have a Scott and Taylor in her hour of need!

As the close of their terms of enlistment drew near, the old volunteer regiments were sent in succession from the field to be mustered out of service at New Orleans. Our home-

---

piles in the shallows; for the low marshes were half buried under water. The legend of its foundation is still commemorated by the device of the Eagle and the Cactus, which form the arms of the modern Mexican republic."

ward march was a joyful one, though over a road then numerously dotted with the skeletons of men and animals. Roofless and ruined ranchos, and many a dark and smoldering heap of ashes, told the disasters in which the people had involved themselves by throwing off their neutrality and entering upon a career of pillage and massacre. Truly "they that plow iniquity and sow wickedness shall reap the same." The hot season had again returned, and in consequence of the low water in the Rio Grande, the land route was lengthened to Reynosa and Matamoros. In the center of the march we met several detachments of troops who had lately arrived in the country; and after exchanging the military salutations usual on such occasions, many a merry laugh would escape from our men, as they contrasted their own burnt visages, flowing beards and soiled and ragged attire with the fresh complexions and perfect appointments of the new levies. But the day after our landing in New Orleans, the barbers and tailors of that city, accomplished such magical changes in their appearance, that it was no uncommon thing for officers and men who had served side by side throughout the campaign to pass each other as strangers in the streets.

In descending the Rio Grande, then diminished to a mere creek, it was difficult to realize that it was the same stream upon whose turbid and swollen current we had floated the previous summer. Its banks relieved from that inundation, appeared quite lofty and wore a more inviting and healthful aspect. It was a bright evening in June, 1847, when our eyes were once more gladdened by the blue waves of the

Gulf. Pitching our last camp upon the breezy beach, we sat down and gazed with delight upon the rolling billows, and the stout transports chafing at their anchors as if impatient and anxious to bear us home. Desert and danger were behind; toils and vigils were o'er, and now the faces and voices of long parted friends began to fill the heart. Soon the full-orbed moon with visage bright, arose in queenly splendor from the deep, and paved a silvery track across the sea; tempting our busy thoughts upward as well as homeward, to that Almighty Spirit who at the beginning "moved upon the face of the waters;" and who had borne us unscathed through all the perils of the march, the camp, the battle-field. We looked from our tents upon the lovely scene,—"the soul, on past and future, foraging for joy"—till the spirits of air and sea assailed us with their slumb'rous spells, while to fairy music chanting—

"Soldier, rest! thy warfare o'er,
Sleep the sleep that knows not breaking;
Dream of fighting-fields no more,
Days of danger, nights of waking."

www.ingramcontent.com/pod-product-compliance
Lightning Source LLC
LaVergne TN
LVHW020209110826
845151LV00003B/656

* 9 7 8 1 4 2 5 5 3 4 8 4 4 *